Beekeeping With

Twenty-Five Hives

My Philosophical Journey
From Passion to Profits:
Taking Your Hobby
to the Next Level

Grant F.C. Gillard

Beekeeping With Twenty-five Hives

By Grant F.C. Gillard

Copyright 2012 Grant F.C. Gillard

For more information:

Grant F.C. Gillard
3721 North High Street
Jackson, MO 63755

gillard5@charter.net

Grant F.C. Gillard has been keeping bees since 1981. He speaks at bee conferences and conventions across the nation. Contact him at gillard5@charter.net to check his availability.

You can find more information about the author at the conclusion of this book, or www.grantgillard.weebly.com

Dedication

In reality, we are the sum of all those saints (and sinners) who have come before us to show us the way and kindle in us a fire for learning.

I was blessed to have stumbled, perhaps providentially, into a course on beekeeping called "Entomology 222" in my sophomore year at Iowa State University. I was merely looking for a guaranteed, no-brainer course where I would get an easy "A" as I sorely needed this kind of a course to raise my grade point average after my freshman year.

My advisor, whose name I can't recall at this time, ran through the course catalog and made several suggestions. Nothing seemed to catch my interest until he mentioned *Entomology 222: Beekeeping*, which he quickly dismissed with a disparaging,

"But this class is for the granola crowd, you know, the nuts and the flakes."

Little did he know that I was one of those "granola"-types. Little did I know my decision would set my life on a marvelous trajectory that would change my future and set in motion an unknown agenda that led me into an apicultural Promised Land.

The classroom instructor was Richard Trump, a retired, high school biology instructor and Presbyterian elder at the Collegiate Presbyterian Church where we both worshipped on Sunday mornings listening to the sermons of Rev. Harry Strong.

"Dr. Trump," as we called him, was a marvelous teacher. He only gave two grades for this course; an "A" or an "F." As we entered the University bee yard to inspect the hives, if we got stung, proving that we were working the hives, we received an "A." If we didn't get stung, we received an "F."

Needless to say, we all got "A's."

For his capable leadership and the incredible investment he placed in us, this book is gratefully dedicated. Mr. Trump passed away at the age of 98 on November 1, 2010.

Beekeeping With Twenty-Five Hives

<u>Table of Contents</u>

Foreword

This manuscript is written to inform, to entertain, to educate, to enlighten. I write to appeal to the reader who thirsts for more information on how to be a more informed and improved beekeeper. The purpose in writing this manuscript is to share my journey into this fascinating subject of keeping honeybees. I want you to become a better beekeeper, and I trust by picking up this manuscript this is your desire as well.

When I was in high school I shared a large garden plot with my aunt, Elaine. Because we lived in a rural area with fertile soil, we were able to put a garden just about anywhere. But all gardens needed water during the long, hot dry spells of summer. With our high water table, water was easily accessible through a hand-dug well.

To install our well, we simply dug down about six feet with a post-hole digger. We easily dug through the fertile, black topsoil, into a layer of clay, then into a layer of sand and gravel. Once we hit the sand and gravel, the water began to seep into our hole.

It was at this level we drove a sand point on the end of a ten foot length of pipe, down an additional four feet. On the top end of this pipe, after filling in the hole with the dirt we removed, we placed a cistern pump, sometimes called a "pitcher" pump. It was a smaller version of those old-style, "pump-handle" pumps made famous back in the old days before electricity ran electric pumps.

We used this cistern pump to draw water out of the ground to water the garden. The only trouble was this pump needed to be "primed" before each use. To prime the pump was no big deal. All you needed to do was to pour about a quart of water down the throat of the pump to lubricate the pump "leather."

Then you began with short, quick strokes on the pump to draw out the air and raise the water level up from the depths of the well. Once those short strokes pulled all the air out of the pipe and you had constant contact with the water, you could start with the long strokes and the water would gush freely with every stroke.

However, when you were done, your last task was to fill the gallon bucket which sat next to the pump. This gallon bucket was filled to provide the water for the next user so they had something to prime the pump. And if that gallon bucket was left empty or if that water was not replaced, there was a lot of complaining going around!

Leaving some water for the next user was the most important aspect of watering the garden from the pump. It gave the next user a little water to prime the pump for their use, and if you failed to replace that water, then it was the ultimate insult to the next person who needed water to prime the pump for their usage. These pumps always needed a little water to get the pump primed at the beginning, and it was the responsibility of the previous user to leave a bucket of water for the next user.

My success in keeping honeybees means nothing to me unless I can help to pass along this information. I think of my experience, as I've noted it in this manuscript, as a bucket of water with which you can prime your own pump. I view all of our collective experiences as buckets of water beside our respective pumps that can be used by others who come along to prime their pumps so they may draw this same water freely.

There will always be those persons who want to drink all the water from the bucket. There are those who never think about the next person needing the water to prime the pump. But remember the well is deep and the water is plentiful. Why shouldn't the thirst of others be fulfilled? It is my hope that this manuscript gives you sufficient water to prime your pump, but it is also my request that you leave a bucket next to your well for the next person.

Though plain and ordinary, the power of this manuscript lies in the information that you take from it and put into practice. What you take and make happen in your bee yard will change your life. The value of this manuscript is in the implementation.

Remember what Arnold Glasgow said, "An idea not coupled with action will never get any bigger than the brain cell it occupied."

The landscape of beekeeping is constantly changing, and this manuscript is but one thought in a larger series I've authored that seeks to address the challenges facing modern beekeepers. And this series is written from, and for, the perspective of the beekeeper. I'm presuming you already know much of the information regarding bee biology and hive management.

You can view most of my books at my web site:

www.grantgillard.weebly.com

Then click on the tab: "My Books"

This manuscript is not the last word by any stretch of the imagination, but hopefully, it will get you thinking in a new direction. More than anything else, I hope you begin to take your beekeeping enterprise seriously. Beekeeping has a potential to become a rather profitable enterprise. Twenty-five hives can be the well from which you draw enough honey to merit a marketing plan. Even one hive can be profitable, but with twenty-five hives, you start entering a level where it seems to make beekeeping worth the time (and the stings)

Even in my own life, I see so many missed opportunities and lost benefits to keeping bees, and yet a large, though untapped potential seems to abound just beyond the reach of so many beekeepers. I hope this manuscript helps you to tap into that potential.

I love what is attributed to Albert Einstein. He is quoted as saying, "We can't solve problems by using the same kind of thinking we used when we created them."

R. Buckminster Fuller added,

"I am enthusiastic over humanity's extraordinary and sometimes very timely ingenuities. If you are in a shipwreck and all the boats are gone, a piano top buoyant enough to keep you afloat may come along and make a fortuitous life preserver. This is not to say, though, that the best way to design a life preserver is in the form of a piano top. I think we are clinging to a great many piano tops in accepting yesterday's fortuitous contrivings as constituting the only means for solving a given problem."

There are days I wake up and I can't wait to discover what new solutions await yesterday's problems. As the hymn writer put it, "Morning by morning new mercies I see." And as one of my church elders is fond of saying, "There has just got to be a way to solve this problem. We just haven't found it yet."

Preface

This manuscript is written for the beekeeper who is hoping to grow to around twenty-five hives, or for the beekeeper who is at the twenty-five hive level and is struggling a little bit to find the available time to effectively manage bees on this level. There is nothing magical about keeping twenty-five hives of bees other than the reality that things begin to change when you reach this level. Twenty-five hives begin to ask you to take your commitment seriously, that these bees now occupy a higher priority in your life.

I also write for the person who is not, and may never, keep enough hives to justify their hobby/sideline as a full-time endeavor with all the aspects of making their operations financially profitable. I really want every beekeeper to find that elusive enjoyment that I found keeping bees, and if the opportunity presents itself, to make a little money along the way.

I hope you're the kind of person who wants to tap into the wonderful potential so many beekeepers miss. This potential, at first blush, is often perceived as a financial potential, and the financial return is there. And there is no doubt in my mind you can make substantial amounts of money keeping honeybees. But there is also a level of satisfaction, meaning, purpose and enjoyment so many beekeepers miss. I hope this book helps you reach that level of personal satisfaction, even if you don't keep but a few hives of bees.

I've also written for the person who would like to grow beyond twenty-five hives, eventually up to one-hundred hives, but recognizes the need to master this twenty-five level first. What follows is what I learned as I started out in Glenville, Minnesota with twenty hives, then after moving to a new part of the country, started over again with four hives, then five, then seven up to twelve, to thirty, to sixty and then upwards (at the time of this writing) to one hundred and fifty hives, plus a bunch of nucs where I raised my own queens and made splits. When asked, I now simply tell people I have "around 200" hives.

You may not want to get this big, and that's okay. We each must choose our level of beekeeping, keeping in mind our other factors such as age and health, family and work obligations, desire (what I like to call the "hunger factor"), your passion for keeping bees, financial stability, land availability, spousal approval, etc., etc., etc. Only then can you really decide how many hives to keep and what level of intensity is right for you.

This manuscript is written with the idea of working up to twenty-five hives. Whether you continue to expand beyond that level is up to you. There are things I learned on the way to twenty-five hives that served me well as I went on up to one-hundred. Then there are a bunch of new things I had to learn at that level.

As you read this manuscript, you will find some duplication of ideas which may have been mentioned in an earlier chapter. I did this because so many things are interrelated in a beekeeping enterprise. You will definitely find ideas repeated, cross-referenced, paraphrased and reiterated, and this was done with a certain degree of intentionality on my part.

For example, the cost of bees is covered in the chapter on finances as well as a separate chapter on expansion. Time management thoughts are also included in a chapter by that same title, as well as in the chapter on record keeping.

As ideas repeat, you may think I've lost my mind (as many of my neighbors wonder), and some days I would not argue that conclusion, but many ideas are repeated because they fit a different context or I come at the same idea from a different perspective because the situation changes or the circumstances are different.

Beekeeping is like a puzzle with many pieces that interlock with other pieces, which in turn, interlock with other pieces. And remember that every piece in the jig-saw puzzles touch four other pieces. Yes, there will be some things that get mentioned over and over again. No, I have not lost my mind! I did it with some intention, and as with most people, sometimes being redundant helps drive home the point of the discussion.

There is nothing really magical about twenty-five hives. It is, however, a level in which things will begin to change in terms of your time commitment to the bees. Time will be your most precious commodity. You will also notice a change in the management of your resources (mostly time and energy) but also your marketing opportunities.

You will also detect a change in your spouse's attitude. My wife lovingly refers to my bees as my "hobby on steroids." My son refers to my bees as "that other family that you spend time with." But it's funny how he seems to enjoy the money from the sale of the honey brought in by "that other family."

You will require a necessary shift in the marketing of your honey. Even if you just want to give your honey away, something has to be done with it. Twenty-five hives produces quite a bit of honey. You will probably need to think about what you need to do to store the honey (I still use five-gallon buckets), and how you'll work with it when a five-gallon bucket granulates.

And while five-gallon buckets seem to be a little tedious, I can manage a dozen five-gallon buckets better than one fifty-five gallon drum. To each their own way, however! There are as many different ways to do things as there are beekeepers.

With twenty-five hives you will find the need to be more efficient. And when you go into a bee yard to feed or medicate or put supers on, your approach changes as well. You will begin to work your hives in "batches" or switch your manipulations to a "systems" approach. Both of those words simply mean that you will find greater productivity of your time when you do one thing to all your hives, all at once. Then you shift to the next thing to do, and you do that next chore to all your hives on the following trip.

As an example, I find it becomes more expedient to do the same thing (or few things once the hive is open) to all the hives in that one trip. It is a more efficient use of my time and energy. I find that if I need to do six things, and if I only do those six things to one-third of the hives in the yard, then the needs of those other two-thirds are always hanging over my head. To do one or two things to all the hives, as time allows, yields a greater feeling of an accomplishment.

Either way, you still need to plan another day in the bee yard, but with a systems approach, you take care of the most important item that all the hives need. And with all my hives, there are tasks that need to be done NOW, and all the hives need it done right now.

In addition, working with fewer tasks forced me to prioritize my to-do list. There are some things that are more important, and I feel better about my beekeeping job if I get those most important things done to all the hives at once. By doing the same thing, or only a few selected things, and do them to all the hives in that trip, I avoid the feeling that something is still hanging over me. And one thing I've learned along the way is that your work is never done. There is always something that needs to be done another day.

Of course, using this systems approach likely means another trip to bee yard on another day, but I'm never sure when that other day might be. But I will sense a greater satisfaction if that prioritized task is off my list. One thing you will learn with twenty-five hives of bees, especially if you have them spread out in two or three different locations, is how much time certain tasks will take and how much time you can afford to give to the more important tasks.

You will also learn **timing** is everything. This is especially true with swarm prevention, supering, mite control, raising your own queens, and, well, just about everything when it comes to bees! Timing is everything. There are selected windows of time during the season when certain tasks absolutely must get done.

And there are times I can only do the things that the weather allows. Opening the hives is best done when the days are mild and sunny. If all I have to do is change feeders or put in entrance reducers, that chore can be done on a cooler day. The old expression of "making hay while the sun shines" also applies to beekeepers. Do what you have to do when the weather allows; then do what can be done when the weather is not so cooperative on those other days.

And for heaven's sake, do not put off today what you **THINK** you can do tomorrow. I can't begin to tell you how I squandered a sunny day thinking I could take care of those other things the next day. The next day comes around and I finish up my office work. I go home and change my clothes. I organize my van with all my tools.

Then I drive out the bee yard, and after I open a few hives a horrendous thunder storm blows up and I'm forced to go home. And some of my bee yards are in low-lying areas and swampy places where the ground has to dry out for three days before I can return after a good rain. Never put off today what you **THINK** you can do tomorrow. Tomorrow is not guaranteed to anyone.

How do we approach this idea of keeping twenty-five hives of bees? Let's look at the three major categories of beekeepers, the hobbyist, the sideliner and the commercial beekeeper.

Traditionally, the industry calls small beekeepers "hobbyists." For the hobbyist, beekeeping is fun, their time commitment may be rather non-committal, limited to sunny days on the weekend or when they feel like it, and any income may be purely coincidental and incidental. As a hobbyist, you may not be looking for any financial return.

If any income is produced, it is likely overshadowed by the costs and your labor. Your commitment to the bees may be more relaxed if it's just a hobby. You get work done when you can, and if you miss doing something this week, next week is still fine. With a few hives, you also devote more time per hive, noting the changes and micro-managing the bees.

As one moves up the scale to twenty-five hives, the hobbyist becomes more involved and the bees are more than just a passing fancy. The exact criteria are kind of loose, but around twenty-five hives you move into that realm of the sideliner beekeeper, sometimes called a "small scale" beekeeper.

At this sideliner level, the finances become sustainable, more than likely moving to a break-even and potentially profitable level. At twenty-five hives, it's not expected that you'll have to hire any seasonal labor, but you'll find the time commitment becomes more serious, and you'll begin to treat your bees with increasing earnestness. You recognize that decisions have consequences, and some of these decisions will greatly affect your honey production. You will find yourself facing specific windows of time in the season when certain tasks must be done. Timing is a critical aspect of keeping bees, and with twenty-five hives, and more time needed to do these tasks, timing becomes more critical and the consequences more grave.

Yet beekeepers with twenty-five hives are definitely not commercial beekeepers, the next level up from sideliner. Commercial beekeepers make a living from their bees; their income (hopefully) exceeds the expenses. In my mind, commercial beekeepers require a large amount of mechanization, lots of heavy equipment and buildings dedicated to their craft. They frequently have to hire seasonal labor.

One commercial beekeeper told me he grossed over $450,000 but his profit was only $15,000 before taxes. Hired labor, workmen's compensation, benefits, higher fuel costs, increased truck repairs all nibbled away at his gross income.

What separates the commercial beekeeper from the sideliner is not always fast and true. Even the hobbyist can hire seasonal labor, but for the commercial beekeeper, it is probably viewed as a necessary expense. The level of commitment for a commercial beekeeper is likely driven by finances rather than by pure enjoyment. And a commercial beekeeper might very well enjoy keeping bees on this level. Be careful not to get too tight in your expectations as we talk about these different categories of beekeepers.

I like to think of the commercial beekeeper as the one who says, "This is what I do for a living. I need to make a profit keeping honeybees." However, even the twenty-five hive sideliner beekeeper is still likely producing a fairly significant stream of income and may look like a miniaturized version of a commercial beekeeper. But the sideliner can sit on his honey all winter long where the commercial beekeeper likely needs to be moving his product.

Somewhere along the way to twenty-five hives, one may need to start considering the full scope of the implications of business accounting practices, including depreciation and tax liabilities.

When you begin approaching twenty-five hives, you begin to look for a dedicated building, or you probably begin to set aside a corner of the garage or basement for this expanded hobby. But this level of intensity doesn't necessarily mean you are a commercial beekeeper. Even a hobbyist can desire to make a profit.

Traditionally, hobbyists are those beekeepers who have under twenty-five hives. This level of twenty-five hives is really pretty arbitrary. But I will also tell you there is a big difference between the beekeeper with four hives and the one who has twelve hives.

There is also a big difference between twelve and twenty-five hives. There is no difference when a beekeeper moves from twenty-four hives to that twenty-fifth hive. The numbers have to be seen with a certain subjective arbitrariness.

Beekeeping with twenty-five hives also begins to compete with your time and energy, family obligations, and unless you are retired, your work and your job. Most beekeepers I know are older persons, mostly men, and working twenty-five hives is physically demanding work. Deeps, or brood boxes, full of honey are heavy. Medium supers full of honey are also heavy, but not as much.

One older beekeeper I know pulls each frame of honey out of the hive and places it in an empty super on his wheel barrow. Then, as he pushes the wheel barrow to the pick-up truck, he lifts one frame at a time into the empty super on the pick-up bed.

This is very time consuming. However, he lacks the physical strength to carry full supers of honey, even mediums or shallows. He trades time for physical strength. He also manages to care for thirty hives, which he still considers to be "just a hobby."

And this may be something he does all day long, technically, "full-time," even though the income generated is not what a younger man or woman could make working the honeybees full-time. Again, take these categories with a grain of salt. We just cannot be that strict in our interpretation.

If you have over three hundred hives the industry considers you to be a commercial beekeeper. And likewise, there are commercial beekeepers with thousands of hives and that's a different ballgame than the beekeeper with three hundred hives, except both fall into this arbitrary category of being designated as "commercial."

And oddly enough, with the increased costs of the larger operation, both may have the same net profit at the end of the season. There is more to life than being the biggest beekeeper in the county.

To me, the idea of being a commercial beekeeper is to make a living at beekeeping. It is your vocation. It's what you do to put a roof over your head and groceries on the table. Beekeeping is meant to pay the bills. It is your primary purpose in life. And yet, like most agricultural endeavors in this day and age, most farmers require a large degree of "off-farm" income to make their livelihood sustainable.

The commercial beekeeper will probably, but not necessarily, sell most of his honey in "bulk," most likely fifty-five gallon drums. He, or she, accepts a wholesale price and likely sells to someone who "packs" the honey and sells wholesale to a retail outlet.

Hobby level beekeepers, on the other hand, will sell largely "retail." They have the luxury of time to bottle what they produce and can accept a higher price per pound of honey to reflect the increased labor that goes into pouring their jars and bottles.

Commercial beekeepers are like large farmers while hobby beekeepers are like large gardeners. Both produce a crop, but the smaller producer has greater options to make more money, but they also have more time to selectively market their crop for a higher income. For the large commercial beekeeper, he or she trades the larger volume of honey for a smaller price per pound (and less labor per pound of honey).

The in-between group, the one who keeps twenty-six hives upwards to two hundred and ninety-nine hives, is traditionally called a sideliner. You are more than a hobbyist, but you don't generate enough income to really consider your income-producing hobby a commercial enterprise. You generate income, but not at a level to tell your boss, or your spouse, or your banker that you're ready to quit your day job and keep bees as your full-time vocation.

But with twenty-five hives, you also find your bees are taking more of your spare time and a greater portion of your passion than when you only had four hives. And I'll also bet you have other things going on in your life and you're not even thinking how to manage three hundred hives.

Being a sideliner is a lot my like my son who is living in that in-between age of adolescence, caught between childhood and adulthood. He, at fifteen years of age, is no longer a child, but he has not yet been granted the full scope of adult responsibilities by our society. He cannot legally drive, drink or vote. Yet as an astute young man he is very aware of many of our social issues, both nationally and locally, and he wishes to participate. Participation is part of the great American democracy. He has great dreams and ideals, yet because he is not of proper age, he still requires his older sister to take him and his friends to the mall.

Society doesn't really know what to do with ambitious young people who have yet to reach the age of majority. They are definitely not a child, but not yet quite an adult. And what do you do with a young person of thirty years of age who is really immature? Does chronological age really have anything to do with maturity?

And so it is with many beekeepers who fall into this level of keeping twenty-five hives of bees. These beekeepers are much more than a hobbyist, yet they are not taken seriously as if their livelihood depended on the bees. And for most sideliners, they really depend on other sources of income though their beekeeping operation may be very lucrative and surprisingly profitable.

This is the middle ground of being what the industry calls a sideliner beekeeper. You are no longer a hobbyist, yet the industry doesn't quite take you seriously enough to think of you as a commercial beekeeper. It's still something you do in addition to your "real" job. And because so much of your income is not really income in the sense of providing for your daily bread, it is likely plowed back into the on-going endeavor of keeping bees or saved for a family vacation.

For my own personal definitions, I view a hobbyist beekeeper as one who spends money on his bees with no intent of getting a financial return. He or she may get a return, but irrespective of the number of hives the hobbyist keeps, a financial return is not expected and it is likely that his hobby ends up costing more money than it generates. This person keeps bees for the sheer pleasure they bring. Joy is their currency. Keeping bees is a diversion from work or something to do on the weekends.

A commercial beekeeper is one who depends on a positive net income from his bees. His or her bees may cost money, as does any business, and require annual investments of time and money, but in the end, there will be a positive cash flow that allows him to feed his family or expand the business. For this person, they keep bees for the money (and no one EVER needs to apologize for making money from keeping bees). Cash is their currency. Bees are this person's work.

The sideliner, in my opinion, is one who runs a sustainable beekeeping enterprise. It will hopefully still be fun and enjoyable, but the expectations are not so high as to make this "hobby-on-steroids" a source of a livable wage. No doubt, like the hobbyist and the commercial beekeeper, sideliners will be spending money and investing financial resources into the enterprise, but their hope is to break even, maybe even make some money so the enterprise is sustainable financially.

The likelihood of producing a positive net income as a sideliner is much greater than a hobbyist, yet it would not necessarily rival that of a commercial beekeeper in terms of gross receipts. I do, however, believe a sideliner's net profit is greater because they have increased options to market their honey at higher prices, prices which reflect their own increased labor costs. We'll have a later chapter devoted to marketing so we'll save most of this discussion for that time.

So for our discussions that follow, think of a hobby level beekeeper as one who keeps a few hives up to around twenty-fives. Think of the commercial operator as one who keeps over three-hundred hives and makes a living from his bees. And those in that "mushy-middle" of twenty-six up to two-hundred and ninety-nine are considered as the sideliners, the passionate ones who have the dedication to take their hobby to the next level and make some money.

This is the group who I write for, and this manuscript is my journey up to twenty-five hives. The lessons I learned as I expanded to this point, served me well as I expanded to my present level of "around" two hundred hives (some of them are over-wintered nucs).

These definitions of hobbyist, sideliner and commercial beekeepers are not hard and fast, but it is my intent and assumption that as you read this manuscript, you are likely a hobbyist looking to expand, or perhaps reverse the annual financial drain and make this hobby a sustainable enterprise.

For some of you, that dream of profitability may be your spouse's hope as well. Or you may be the beekeeper with twenty-five hives or so and you're looking to discover and master the efficiencies to expand further. You like the money that is coming in and you know you can do better.

I write this manuscript as one who has made that journey. This is my bucket at the side of the well to prime your own pump. There is a great deal of money to be made in keeping bees, but there is a large degree of time, energy and commitment that must be invested before you start raking in all that money. I hope this manuscript helps you navigate and negotiate your journey into this wonderful endeavor we call beekeeping.

Beekeeping with Twenty-five Hives

Background and Introduction

As I sit down to revise write this manuscript, it is the winter of 2012-2013. Seven years has past since I wrote the original manuscript in that winter of 2005 – 2006. I eagerly await the coming spring, and I confess I'm a little nervous. I think I was nervous back in 2006, as well.

I have already been out to see my hives on some of the warmer days of January, and the bees are looking good, at least from my external observations. This is a relief as we had some horribly, bitter cold days in December. Our summer was one of drought, and the long, gentle fall was warm with the bees active and eagerly consuming their stored honey. My hives feel light, and I'm nervous.

I went into this winter with 179 hives and about two dozen 6-frame nucs (yeah, close to 200, give or take). My nucs look good as I walk through the bee yards. These are splits I made with my summer-raised queens from my survivor stock. Some of the hives, however, are a different story.

I can count about five hives that have not survived the winter—so far. These hives are the smaller hives that should have been combined with another smaller hive. Most beekeepers believe in an old adage of "taking your losses in the fall, making your increases in the spring."

This means combining your weaker hives in the fall, taking a loss on paper in the physical number of hives you carry through the winter. Then, in the spring, in a manner of swarm prevention, you can order some queens and make splits.

But there are many beekeepers like me who resist the intelligence of combining hives. We stubbornly refuse to follow the wisdom of that time-tested advice. And somewhere along the way, you would think I would learn. Because the clusters are smaller, they just cannot generate enough heat to keep the hive warm enough to survive. In addition to small clusters, I like to keep an open bottom on the screen bottom boards (SBB) to improve ventilation.

But more and more, I'm questioning if that is a realistic practice for all winter long in Southeast Missouri. The flip side, however, is the high humidity in our area, even during the winter. We suffer from a "damp cold," nothing like the drier, and more tolerable freezing temperatures I remember from my childhood in Minnesota.

As I sit down to put some thoughts on paper, I've taken a few moments to reflect on how I came to this place of keeping around 200 hives. I have hopes and goals of growing to 350 hives for next winter. I've spread my hives over multiple locations. I catch feral swarms and raise my own queens. I make most of my own equipment in my garage from scrap lumber I pick up from a variety of sources.

However, with more and more bees, and selling more and more honey, time is beginning to run short. I find I am buying more and more equipment, ready to assemble...then I find I have to hire the neighbor kid to put it together and paint.

I sell honey both retail and wholesale, mostly in jars and bottles, in my driveway with an "honor box" and seasonally at the local farmers' markets. Lately I've cracked into the locally-owned, retail grocery stores where I sell my honey at a discounted "wholesale" price. One year my income from the honey paid for a seven-day cruise for my wife. She even let me come along. Bees are a big part of my life. But it has not always been so. This "hobby on steroids," as my wife likes to call it, has grown little by little every year into a very profitable business.

I've kept bees off and on for around 30+ years, ever since my college graduation from Iowa State University in 1981. Every time my family has made a move or I've changed vocations, or when I sought to further my education, the beekeeping endeavors were interrupted. I never sold my equipment (which would be self-defeating), but the bees died from neglect and my absence.

So I put the equipment away in storage or hauled it along to the next location. I never gave up thinking about the bees, even though during some of those times, I didn't actually have bees. Then somewhere in this fallow gap of not having bees, I quit fighting that overwhelming urge and I got bees. For me, it's like a sickness that cannot be cured. I just have to have a few hives of bees around.

In those fallow times, I always knew in my heart that I would get bees again. I just needed the time and the place. This is what I believe really makes a person a beekeeper: the intense desire, even passion, to pursue the elusive perfection of keeping bees.

And it happens on different levels. Keeping bees may be something you do for fun or enjoyment. You may want bees to pollinate the garden or you have dreams of making a little money along the way.

But in your heart, you know you are a beekeeper. It is a calling, and NOT keeping bees is harder than the actual work of keeping them. You just have to keep bees. You are a beekeeper, a keeper of the bees. It's in your blood that circulates with every beat of your heart.

The old-timers used to call it, "bee fever." To them, it was this itch that could not be scratched without keeping some bees in the backyard. And even if something comes along to wipe you out, even when the days are hot or drought stalls the nectar flow, the frustrations are only overcome by the presence of bees in those boxes.

It's like you were meant to keep bees. Call it fate; call it karma. It is a calling. It is your passion. It is your destiny. And those who are called to be a beekeeper must keep bees. There is no rest until you have those little ladies in the box and a jar of your own honey on the table.

My initial foray into beekeeping came after my college graduation where I bought enough bees and boxes/frames for 20 hives. My full intent was to be a commercial beekeeper, though at that time, beekeeping would be but one of several enterprises on the family farm. I loved the idea of being diversified, so along with other farming ventures, I also kept honeybees.

But then, after three years, my plans changed. At the time of this transition, I put the hive bodies in the barn, went on to graduate school, got married, had children, went to work, and basically became a productive member of society like everyone else.

For many years, I shelved my aspirations of being a beekeeper, but the thoughts, hopes and dreams never left me. And sooner or later, when the opportunity presented itself, I cleaned up my old equipment, ordered some packages, and the next thing I knew, I was back. I was once again a beekeeper.

Up until the last five or six years, beekeeping for me has always been more of a very part-time hobby as room for the hives and time to work them allowed. Moving and other interruptions, as well as the normal family obligations with my small children and other challenges, limited the number of hives I kept to four, which I mostly kept along the back fence line near my garden. But my heart was back on the family farm with twenty hives. My imagination was not satisfied with four hives. My quest for a challenge was not met with four hives. I didn't think I was pursuing the vocation of a beekeeper with just four hives (but don't let me disparage the small beekeeper. Even one hive makes you a legitimate beekeeper!).

My present situation grew out of those humble re-beginnings with four hives after an initial and somewhat futile attempt at twenty hives. I continued to keep a few bees as a hobby as time allowed. It was, in reality, more of a distraction, something to "mess with" after I came home from work. My wife worried about what the neighbors would think, how our young children would react, and if I had enough time for one more activity in my hectic, harried life.

In reality, I didn't have more time with three small children. But it's not what you **have** time for; it's what you **make** time for as decide what is your priority and mission in life. I could still be a good father, a loving husband and a dedicated beekeeper.

As the years went on, I kept increasing slowly, little by little. Someone called and they had a swarm on their rose bush. They knew I kept bees. Did I want them? (And what kind of question is that to ask of a beekeeper? Of course I wanted them!) That was one more hive.

Then another person had another swarm. I needed some more hive bodies. And I needed bottom boards and tops and frames and foundation. Every trip back home to Minnesota meant I was bringing back some of the equipment I had in storage. But then some things needed to be purchased. This meant I also needed more money. But with three young children, money was tight. But the bees from the swarms were free and so I made the move to expand.

I started cruising the back alleys of large retailers scalping scrap pallets out of the dumpsters to build my boxes. While it seems like this is a less-expensive way to go, it requires a lot more labor.

But at that time in my life, I had more time than money. So I kept an eye out for scrap lumber that I could convert into hive bodies. With a garage full of old, broken pallets, my wife was beginning to think I had lost my mind. At times, I wondered as well, but I had before me a vision of being a beekeeper with a positive stream of income. And I was looking for extra income to meet my growing family's expenses.

With more hives came increased amounts of honey. I stored my honey in 5-gallon buckets I got from the local bakery. They were free, and aspiring beekeepers are pretty good at playing the frugal card.

At first I gave my honey away as gifts and presents. I confess I was a little embarrassed charging my friends and relatives for my honey. Then I started selling it annually at a local "harvest" festival held every fall at the local apple orchard. Pretty soon the word spread and the demand for local honey was more than I could produce with five or six hives. So over the winter, I cobbled together some scrap lumber and built some more hives.

Initially, I tried to reinvent the wheel with what seemed to be innovative designs on an old idea. But more and more, I kept coming back to the conventional configuration of the Langstroth hive. I would always build a few more hives than I had bees, then I would order a couple of packages in the spring.

Then I'd get a swarm call. Soon I had twelve hives. My wife was getting nervous. Did we have room for twelve hives? Was this becoming an addiction or just a mild obsession?

Then doors started opening for me. I expanded my hives, in part because several local farmers requested bees on their property. These were not paid pollination situations, but rather some local farmers, basically some "good ol' boys" that remembered the old days of bee trees and wild honey. To them, it just felt good to have a few bees around the farm. They enjoyed watching them work, flying back and forth carrying nectar and pollen.

All they wanted was a couple of quarts of honey a year for "rent." I never charged them for any pollination. I got to keep all the honey the hives produced, and much of our agreement was the old-fashioned "gentlemen's handshake." In turn they gave me access to wonderful fields of flowers that yielded buckets and buckets of honey.

As the price of package bees kept going up (and back in those days, $30 for a package was outrageous!),

I turned to pheromone-baited swarm traps. I started catching feral swarms and the swarm calls started to multiply as word spread that I was a beekeeper. Then the newspaper did a small article spreading my notoriety. More calls came in, allowing me to retrieve more swarms.

Pretty soon I was at thirty-three hives, then sixty-four hives. And then the real question I faced became, "I just caught and hived that swarm, but it won't produce any honey this year, so is it a real hive when I sit down and tell someone the number of hives I work with?" And how about nucs and splits? Do they count when I number my hives?

One year I was planning on making nucs to sell, but I got a bad batch of southern-raised queens, poorly mated and they were hardly accepted. So I started raising my own queens and making late summer splits. Now I had more hives, or more correctly, nuc boxes.

Then came a rather remarkable year in which my job rewarded me with some traveling opportunities. I took some continuing education courses and I was away from home for about a month. It was that summer that the garden just got out of hand.

That summer we had ample rain, unusual for Southeast Missouri. Then, while I was away getting an education, the weeds exploded and the garden looked like a jungle. This was, in part, due to my domestic neglect as I traveled, but also a result of my annual organic fertilizer program. Every year I would I dump several loads of manure on my garden (inoculated with more weed seed). The garden got so bad that summer that even the neighbors complained.

My wife said I had a choice. Either I choose to garden and get rid of the bees or I keep the bees and I mow off the garden. My son was overjoyed! He had great visions of turning the garden into a football version of his personal "field of dreams." He encouraged me to dump the gardening and go for the bees! And yes, it was a very large garden and it fed my family very well. But it also took a lot of time, which I used to have before I escalated the number of hives I kept.

My twin hobbies of gardening and beekeeping were competing for my time and energy. And there is great truth in that you can only serve one master. Try to serve both masters and one will despise the other. And sometimes your spouse will despise the other one anyway.

But I wanted to do both. I thought I could do both. I tried to do both. But my protests went unheeded. My wife told me to choose. I chose the bees, but under protest. The garden got mowed off. Even the lawn mower protested under the choking growth to no avail. My lot was cast. I was a beekeeper. The garden was history. And I have come to realize that everything happens for a reason. The time I tried to put into the garden was now redirected into keeping bees, or I might more accurately say, MORE bees.

This is one of the unspoken aspects of keeping twenty-five hives of bees they never tell you about in all those informative articles in the wonderful bee magazines. We only have so much time, not just in a day, but also our lives are limited. Every day I feel time slipping away and my quest to do something noble with my life. But time is limited. So is your energy. So is your spouse's patience. I had to make a choice.

With my son overhearing the "conversation" my wife was having with me, my son began chanting, "Bees! Bees! Bees!" He loved the idea of my choice of bees. I made the choice to give up the garden and redirect my energies to the bees.

My son played "touch" football with the neighbors where tomatoes once yielded their bountiful harvest. He complained how the stump from the old peach trees messed up the sod, but soon it rotted away. He got his football field. I got my bees. My wife got her wish. I still miss my garden. But I just can't worry about what was lost; I give thanks for what's left. I have my bees.

As I reflect on my ascent to 100 hives, then on to my present level of 200 hives, everything came pretty naturally, logically and somewhat rapidly. Along the way, I can detect certain levels of beekeeping expertise that mandated changes in my perception and perspective. While not set in stone, there are levels of beekeeping that change your approach. Some levels force your approach to change; other levels encourage creative thinking.

My advice is to master one level before moving up to the next. Mistakes become amplified with more hives. The consequences of those mistakes (like swarming and mite infestations) also become more costly. If you have to buy all your inputs (like hive bodies and packages of bees) the consequences have huge implications if you don't manage them well.

I can see a definable level for the person who keeps two to four hives. These hives don't take much time, and there are times when it just seemed like a lot of work to get the smoker going for such a brief time of working with the bees.

But looking at the hives, opening them up, analyzing frame by frame and finding the queen was very relaxing for me. I enjoyed those days of four hives. You get to give them a lot of TLC and attention...sometimes opening the hives too much.

But when you broach a level with a dozen hives, your time commitment and interest changes. You begin to buy larger purchases, which of course, take more money. I began to wonder if it is easier to buy the hive bodies than to cut them out of wood from the pallets I picked up from the dumpster at the home-improvement store. You run out of room in the garage for your empty hive bodies and the scrap pallets now sit outside (much to my wife's consternation).

People begin to actually call you a beekeeper. They ask you for honey, and at this point, they balk at the idea of paying you for honey, or at least, paying a respectable amount that is close to the going retail price of honey. They still treat you like a hobbyist who just keeps bees for fun as if there was no investment in the equipment. And at this point, much of your investment is personal.

As you expand from twelve hives upward to twenty or twenty-five hives, you will begin to find things changing. You are probably looking for a new place to expand, or perhaps, as in my case, people come to you and ask if you want to put bees on their property. And since it isn't really economical to drive six miles to care for two hives, you negotiate and put eight hives on their farm. Fields seem to open before you. And at twenty-five hives, you are either a serious hobbyist, or perhaps in reality, a small-time, semi-commercial beekeeper. In essence, you are the serious sideliner and your bees are important to you. Your motives now change from tickles and giggles to marketing and profits.

And I'll say it again: never apologize for making money at this incredible hobby of beekeeping!

I found myself, as I was moving from twelve upwards to thirty-three hives, as needing to be more efficient, better organized and more informed as a beekeeper. Mites were the biggest problem, and resistance to chemicals was beginning to rise to the surface of our concern. I wanted to go a more natural route. Chemicals were costly, but natural methods took more labor, more time and a closer level of monitoring your hives. It was not uncommon to have hives die out as I resisted becoming a "chemical" beekeeper.

I also began to recognize my need to wear more "hats" and become a better beekeeper, a more efficient producer and a more aggressive marketer.

At this level of twenty-five hives, you need to start developing new markets for your honey. At this level, your capital investment begins to grow and you're likely looking for a financial return...as might your spouse! Because of the limits of time, you are likely to shift to buying your woodware instead of scalping scrap pallets. Profits would be nice, but even a break-even sustainability would be most welcome.

When I was climbing through this level, I saw my purchased inputs as an investment that might not pay off for a couple more years. But it is not uncommon to invest $500 today and have $1000 to show for it in two years. Now that's a better return than you can get at the bank, and it's more fun!

Your marketing will need to become a bit more professional. Putting honey in old mayonnaise jars and limed-up canning jars isn't quite good enough, and not everyone likes to buy that much honey at a time (fearing it will "go to sugar"). At this point I started to look for smaller squeeze bottles and bears. These cost money.

You probably need to start looking closer at designing your own unique label and the kitchen in the house is no longer the best place to extract honey (unless your wife is away for the entire weekend). The time commitment to get away from your job and slip out of family obligations is also harder to schedule. The weather is the hardest to schedule. Working the bees, well, it becomes work. It takes a different level of commitment.

The number one rule I've discovered when it comes to managing twenty-five hives is that ***beekeeping at this level is not for procrastinators.*** If you only have four hives, and they swarm because you were doing other things, you get discouraged but you still survive.

If three of those four die out, buying replacement packages again in the spring is something you can easily live with. If you don't treat for mites on time or fail to get the supers on to catch the honey flow, the consequences of your actions are easily overcome. After all, keeping four hives is just a hobby.

But at twenty-five hives, your hobby must become a greater priority in your life. At this level, most beekeepers find they don't have the time, the motivation, the perseverance, the discipline, the energy, the interest, or their loved ones begin to resent the time their hobby takes away from the family time. (My attempts have been to try and get the kids involved, but I've not been successful).

Twenty-five hives seems to make or break a beekeeper. Either they move on up beyond twenty-five hives, as I did, or they drop back to four really productive hives as a hobby that becomes something like a family pet. A few beekeepers will quit all together and sell their equipment. Some beekeepers will put everything in the shed, taking a break until they "find" the time to "someday" get back into their hobby.

But as you expand, you'll find it's not always about the time. It's also about energy, devotion, commitment and a strangely wonderful character that no one else can understand: ***passion***. Sometimes I wonder if beekeepers are made or are they born to keep bees. The most successful beekeepers I know have passion about their bees and pride in the honey they produce.

Expanding from twenty-five to a hundred hives is easy if you can master the twenty-five hive level. Keeping bees in one hundred hives is a lot like keeping four units of twenty-five bees. You begin to streamline your processes and look for efficiencies and economies of scale. I used to find the need to drive to a bee yard and take care of all the hives that trip, and then I find I didn't bring enough of whatever it is I need that day. You soon learn. Necessity becomes the mother of inventiveness. Experience helps you to become efficient.

At twenty-five hives you want to universalize your equipment, say moving to a standard size of mediums instead of a mix of mediums and shallow supers. You may want to use mediums for everything, brood and honey. Your personal interest and time spent on each individual hive decreases because you have more hives to visit. And you notice more income. Your hobby begins to bring in more money than it costs.

As you move to twenty-five hives, you'll also notice some elements of beekeeping take on a new priority. You'll find, or even discover, "niches" of special interest. In my ascent to one hundred hives, I started producing more comb honey. I sell a few queens and a handful of nucs, but most of these projects are for my own consumption. Yet there are some beekeepers who make a nice profit raising queens and selling nucs.

In order to diversity and maximize profits, I want to develop other products using wax and propolis. Presently, I sell a honey and beeswax, plain lye soap at the farmer's markets, but the "potions and lotions" venue is still wide open. My wife is taking a larger role in marketing, yielding my time to production. I find myself settling into a niche other than just keeping bees (though if keeping the bees is what you wanted to do, then letting a spouse or child market your products is just fine).

Perhaps you only have four hives but wonder what it would take to "get serious" about keeping bees. You may dream about the income potential or the possible enjoyment of keeping more bees. More bees will mean more work. But I remember an old expression that says, ***"Those who enjoy what they do never have to go to work."*** Yes, bees will require more labor, but it doesn't have to be work. It's never work if you really enjoy what you are doing.

Maybe you are presently at twenty-five hives and you're having a hard time getting away from work to care for your bees to prevent swarming, treat for mites, get the supers on, or harvest all that honey. Twenty-five hives seems to be a significant plateau.

You may not want to go beyond this level. You may wonder if you even want to get this "serious" about your bees in the first place. Your spouse or family may wonder why you want to get involved in a hobby at this level. They may not want you to get that involved as you're gone too much of the time. The decision is not yours alone, but you're the one who's going to have to make it. I hope to present enough of what I know and what I've experienced to help you make that decision with a degree of integrity to your own personal situation.

At two hundred hives, keeping bees is still fun for me, but it is also more work and my time is always scarce. The weather is seldom cooperative. As the hobbyist can say, "Well the weather is a little overcast today, so I'll not worry about working with my bees as they're going to be a little testy today." At twenty-five hives, you'll find there are some days you have to take care of the bees irrespective of their weather-related disposition.

I've had to become more efficient at my "real" work as well as in the bee yard. One hundred hives has made a better beekeeper out of me, but it's because I've made numerous mistakes and stupid assumptions along the way. I also learned to manage my time more effectively and juggle my family and work responsibilities better, but this will always be a challenge, and it probably always will.

Keeping four hives is one thing; keeping twelve is different; keeping twenty-five hives requires a whole different philosophy and dedication. It will also give you a whole new education. I'm beginning to appreciate the time that one hundred hives required, which set me up for where I am today. I also like the money that these hives generate for me. So does my wife. When my wife and children began to see the special things the bees provided for them from the sales of honey, they really started to encourage my hobby.

I highly recommend keeping your family's support through your expansion process. Still, the snakes, ticks, chiggers and poison ivy, not to mention the stings, kept my children from fully embracing my hobby.

Whether you want to grow to twenty-five hives, or even if you're at twenty-five hives trying to figure it out, or if you think you want to move upward beyond twenty-five hives, this manuscript is for you. Come along with me on my journey and we'll learn together.

My intent is not to have the last word or even show you how much I know. See what I've done. Challenge my assumptions and conclusions. Take my education in the school of hard-knocks and bee stings and climb the learning curve. I've left you a bucket by the side of the well to prime your pump.

I wish you the best of luck, but remember that luck is nothing more than experience and preparation meeting opportunity. And preparation is really about passion. Luck is also what's leftover after you've already given 100% to your efforts.

Beekeeping with Twenty-five Hives

Chapter One:

Where do you want to go?

When I travel to distant parts of the country, I prefer to drive. I prefer to drive mostly because I hate flying. I hate flying because I don't have a car at my disposal when the plane lands (unless, of course, I spring for a rental which has become increasingly expensive these past years). Without a car, I'm dependent upon other means of transportation, which often isn't that dependable. Plus, I hate the wait at the airport when you need to arrive two hours before your flight departs.

I despise the long-term parking where I leave my car because parking is outrageously expensive, and then I have to wait for the shuttle service. And if you've ever had to wait for a shuttle service, you begin to worry about reaching your gate on time. Using long-term parking, and the shuttle service, I plan on arriving at this parking lot three hours before my flight takes off. Then I start thinking how far I could drive in those three hours.

I also hate to fly because I find the security checks to be a huge bottleneck (and each day the security becomes more rigorous and ridiculous—and have you noticed how most of these airline security people seem to despise their jobs?). This is especially true when they make you take off your shoes to enter the metal detector. They are so impatient. And how come I never get frisked by the pretty TSA agent? I always get the curmudgeonly old man that reminds me of my uncle Charlie.

It's a hassle to fly. Then I always seem to be seated next to some chatty person who requires a constant interjection of small talk. I prefer to read when I fly. If I have to fly, and you're seated next to me, just leave me alone. It will make your flight, and mine, that much more enjoyable.

On one of my continuing education trips, I flew to Atlanta and got into a taxi at the airport. One good thing about airports is that they attract taxi cabs like honeybees to hummingbird feeders. There is always one waiting for you and I find them to be a cheap alternative to a rental car. But the downside is I'm usually stranded when I reach my destination within the city.

"Where to?" the cab driver inquired. I gave him the name of the school where the conference was being held. He asked, "Do you want to take the express way or take your chances with the downtown traffic?"

I asked, "What's the difference?"

He told me the express way was longer, but quicker. The downtown route was shorter, but may take more time depending upon the traffic. So I asked again, "What's the difference in terms of the fare?"

"About the same," he replied. I told him I would take my chances with the downtown traffic and off we went. I arrived in good time and the fare was not too bad. But secretly, I was still wishing that I had my own car.

The beauty of life is that it often offers alternatives. Alternatives hold different benefits and advantages. Sometimes it's just a wash either way, or as my mother used to say, "Six of one; half-dozen of the other." It doesn't make one way right and the other way wrong. You have choices.

When it comes to keeping bees, where do you want to go? How do you want to get there? Do you want to keep bees just for fun, or is there a profit motive behind your beekeeping? Do you want to invest your money in purchased packages and equipment, or do you want to make your own equipment, capture feral swarms in pheromone-lured traps and then requeen later with known genetics?

Do you want to wholesale your honey in five-gallon buckets or sell it in little squeeze bottles at the farmer's markets? Do you want to develop the markets and sell it yourself or do you want to wholesale it to another retailer, or even to another beekeeper who will put it in small bottles and sell it at the farmer's markets at their booth?

Where do you want to go? Until you answer this question, you may be spinning your wheels. You may find yourself headed in a wrong direction unless you know pretty much where you want to go. In every endeavor, it is vitally important to know your intended destination. You may change your mind along the way, but those who wander through life seldom get to where they hope to be. Every trip needs a map, but more importantly, you need a destination. Once the destination is set, you need to figure out how you want to get there, and rest assured, you'll find multiple routes and alternatives paths. The hard part is deciding which path is the best one for you.

As I put this manuscript together, it is my presumption that you want to keep bees. By the title, this manuscript is for those who are thinking about a destination of twenty-five hives, although many of the things I talk about fit the beekeeper with four hives as well as four-hundred hives. I gather that somewhere in your mind, you have thoughts of keeping a few more hives than you presently have, or perhaps like a lot of beekeepers, you want to expand to the point where you can increase your income over the expenses.

Profitability is a destination as well.

In my heart, in the unspoken recesses of my spirit, I have always wanted to keep bees. I have dreams of doing nothing but keeping bees making it the full-time endeavor of my labor, though with three teen-age children and a mortgage, my dream is not very practical, at least that's how my wife sees it. But at what level does my beekeeping sustain a lifestyle I've grown accustomed to?

When I started out keeping bees and quickly grew to twenty hives, there was no where else to go in my mind but up. But up to where? What level? I had great expectations to expand. As long as I could expand each year, and without incurring too many additional expenses, I wanted to move up. But then I moved residences and my plans changed. I lost my bees and put the hives in storage.

After my life settled down I got bees again, starting back up with four hives in the back yard. And with my life as it was in this new town with this new job, there was no practical means of expanding beyond this point of four hives. I had small children to raise and a new job to figure out. I didn't have any connections or locations to put my hives nor did I realize what markets existed to sell my honey. My dreams were temporarily deferred.

But I always felt in my heart that I was a large-scale beekeeper looking for a new out yard to expand. Never mind I had no idea of the work load, the time commitment, or even what constitutes a "large-scale" operation in the beekeeping world. I just had this gnawing hope to enlarge my operation.

This urging I felt in my heart is an element of keeping bees I call, "vision." Everyone needs to have a vision. A vision is your destination, and like my taxi cab ride from the Atlanta airport, there are several routes to choose from. Your vision shapes all the other factors in keeping bees. And maybe your vision is to keep four hives. If that's the case, then more power to you.

Your vision is your destination. Everything you do should move you one step closer to arriving at this destination. More than anything else, you need to decide, and decide for yourself, what your beekeeping vision is to become. What is your destination? And don't think too far out in the future. Sometimes you just need to think where you want to be in five years. Or for some people, they just want a one-year plan. Then when they reach that one-year plan, they can revise their vision for the next level. Or they can decide to stay at this level.

The most important thing is to have a vision, work with a destination in mind. Remember what the Bible says, that without a vision, the people perish (Proverbs 29:18 KJV).

Translating that into a context of keeping bees, if you are unsure of your destination, then you will likely spend a lot of time and energy doing things that will not contribute to your vision. If your vision is keeping bees, then you don't want to spend your time, energy and money on other pursuits. Not that those other pursuits aren't worthy of your time, but if they get in the way of what you want to do (i.e. keep bees), then you need to decide what is your real vision, what is your ultimate destination. This is where my wife did me a HUGE favor when she said the garden had to go. My vision was divided and she helped me to clarify where I wanted to go.

And sometimes your vision is put on hold and sometimes the doors open easily to make it a reality. In my vision of becoming a large-scale beekeeper, I really had no plan on which route to take. In a sense, I was perishing, wasting my energy and unable to move forward, or if I moved forward, I was unsure of the correct direction. I was still struggling to find a path, any path, that would lead me to expand. So with four hives, I never gave up my vision, but it was getting discouraging waiting. I'm not very good at being patient.

But amazingly, the proverbial brick walls began to yield. I believe everything has its own time, and that everything happens for a reason, in its own season. Soon opportunity knocked, the door to keeping more colonies opened a crack, then widened. Someone called who had a swarm, so I added a couple more hives. This started me on my way, like being able to take that first step. When I was at four hives, I always believe I wanted more hives, but it was always a "someday" hope: someday when I get more money; someday when I have more time; someday when the children are old enough to help me. Then someday came! Forward!

And you have to be ready when opportunity knocks. There is a belief that opportunity only knocks but once. I'm not sure I necessarily believe it as every day is filled with opportunities (some better than others). There is also a belief that "luck" is nothing more than opportunity meeting our preparation. If that belief holds true, then we need to be prepared. We need to take steps toward this destination.

While I never specifically set out to be a beekeeper with two hundred hives, here I am. It just seemed to happen, or more realistically, I let it happen, maybe subconsciously or unintentionally. While I never set 200 as a goal, I didn't do anything to prevent it from happening. I never turned down an opportunity to expand or retrieve another swarm even though I was fully conscious of having more bees than I had the time to look after. And with each swarm call, I had to build another box and assemble another ten frames. It was like I got in the taxi cab and told the driver, "Oh, I don't know. Let's just drive around a while." And then someday he drove past the school and I said, "Oh, look! I want to get out here."

So here I am. I didn't really plan to be here, but here I am. I always used that nebulous vision of a large beekeeping operation to guide my steps, but I had no specific goals. I had no specific targets. In retrospect, if I had specific goals, I would probably have reached this level quicker, and with more efficient results. Instead, I kind of drifted toward my present location, but I think in the back of my mind, I am where I am supposed to be.

While this 200 hive level was not my specific goal in those early years, I didn't do anything to resist reaching this point either. But now I find myself asking, "Do I want to continue to expand? Do I have the resources (time and energy) to expand? While I now have the money to expand, is this the best way to increase my number of hives? Do I want to spend the money to buy more nucs/packages? Should I now be buying my equipment rather than making it? Is buying equipment a better use of my time? Do I just want to stay at two hundred hives and diversify into queens and nucs, or do I want more hives in more locations? How am I going to find more locations? How am I going to find more time? Should I wait until I'm retired?"

In these dreary winter months of 2012-2013, I'm making plans for 350 hives. These plans, as I've learned from my meanderings, have <u>written</u> goals. I've plotted out a timeline for splits, raising my own queens, setting out swarm traps. I have intention. I have plans. I have priorities. Thanks to my wife's employment transition (a euphemistic interpretation of being, "let go"), she now has time to spend at the farmer's market. In addition, as she was unceremoniously let go from her full-time employment, she picked up a part-time job that allows her the opportunity to work the farmer's markets, which frees me up to expand to my written ideal of 350 hives. Nancy does not care for working the bees and being outdoors, but she likes selling. And on top of all this, she knows we need to find a way to make up for the lost income from her previous full-time job. The beauty of all these changes is how we are working together.

My earlier journey, up to about a year ago, as fuzzy and nebulous as it was, never had a strong commitment where I invested huge amounts of money or capital. I never borrowed money to buy equipment. This is good. If I had changed my mind somewhere along the way, I would hope to gather some of those resources back. But then if I had clarified distinct goals, I might have made better use of the resources at my disposal.

As you sit down to read this manuscript, you may be keeping four hives. You've had some luck selling honey and you want to get bigger. You want to expand but how? How big? Do you have a set, definable goal? Is it a measurable goal? Does your goal have a timetable? Do you have a long-term vision? Is it just a fuzzy dream of where you think you might want to be?

There is an old saying that people don't plan to fail; they simply fail to plan. Does your dream have a deadline? Have you asked all the hard questions? Do you want the hard questions asked (I never did!). Are you comfortable with the possibilities that you may fail? Are you comfortable that some of the questions may not have answers? Is your spouse comfortable with not having the answers?

If I had to do it all over again, I would put more planning into the growth of my beekeeping enterprise. My growth has been slow and steady, somewhat accidental or providential. I've bought a few things along the way, but mostly made my equipment out of scrap lumber. It was free, but I spent a lot of time and energy (sweat equity) that may have equaled the price of the good lumber in the long run.

I found an ad for cheap, used shelving lumber (1 x 12's) in one of those free "shopper" type newspapers given away at the supermarket and convenience stores. I bought a couple hundred boards at fifty cents each. Then I went back and bought some more. I firmly believe that opportunity only knocks a couple of times. Rather than be a day late and a dollar short, I went back, again, and bought all that remained. I have yet to use them all up, but I knew if I wanted to expand in an inexpensive way, these boards would not always be available. At least my experience has been that later, when I needed them or wanted them, they would be gone. Carpe Diem!

At one point, I advertised for used beekeeping equipment. I ran an ad in one of the free "shopper" newspaper from the supermarket. I got the strangest phone calls in response to that ad. I went and looked at a lot of used bee equipment. Some of it was junk, rotted and falling apart. Some was worth salvaging, but it cost quite a bit of my time and labor to repair it.

Most of the people with used bee equipment for sale want to sell you all of it. They want you to buy the whole lot. I probably paid too much cash for a few good items, as these whole lots also include great quantities of semi-useful junk, worn out items of little further use, duplicate items I already had, and some home-made orphans that were of no use to me. In the end, I would have been money ahead if I bought the items I really wanted and could use, even if I had to pay brand-new prices.

I've purchased a few packages along the way and even a few queens, but I find more and more, it is far more economical for me to catch feral swarms, raise my own queens and make my own splits. I haven't borrowed any money on my beekeeping endeavor so I'm debt-free (I wish I could say that about the rest of my life). While I didn't set out to plan to be at two hundred hives, here I am. I may have reached this point in spite of myself!

Where do you want to go? My recommendation is to make some goals. Write down some targets you hope to reach and when you want to reach them. Put a deadline on these goals. Don't just keep thinking "some day," because some day will never come and one day you'll be at the nursing home wishing you had. Shoulda, coulda, woulda: the triplet siblings of "someday." Regret is a horrible burden to bear. Be sure and include what things you need to reach these goals. And as I've followed the advice of the productivity experts, written goals stir the creativity of the subconscious mind. Written goals tell your mind you are serious about this expansion.

Break down the larger goals into smaller steps. Then ask yourself what you need to do TODAY to get, or keep, the ball rolling. There is an old saying that says, "Don't count your days; make your days count."

Beekeeping is seasonal. All winter long many people say, "I can't wait until spring is here so I can keep bees." Then spring arrives and they haven't ordered their equipment, or they have ordered it and it's on back-order. This is so true with package bees. You have to get your order in early.

And then I get a call from a nervous person who wanted to start keeping bees. They ordered their packages and their equipment. Sometimes the equipment arrives on time, sometimes it arrives after the packages came, sometimes critical parts (like foundation) has been back-ordered. And most bee supply companies will not ship wax foundation while the weather is still cold. That wax will crack and break if it gets too cold.

That's when I get a nervous call from these beginners asking what do I think they need to do? Do I have any extra parts (like foundation) I could sell them? And sometimes I do but most times I don't have any "extra" equipment. Most of my equipment is in use. And they fail to remember how equipment has to be assembled and painted. Do you know how unfavorable the weather is for painting in the early spring? And then most of my used equipment is really worn out. I'm not sure I feel comfortable selling it, and then if I sell my used equipment, then I have to replace it with new.

The key to keeping bees is planning, preparation and passion. Make your plans. Prepare your day. Then attack with passion. But make each day count. Do not procrastinate.

Each day ask yourself, "If my larger, longer term goal is "XYZ," what little thing am I doing today to move me closer to attaining that goal?" Each day, each week, make a little progress toward the larger goal. Before you know it, spring has arrived and the weather will not wait for you. Be prepared. Do not procrastinate. Be ready.

Then go slow and grow steady, and a good rule of thumb is to only double what you have each year. So if you are at four hives, don't expand beyond eight the next year. If you are at eight hives, don't expand beyond sixteen the next year. With each level of expansion comes added responsibilities and increased attention to detail. With more experience, the process becomes smoother and easier, but it's still work and the work takes time.

So where do you want to go? Where to? And what do you want to do once you get there? There was a story when I was in college back in the late 1970's and early 1980's about a son who came home from college. His father was from a long line of farmers and the family farm was paid for, handed down from one generation to the next. Dad raised hogs in a dirt lot, sheltering them in an old barn with straw bedding, mixing his feed in a series of five-gallon buckets. This was the manner of how his father, and his father before him, kept hogs. This practice of raising hogs was labor-intensive, but it was cheap and debt-free, and most of all, profitable. But it was also hard work. Because time and energy was always in demand, there was a limit as to how many hogs this farm could produce.

The son comes home from college and tells his dad of the great ideas they talk about at the university, ideas like concrete manure pits and feeding hogs on concrete slats covered by large metal buildings. There is no straw to bale, no manure to shovel, no weather to contend with and everything is automated. And ten times more hogs can be raised from the same amount of land. The son sees dollar signs in his dream.

So the father and son take an excited trip into town. They talk to the banker, and mortgage the farm to build a large farrow-to-finish, hog confinement facility. They buy new breeding stock. Everything is financed with borrowed money. Everything looks good until the bottom of the hog market drops out from underneath them. Through no fault of their own, the enterprise becomes hugely unprofitable. But because they owe so much money on the new buildings, the banker says they cannot afford to quit. They have to raise the hogs to meet the interest payments, and basically they will be working without an income. The son has to take a job in town, plus work the farm when he gets off of his income-producing job.

The enterprise continues to lose money and the farm must be sold to meet the mortgaged debt. Now back in the 1980's, this was a common occurrence. Debt, outrageously high interest rates and slim margins in a falling market forced farmers off the farm in droves. And many of these operations were rapid expansions with the idea that high prices were here to stay. So what has this sad story to do with beekeeping?

My point of this story is asking the two-part question: where do you want to go and how are you going to get there? You need to think about where you want to go, as there are different places to go. There are different ways to get to the place you think you want to go, and once you reach that place, you may find you want to go somewhere else. Every decision has consequences. Some commitments come with long-term, very expensive costs. We always need to be thinking ahead.

To return to my taxi trip through Atlanta, there is the express way which is longer but quicker. In beekeeping, you can borrow the money, achieve your level of hives you wish to keep almost immediately, but you have a long road of debt to pay down. You can take the downtown route, which is shorter, but it may also take longer depending upon the traffic, and the traffic is often unpredictable. There are different places to go and a host of different routes to take you there.

And along the lines of expanding your bee colonies, you may think in terms of a series of smaller steps. You may have four hives and you can afford to expand to eight this year. Next year you can take the jump to sixteen. The year after, expand some more. You don't have to grow to your end number all at once, all in one year. I can speak from experience that my expansion from thirty hives to sixty-some hives in one year really taxed my mental ability to keep everything organized. That's when I developed my record keeping system. That's in another chapter down the road.

I've met some earnest beekeepers in our bee club who articulated dreams of a hundred colonies. And I say, "Good for you!"

But when they reached twenty hives, they found out just how much time it took and they were lost as to where to sell their honey. I ended up buying it wholesale in five-gallon buckets and marketed it through my farmer's market stand. This is a common occurrence. They never reached their hundred-colony goal, and that's okay. Can you imagine where they might be if they borrowed the money and bought a hundred hives worth of equipment and bees? But the beauty of these beekeepers is they set goals and wanted to work their way to that level.

Most beekeepers I know never set goals, never set out to attain specific levels of production. The whole thing just grew on them and they grew with it. They had four hives and added a couple more hives, and they may order a couple of packages this next year, or not. They're not sure. Or they started with four hives and they have no dreams of getting any larger. And that's okay too. Each of us must take stock of our time, energy, priorities, family commitments and work obligations and determine where we want to be. Many beekeepers look to me and my 200 colonies and think I'm a glutton for punishment. Maybe so, but I've having the time of my life. I'm in a good place.

If four is the number of hives you can handle, than work those four hives with diligence and pride. If twenty-five hives is your goal, then work toward that goal with diligence and pride. If you want a hundred hives, then, "you go, girl!" (We have a growing interest from young women in beekeeping).

When I got out of college, one of my goals was to have a bunch of hives. But how many? I wanted hives to make money for me. But how much was possible? I had some money upon my graduation so I bought the appropriate number of boxes and bees for twenty hives. My goal was to have more, but twenty was my initial stepping stone into the massive world of large-scale beekeeping. I thought all I needed to do was buy these nucs, put the bees in boxes with new foundation and the honey would literally be rolling out the front entrance by the end of June. Then I'd simply put the honey in jars and everyone would come clamoring to my farm wanting to buy my honey at full retail prices. This is what they call fantasy. In real life, it is very different than what we imagine in our minds. Still, I had some aspect of a vision, though it was pretty fuzzy!

After I got all my boxes built and nucs delivered, about half the colonies swarmed two weeks after everything was set up. I introduced the bees to brand new, plastic foundation (new and innovative at the time). They balked at drawing it out. Then they ran out of drawn comb space, the available space became congested, and this condition initiated the swarming impulse. I didn't understand what made them swarm when they had all this room. But "room," or open space and available cell space on the drawn comb are two different things.

The first year with twenty hives yielded no harvest, much to my surprise. I would have done better starting out with four hives and learning what keeping bees was all about. But instead I wanted to start out with a bang, become rich overnight, then expand explosively the next year.

Yeah, right.

I also wanted to raise sheep at this time, part of an integrated farming enterprise. What I should have done was bought a few ewes and retained the young females for breeding stock. But instead, I was buying every kid's former 4-H project and any old, broken mouth ewe shipped in from Montana to the sale barn. I didn't have enough barn space for all the ewes, and I needed more room when the lambs were born in April. I ran short of feed and had to buy it. In a nutshell, I expanded beyond my means and I could not support the enterprise.

In addition to the simple logistics of keeping all those ewes fed and sheltered, problems kept popping up. These were problems that I could not foresee because I didn't have the experience. These problems also arose because I didn't have the insights to know when they would pop up, nor did I have the experience to keep them from getting worse. They don't tell you all these things in those nice books you read.

With keeping honeybees, it is obvious that my mistake was assuming I could expand so fast. Many beekeepers never expand. They remain as hobbyists, and I will reiterate over and over, keeping four hives and doing a good job of it is a good thing. Do not think of yourself as somehow inadequate if you don't have (or don't want) more hives. But a lot of us start with four hives and move on.

I don't know of any beekeeper that goes in and buys a large operation without a goodly amount of experience behind them. Most require an on-going enterprise to support them during this time of expansion. Most of us have something else going for us to put food on the table and any beekeeping enterprise is of secondary importance. I never raised sheep in my life but I was up to over one hundred ewes my first winter. I was young, energetic, and quite foolish. And I knew everything there was to know, right?

Growth and expansion is something that is best taken slowly. When expansion comes too fast, you never really catch up. Success always is elusive and failure is constantly nipping at your heels.

So what are your goals? Most people do not set goals because it is too painful to wake up and realize our goals are either too ambitious or we are not qualified to attain them. In most circles, this is called "failure." When we don't reach our goals, our culture tells us we failed. So it is better, or so we think, not to have any goals at all. That way, I never fail if I don't reach my non-existent goals.

However, I will contend, if we have goals, then we need to begin to develop a means of reaching those goals. Some people do not want to even mention goals because that requires them to develop the means of reaching those goals. "It's too much work!" they complain. Or we fear someone else who tells us, "What? You're crazy to want those goals!" We would rather wander aimlessly, driving around the streets of Atlanta hoping to arrive at our destination without articulating any desire on where we want to go. This just wastes time and energy.

But goal setting is a good thing. Setting goals moves you in a positive direction, even if that direction will change later on. We look at the larger goal and strategize smaller steps to reach the larger, longer-term goal. We don't count our days but we make our days count. And every day we need to ask ourselves: "What did I do today to move me closer to achieving my goals?" What little step today propels me a little further down the path?

In my journey toward the level of one hundred bee hives, I don't think I ever sat down and said, "This year I will have sixty hives. I will develop two new farms on which to locate my hives. I will expand with the purchase of twenty packages. I will order queens and split twenty of my other hives. I will sell my honey at one new market with a new line of squeeze bears. Then with the profits, I will buy twenty new beehives for next year's expansion."

I never thought those thoughts. In retrospect, I should have. And so much of my encouragement in this manuscript is to jump over the puddles of my mistakes. There is no sense in getting your feet muddy. I'm hoping you will be able to go around my puddles.

Should I have set goals? Yes! Did I set goals? Nope. But in the back of my mind, I was always thinking, dreaming, scheming, visualizing my way to more hives. In a sense, <u>my vision was my long-term goal</u>. But did I spend each day planning how to systematically and efficiently reach my fuzzy vision? Nope. I just kept working, sometimes rather inefficiently, toward the general direction of my vision. I got to see a lot of scenery in downtown Atlanta.

Now that I've reached this level of two hundred hives, where do I want to go? I honestly don't know what my limits might be, but I'm aiming at 350 hives to carry into next winter. Last fall, when things were winding down, I purposefully and intentionally sat down to catch my breath. I poured myself a nice cup of tea (with honey), relaxed my frenetic thought process in order to ponder the future and contemplate the opportunities and possibilities.

Despite my bad habits in the past, I wrote down some written goals. Am I at the place I want to be, right now? Is this expansion to 350 reasonable? Is it challenging? What do I need to rise to this challenge? Is my spouse on board with me? Do I have the resources, and the plan on how to expand? Is this where I want to be next year?

Taking the time to sit down and write this manuscript has granted me the opportunity to ponder my future. This past year, with the new swarms I caught and the new queens I raised, I have around two hundred hives. Is this my limit or do I have the time and energy to do more?

There are two old clichés that come to mind. One that I mentioned earlier is that "People never plan to fail, they just fail to plan." The other one is, "If you don't know where you are going, you're bound to end up somewhere else."

Both of these clichés speak about the importance of planning, with a hope and a dream of getting **where** you want to go and knowing **how** you're going to get there. But most people don't really know where they want to go. Some people know where they hope to be, but they are afraid to articulate it. They fear sharing their plans because there is someone (usually a parental-type figure) around who is quick to say, "You'll never do it. You'll fail. Where did you get this crazy idea?"

And there are a host of people around who tried and failed. They find themselves surrounded with "Job's comforters" who continue to tell them, "I told you so." Many times they never actually told you but they think they told you or they were going to tell you.

This kind of fear has an affect on your professional life, your personal life, your financial life. Some people reject planning and goal setting because life is full of so many contingencies. And let's face it, life itself is a contingency. You cannot predict the future. You can only adjust your plans accordingly. So we wake up each day and do what we can do, taking life's lumps along the way, then hope tomorrow is a better day. But planning is a better way. You can always change your plans.

I trap feral swarms to expand my bees and refill my winter dead-outs. I set out around eighty traps in around thirty locations. One day, as I was bringing home three traps of swarms and putting them in hives, my beekeeping buddy, Herb, stopped by the bee yard. He saw my van parked in the grass by the bee yard and pulled in to see what I was up to. When he saw my three swarm traps loaded with swarms and my three new hives, Herb said with a slight note of envious disgust, "You are the luckiest man alive."

My response was a cool, "Luck has nothing to do with it. Luck is nothing more than experience and preparation meeting opportunity. I prepared and opportunity rewarded my plan."

When you're prepared, you can take advantage of opportunities. When you are not prepared, sometimes you don't even recognize the opportunity when it comes along and bonks you on the head. Or as someone else once said, "Sometimes opportunity comes along dressed in work clothes disguised as hard work."

I now make plans every year to put up traps and make my name known that I handle swarms. But I don't set out to define the number of swarms I hope to catch. I've purposely left it open to catch as many as I have time for, but I also make sure I've got the boxes and frames to put them in. But on the end of preparation, you have to set the traps in advance of the swarm season. You have to be ready to go before the season slips past you. Then, once you catch a swarm, you have to have the boxes ready (assembled and painted) plus the frames ready to put in the box (be sure an order your wax foundation early—they cannot ship it in cold weather). You have to have a hive stand in a bee yard somewhere, ready to accept the swarm.

Luck? Hardly! Luck is nothing more than experience and preparation waiting for opportunity. Sometimes those opportunities never come, but if you're not prepared, then maybe it's best if they never came at all. And always remember that opportunity, like time, waits for no man (or no woman, for that matter).

In one of my early years, I had several swarm calls, one right after another. I was caught short of equipment and didn't even have the frames assembled. I tried calling some of my beekeeping buddies to divert the swarms their way. They were not prepared. They wanted the bees but they were not ready to receive them. They had to pass. Some of the swarms I dumped into plain wood boxes and allowed the bees to draw out their own comb pattern (this was a big mistake!). Then I hoped to top them with standard boxes with Langstroth frames. This didn't work out so well.

Since that time, I always build extra boxes and I always have extra frames ready. I have hive stands leveled up ready to accept those swarms. And offering to catch and retrieve swarms is not something you can arrange by appointment. You have to be ready at a moment's notice. You have to invest the time and energy to be ready not knowing when (or if) your investment will ever pay off.

Perhaps growing your number of bee hives is not so much about planning as it is being ready to take advantage of life's opportunities. Flexibility is a big advantage. Readiness is a virtue. Availability is a key component. But then a lot of people have regular work hours and this is not an option. Beekeeping is something you have to do as you work around the weather. And many times the weather will not cooperate.

From time to time, I am approached by old-timers who have long since given up their beekeeping days. When mites wiped out their bees and the chemical strips were not fully understood, a lot of beekeepers put the equipment away to wait until "someday." I buy a fair share of used equipment, but a lot of it is chewed by mice, stuck together by moth cocoons and horribly dirty, not to mention slightly rotted.

More often than not, my purchase is an exercise in generosity in exchange for some stories of the good old days. Much of what I buy I should simply refuse. Some of what I buy I end up burning. And it still costs money. And when I look at what I bought that was still quite usable after I throw away the junk, the cost is quite expensive for what is left. I should have simply bought new.

Then there are a couple of small-time beekeepers who approached me to buy their hives, complete with bees. They are either tired, short on time, or they became allergic to bee stings. At this point, a hive of bees is worth around $150, plus it has to be moved. Moving hives is something I absolutely detest. It is a lot of work and the bees hate it as well. In addition, it has to be done at night. Have you ever set down an indispensable tool at night in the long grass? Plus, if the former beekeeper has been busy, it's very likely these hives have not had the treatments for mites, room for proper expansion, etc. I find it way too expensive to buy a fully functional hive from a neglectful beekeeper.

A local beekeeper had four hives and was going to sell his acreage. The bees had to be moved in order to sell the property. All four hives had bees and a full crop of honey on them. They looked healthy to me when I looked at them. He didn't want too much money for the bee hives, around $100 for each of them, then he also had some extra boxes and bottom boards for an additional $100. I started figuring that maybe the honey on the hives would greatly offset the cost of the equipment. But it was late October and things in Southeast Missouri were getting ready for fall. I decided to pass.

One of my friends, a fellow who had no bees and no experience but wanted to get into the bee business, ended up buying all four hives. He moved them with great effort as they were very heavy. He didn't bother to open the hives for any real inspection other than separating a few hive bodies and looking between the boxes. But the next spring all four hives were dead. I never knew if it was starvation or a mite infestation. The wax moths soon moved in and the colonies were history. While $500 for the four hives and the used equipment didn't push this fellow into bankruptcy, it did have a great impact on his family's financial standing, and his wife's patience with his next venture.

My preference is to go slow and steady. But slow to me may be fast to someone else. What my spouse tolerates would drive another wife to justifiable homicide if not marital infidelity. When I tell people I now have two hundred hives, they look at me like I've lost my mind. To them, six hives is all they can care for at this time with their other commitments.

But the good news is that with more hives, you learn how to make more efficient use of your time. You also know how to make your days count, especially in the winter when things are slow. It's when things are slow that you can prepare for the rush of the spring time when there is never enough time to do anything.

Everyone is different. In this chapter I want to pose three really significant questions. **First**, where do you want to go? What level of beekeeping is your goal? Recognizing that goals are flexible, this goal may be temporary or a stepping stone to another level. But where do you want to go this next year?

Second, how are you going to get there? Do you want to go the express route or are you ready to take your chances and maybe fight the traffic through downtown? Both ways will reach the same destination. How do you want to get there?

Third, what will it take to get there? Will you borrow money or will you use your savings? Do you want to buy used equipment or are you willing to pay for new equipment (and the delivery charge). In the long run, as I look back wistfully, I paid too much for worn out equipment. I would have been better to buy new. But then the new equipment also had to be assembled.

One of the things I like about keeping bees is the idea that I'm in charge. Or at least I <u>think</u> I'm in charge. The decisions are up to me, but likewise, I bear the full responsibility of the consequences. In retrospect, I wish I had put more emphasis on planning and goal setting. But then I also wonder if I really stuck with my plan, would I end up where I am today? Would my goals have limited my growth? Or would I be at five-hundred hives if I followed my goals?

The world may never know. All I know for sure is where I'm at today. The future remains to be open. I like to live life as if it had no limits, but in reality, my real limits come in the form of my time and energy.

As you read the rest of this manuscript, as you hope and dream, ponder and contemplate your potential and opportunities, give some thought to why you are keeping bees today, or why you want to keep bees in the first place if you don't have bees just yet.

When you can answer that question, it will guide you in the direction you must go.

I wish you great success in this journey. But buckle up. I can be a bumpy ride.

Beekeeping with Twenty-Five Hives

Chapter Two:

Markets and Marketing

Before we get too far along about keeping twenty-five hives of bees, let's pause and reflect on an old adage that has served me well:

"Start with the end in mind."

This old adage means that on any given task or proposed project, you start with the vision of where you want to go. What is your destination? You want to visualize the end product or what things look like when you finish. You want to identify what it looks like when you're done. You want to know, with some openness to contingencies, where all your present steps are going to lead you.

With keeping twenty-five hives of bees, before we get into too much more "nuts and bolts" about keeping bees and the practical management of the hive at this level, let's talk a little bit about the end, selling honey. Now we could also look at this "end" as growing and expanding to twenty-five hives and how you're going to get there, but realistically, I'd hate to have you get to twenty-five hives and not know what you're going to do with all that honey.

And if you are under some financial pressure to sell that honey or to recoup your monetary investment you sunk into your operation, then it becomes more critical to look at the real end, selling honey.

I confess my greatest joy comes from keeping bees. I love to watch them and observe them work. But I also have a lot of honey that needs to find a home. Since a lot of my friends love honey, I could give it all away. I could donate it to worthy causes like the local food pantry. But I also have a desire to make some money along the way. This means I need to sell my honey.

Selling honey means *marketing* your honey, and that means finding markets. Sometimes you'll need to be creating new markets or developing potential markets. But in the end, your goal will be to market and sell your honey, and come out with cash in your hand. This is the end that we're going to start with. This is where I want to go with my bees.

And as you think about the end, that is, marketing and selling your honey, it is a grand temptation to begin thinking and dreaming about those giant piles of money you're going to rake in. There are three rules I've learned to live by when I've contemplated selling honey and making great gobs of money.

And by the way, making money is my ultimate end that I always keep in mind, and secondly, I will preach this message over and over and over: *It is not a sin to make money.* It is not immoral to desire to make a profit keeping your bees. We operate in a capitalistic, consumer-driven society. We measure things in dollars and cents. If you want to barter your honey or give it away, that's okay, too, but let's not get wrapped up in a guilt trip about making money.

Yes, there are those who will sell their soul for the almighty dollar allowing themselves to be driven by greed and avarice, but I hardly think this will be a problem for you if you keep bees.

Here are my three key ideas about marketing honey and making money:

1. You're not going to get rich selling honey, at least not overnight.

2. However, there is a lot of respectable money to be made selling honey.

3. The amount of money you will make is directly proportional to amount of labor, energy and creativity you invest in marketing your honey...and how diligently you take care of your bees.

To sum up those three rules, the more you work at marketing your honey, finding those little "niche" markets, the more money you will make. However, these methods take more work and more creativity. If you want to "bulk" your honey in 55-gallon drums or even 5-gallon buckets, you will make less money. But these methods take a lot less work. Marketing honey is a trade-off between the money you want to make and the energy you are willing to put into creatively marketing your honey.

But let me clarify: You will make less money per pound selling bulk honey, but your total gross income may be higher. While bulk methods take a whole lot less time and labor, selling 5-gallon buckets of honey will allow you to market a greater volume of honey. Selling wholesale allows you more time with your bees.

With a greater volume, you could gross more income, but the price per pound that you receive for your honey will be less. If you take the time to pour and pack small bottles of honey, it will take more time and energy, but your price per pound will be substantially higher when you sell them with a little creativity.

Somewhere in your plans to grow to twenty-five hives of bees, you will need to sit down and determine how and where you want to market your honey. If these markets are not yet developed or unavailable, it may take a little more energy than you realize to crack into the realm of selling your honey.

As an example, as I write this manuscript, I can sell a pint jar of cut-comb honey for $8.50 (this is my retail price to the consumer). Cut comb honey is where I take a frame of honey that was started with unwired, thin surplus foundation. I cut out a section of the comb, drop it into a wide-mouth pint jar, then fill the rest of the jar with honey. In my area, this is a very popular method of selling comb honey. I ask $8.50 which represents my extra labor. I sell regular pints for $6.50 a jar. As a comparison, I retail my quart jars for $12 (without comb, just plain extracted honey). For my local area, this is on the low side. Some beekeepers are fetching $15 per quart and even upwards of $18 per quart in the more urban, upscale markets.

To reduce my work and energy, I can sell this quart jar wholesale to a grocery store for $10 which will, in turn, sell it for a retail store price of $14.50 (that's the difference between wholesale and retail). However, if I wholesale my honey to the grocery store, they have more time to sell more jars, and they have more overhead. My honey has more exposure to potential customers than if I tried to sell it myself.

There are all kinds of trade-offs. I suspect that if you've been keeping bees for a few years, you have an idea of where you can sell your honey and what you can get for it.

When I interview the larger beekeepers, most of them do not have the time to market all their honey at retail prices. I observe them selling a small portion to friends and family at retail prices. They wholesale a larger portion to the local grocery store that they have packed in quarts and pints, then they bulk the majority of their honey to the commercial markets, some of which is used in baking and manufacturing of cereal, salad dressing, etc.

But there is also a person who will buy that 55-gallon drum at a bulk price, then take their time and energy to pack it into quart and pint jars. These jars are either retailed or wholesaled, but the price will reflect their time and energy and marketing costs.

Under these methods, the best price per pound will definitely come from the direct retail sales. The lowest price comes from the bulk sales. In the end, however, it is not always the price per pound you receive but how much honey you can move at those prices. Ideally, if we could all sell retail we would all receive the greatest price per pound, but time would limit how many pounds of honey we can move.

This is a dilemma I face every year. I market some of my honey at the farmer's markets at a retail price. But to set up, sell, and break down my booth takes about five hours. I often wrestle with the time spent at the market and my need to tend to my bees. This is what makes bulk marketing of honey so attractive. I can basically sell my honey at a lower price so I can spend more time with my bees and potentially produce more honey. If I want to receive more money per pound, then I won't have that time to spend with my bees.

This is what will make marketing honey from twenty-five hives so difficult. The smaller hobby-level beekeeper has fewer hives and can spend great amounts of time marketing their honey. The larger commercial beekeeper has more bees that require more attention and thus they cannot devote enough time to marketing their honey at retail prices. At twenty-five hives, you will be in that murky middle. You will feel caught in the middle of needing to spend more time with the bees while you try and maximize your price on your honey. Every day at the farmer's markets when sales are slow, all I can think about is the work that awaits me in the bee yard. But once in the bee yard, I remember how I need to get out and sell more honey.

One of the things I'm looking forward to as this new year rolls around is my wife's involvement in the farmer's markets which basically frees me up to tend bees.

And here's another good thought: honey never spoils. It will granulate and you'll have to think of some method of gently warming your honey back to a liquid state. But it never goes bad. If you can store your honey in 5-gallon buckets, you can wait for your markets to materialize. You don't have to rush into selling your honey and getting rid of it. If your honey is light and marketable, then it will pay to wait for the right price.

The right price will be different for different people. If I don't, or can't, invest the energy in marketing my honey in this manner, and I want to opt into selling it "bulk" in a 5-gallon bucket, I can rather easily sell that 5-gallon bucket for $125 upwards to $150 (and at 60 pounds per bucket, it works out to a bit more than $2.00 per pound up to $2.50 a pound). That's the going price as I put this manuscript together.

Recognize also, with my cut-comb honey, I have the cost of a wide-mouth pint jar, which at this writing is around 90 cents. If I were to buy my jars by the pallet, I could probably work that price down to around 80 cents. But that's also a huge investment, all at once, for a supply of jars that may take me all year (or more) to fill and sell.

Again, think about marketing. How much honey can you sell? How much demand for your honey must be created or stimulated? How much education of the consumer am I willing to develop? I have found that setting up a table at the farmer's markets and giving away samples, what I call my "taste challenge," stimulates demand. When people find out how my honey, fresh and unpasteurized, differs in taste to that foreign store-brand honey, they buy several jars. But this takes time and energy. If you're not a "people" person, then maybe the farmer's markets are not for you.

Also keep in mind that there is a limit as to how many pint jars of cut-comb honey I can reasonably sell. Each 5-gallon bucket represents forty pint jars, and there are some of my honey customers who do a lot of baking. They'll buy a 5-gallon bucket of honey from me every year. They don't want all those jars, and they want a discounted bulk price! I also have a few customers that want a gallon jug of honey. My current price for a gallon is $40.

Do you begin to see how my lack of labor with a 5-gallon bucket (selling for $125) compares with my extra energy selling a gallon jug (making that 5-gallon bucket now worth $200). Even when you take out the cost of the gallon jugs ($2 each), it pays to sell smaller units of honey for more money. If I were to take that same 5-gallon bucket and pour it into pint jars, I would have a return of $260 (forty pints at $6.50 each) with a cost of approximately $28 for the jars. Twenty quart jars yields $240 (at $12 per jar) with a cost of around $16 for the jars.

But here is a very important note to remember: When you sell in bulk/wholesale, you are responding to the market price of what someone else is willing to pay for your honey. When you retail your honey, you are in charge of setting price, and most of us will charge a reasonable price up to what the market can bear.

Here's what I want you to remember: When you bulk/wholesale your honey, you are a ***price taker***. That is, you take what someone else is willing to offer you. Now bear in mind, you don't have to sell to that person at that price. There is always room for negotiation and you can definitely hold out for a higher price. In a very general sense, you are a ***price taker***, you take the price someone else is willing to offer you for your honey.

However, when you retail the honey, you set the price. And bear in mind, you can only set the best reasonable price that the market will bear. I would love to sell my honey for $50 per quart, but at the time of this writing, $12.00 is a reasonable price. I am a ***price maker***, that is, I make the price. I set the level at which I am willing to trade my honey for your cash.

Further to the west of me, there are beekeepers who are getting $10 for a quart. I've seen pictures of farmer's markets where a quart goes for $18.00 (at more suburban settings). I talked with a beekeeper in the bootheel region of Missouri, an economically depressed area, and they are lucky to get $6 or $7 per quart. Folks in the area just cannot, and will not, pay more.

And I suppose I could set my price at $50. After all, I am a ***price maker***! But then I have to be willing to sit on my honey until the world runs out of honey and the scarcity of supply and demand raises the price to $50 per quart. This year, many of the smaller hobby beekeepers are completely sold out of honey. A mid-sized beekeeper in my area has taken his honey off the market. He believes the demand will drive up the price. When the price goes up, he says he'll ready to sell his honey. Price makers can afford to be flexible...and patient.

Is this wishful thinking on his part? Does he sound notoriously greedy? This is the way things go in any market, and a student of history who knows of the great Tulip bulb shortage in the middle ages knows that prices and speculation are all part of the game. Then there is the world honey market and prices that fluctuate with the global economy.

Will this mid-sized beekeeper get his desired price? It may be a long time. Every beekeeper needs to set his prices. At one farmer's market a number of years ago, a person approached me and asked me what I wanted for a 5-gallon bucket. Prices that year had risen to $90 for a 5-gallon bucket. There was a shortage of honey due to importation problems with cheap, Chinese honey.

Since that $90 was the going price, that's what I quoted her. She got a little upset and thought my prices were too high. She said she remembered the last bucket of honey she bought only cost her $40, but she also conceded it was a long time ago. So I told her to shop around, explaining how the global market had pushed up our domestic prices. She checked around and came back the next week offering me $90 for the 5-gallon bucket. And she seemed quite happy to get it for that price.

Since that time, and since I've developed other markets for quarts, pints and squeeze bottles, I am less interested in selling a 5-gallon bucket at current prices of $125, even $150 in a bulk/wholesale container. I can make more money selling quarts and pints, and the extra money I make basically goes to reward my time and energy. You will have to decide how you want to sell your honey. There is one old beekeeper in St. Louis who sells nothing but 5-gallon buckets. And every year, he sells out. But he has confessed he doesn't like to sell honey and he's set in his retirement with a nice pension so he's not in beekeeping for the money. He just loves keeping bees.

When you sell your own honey, you are in control of setting the price. My quarts currently sell for $12.00 locally. I could, however, sell my quarts for $10.00 and probably sell more, but even at $12.00 I have no trouble of moving my honey. There is another farmer's market in Illinois where a lady sells her honey for $5.00 per quart. She sells out fast. People seek her out because she sells her honey so cheaply. But then again, she is a ***price maker*** and she makes the price so her honey sells, and it sells fast. I feel she is too cheap, but then again, maybe she thinks I'm too greedy.

What you will learn along the way is that marketing is greatly subject to supply and demand, but also quality. I sell a quality honey produced locally and naturally with no chemicals. I advertise it as "local, raw honey." People in my area want this kind of honey. Those who don't run to the large wholesale warehouse and buy their jug of imported, pasteurized, highly filtered honey for $5.00 per quart. Though few of these consumers know where it comes from or what's been done to it, they use price as the criteria for their selection.

Over and over again, I am reminded that people perceive quality and they are willing to pay (to a certain extent) for that quality. If you price your honey too cheap, they suspect something is wrong with it. If you price it too high, they'll scoff and buy the store-brand honey. The real question becomes: how high will I be able to go before I turn business back to the store-brand honey? And in terms of consumer education, can I demonstrate how my local honey justifies the price I am asking?

Marketing is largely governed by supply and demand, but also quality, which also requires a bit of consumer education. I was working at one of the farmer's markets where I had a selection of squeeze bears, the one's with the pointy nozzle tops. They were priced at $3.50 for 12 ounces. Then I also had a selection of other squeeze bottles and glass jars.

Along comes a couple of ladies who look over my honey. One picks up a quart jar with my large label that says, "Local, Raw Honey." She *oohs* and *aahs* about the quality and benefits of locally produced, raw honey. She holds it up to the sunlight and marvels at the color. I'm already anticipating a sale. She appears to know what she's talking about.

Her friend who is with her looks over her shoulder. All she sees is my $12.00 price tag. So she picks up a 12-ounce squeeze bear for $3.50, but her friend (the one holding the quart jar) says, "Oh don't buy that. You can get that in the grocery store."

Now it was the same honey, only a different size container and different label. But what is the perception? Two people looked at the same product in different containers and formulated differing opinions.

After I corrected her to say it was all locally produced, she simply said, "Uh-huh." People are funny and marketing your honey will take a great measure of education, and often a bit of creativity with large doses of energy. Then you will be approached by the old-timer who remembers when they had bees on their farm and sold honey for $2.50 a gallon and a $1 per quart back in the depression. Or they want to know why you charge $12.00 for a quart and the grocery store sells their honey at $9.99 for the same size jar?

Here's where I launch into my "locally produced" speech and the benefits of local honey. Some people don't realize the difference until you show them the difference. There are a lot of ignorant people out there!

As we continue in this chapter on marketing, keep in mind there are a hundred different ways to sell your honey. As a rule of thumb, the more energy you put into marketing your honey, the greater the value per pound you will receive. If you have great quantities of honey you need to market, then bulking it may be the best way to do it, but overall, the price you receive for a pound of honey will decrease with the larger volume. This is because larger volumes require less labor to bottle and market.

With that said, and the caveats given about getting rich, let's proceed with the end in mind: marketing your honey. As you build your apiaries and grow to twenty-five hives, it may become more and more apparent that you will continue to harvest quite a bit of honey! Somewhere, some how you need to get rid of your honey.

My ideas of marketing honey in my initial foray into beekeeping were totally ludicrous. I was clueless, driven by a financial dream of making my bees an income-producing venture. Thankfully, that portion of my beekeeping life was interrupted and I had time to rethink my marketing plans.

In my early days when I got restarted with just four hives, it was fun to give my honey away to friends and family. My bees were considered to be a novelty. I bought some cases of squeeze bears and it was fun to give them away. My wife and I lead a couple of religious retreats every year, and guess what the other leaders receive as a gift for their participation? HONEY!

And oddly enough, it seemed like a lot of people would look at me quizzically and say, "You have bees?" The notion of keeping bees is so foreign to today's consumer; they seem to think honey originates on the store shelf. Lots of people think our vegetables magically materialize in the produce section of the grocery store as well.

But giving honey away, though fun and rewarding in its own right, is a financial drain. But as I was just a small operator, this financial drain was not going to pull me under. Still, jars and lids cost money. When you only buy a single case of squeeze bears at a time, they are expensive. When you can buy containers in bulk, they get cheaper.

Further, your time is worth something. As one expands, equipment costs continue to rise. It's nice to see some financial return, even if you only have a few hives. Somewhere you have to make a break between giving your honey away and establishing some kind of marketing plan to recoup your expenses. Or you need a regular job to subsidize your hobby. And a lot of beekeepers do this and there is nothing wrong with it.

But this gets back to my initial questions: Why do you keep bees? What do you want out of your beekeeping? Where do you want to go? How are you going to get there?

There are two things I want out of my bees. One is an outlet for my creativity which acts as a therapeutic diversion from my "real" job. But the second thing I want from my bees is money. And as I said earlier, I don't think one needs to apologize for this desire. It's not money that is evil; rather it is the covetous desire (a misguided and inappropriate love) of money that is the

root of all kinds of evil. And some of these evils are cloaked in socially acceptable intentions.

But money is not evil, in and of itself. It is the inordinate desire for what you think money will do for you is from which all kinds of problems originate. But money, in and of itself is not bad. Do not apologize for making money. Do not apologize for wanting to make money. We live in a commercially driven, consumer-oriented, capitalistic society and money is the means by which we buy, sell and trade...and keep score.

I sell my honey and take in money. Unfortunately, I'm not getting rich overnight, but I am recognizing a nice, steady stream of income. I admit I'm not ready to quit my "real" job, but for the energy and money I've invested in my bees, for my time and efforts in marketing my honey, I'd like to see some greater financial considerations. It goes back to rule #3 previously mentioned above, the more time and creativity you put into marketing your honey, the more money you will realize.

And this is where a lot of people fail in keeping bees. They want the money without the work. It's not wrong to want the money, if your desire is kept in touch with reality, but the only time "success" comes before "work" is in the dictionary.

If you want to give away your honey as gifts or barter your honey to the neighbor boy for mowing your grass, that's fine. But if you want to make money by selling your honey, there's nothing wrong with this desire. Money is nothing more than pieces of green paper with numbers on it. It is our way of keeping score in the market place. It is how we do business.

I want to see a financial return from my beekeeping. I like to see more money coming in than I have to expend to keep my bees healthy and productive. I then use this money to do some fun stuff with my family and to expand my bee operation.

It is my intent to make my beekeeping enterprise a self-sustaining, income-producing "sideline." And I use that word "sideline" in the vein that I do not depend upon this enterprise to fully fund my family's living expenses.

But I do intend to manage my bees such that I'm willing to invest the necessary inputs and resources to keep them healthy and productive, and I'm also looking for a positive cash flow when I'm all done. The amount of this cash flow is not necessarily a prime concern of mine, as I still have a real job. But I do hope my bees make me some money, hopefully more money than what I need to spend on them to keep them healthy and productive.

Let me give you an example. Every spring, thousands of beekeepers buy packages of bees to replace their winter "dead outs." A dead out is a hive that dies out during the winter. What is the number one reason bees die during the winter? Mostly it is the lack of sufficient stores of honey. The bees basically starve to death. This may result from a drought or it may be the result when the beekeeper gets too greedy and harvests too much honey thinking the bees will make it up on the fall flow. I've learned you can never depend on what might happen.

Every fall I get calls from people asking me what they should do with their bees. The beekeepers feel the bees may be a little light on their honey stores going into the winter. Previously that summer, the beekeeper harvested his honey, hoping and banking on a nice fall honey flow to fill up the hive for the winter. But a lot of summers are hot and dry here in Missouri, and the nectar is just not available and the bees eat up the honey left from earlier nectar flows.

So what do the beekeepers need to do as they enter the fall? I tell them they need to go and buy sugar, mix it up in a 2:1 concentration and feed it to their bees. The most common response is this: "But I can't afford to feed my bees!"

I argue they can't afford NOT to feed them. Let's look at the math: If you were to buy a 25-pound bag of sugar and feed it to one hive, it's going to cost you around $13 at today's prices.

Next spring, if prices stay in line with what they were this past spring, that replacement package is going to cost $70, and not everyone is going to have packages available. Presently, there are shortages of honeybees in the spring thanks to an abundant demand for bees to pollinate California almonds. We used to import packages from Australia to fill the demand for almond pollination, and with the airfare, those packages cost $110 each. Domestic packages run around $70, but you might be able to find some for $60 if you are willing to drive and pick them up.

So do the math: Spend $13 today or $70 next spring. And yes, it is still a gamble if those bees will live through the winter, even if you feed them. You're still going to have to spend some money on miticides and other fall treatments. And a best guess as to those costs will be around $10 per hive.

My point is this: keeping bees costs money. How do you want to cover those costs? You can easily subsidize a small hobby from your real job. And this is not too bad if you only have a few hives. My goal, however, is to make money, and hopefully I have more money coming in then I'm going to pay out. That is what I call a positive cash flow.

So how are you going to make money with your bees? The principal product you'll have to generate a positive flow of income is honey. How do you want to convert your honey into money? Will you wholesale the honey to some other beekeeper so they can "pack" it in smaller jars and sell it retail? Will you "pack" it yourself, that is, pour it in jars and bottles? Will you then wholesale these packages to a retail store or will you retail it yourself? Where will you sell it retail, a farmer's market or from your house? How about selling it by the five-gallon bucket for bulk, wholesale prices? Are there commercial businesses that would buy your bulk honey (bakeries, restaurants, etc.)?

The good news is this: honey is not a perishable product. You can store it until you have a market developed. Another piece of good news is that honey is not something that requires an introduction. Everyone knows what honey is, and if you have a good tasting, locally-produced honey, people just need to find you or you need to find those customers.

There is also a growing trend among health-conscious people for local, "raw," honey. But you don't need to tell them how most smaller beekeepers don't have the equipment to pasteurize their honey anyway, so it really is "raw." Let them think you make this honey and keep it raw for the quality.

So will you advertise? Hand out samples? Put a sign in the yard? Visit a local business and see if they will give you some shelf space? The principal idea is to sell your honey. People just need to know you have it and you need to get it to them, or get them to your honey. And if you have a bunch of honey from twenty-five hives, it may take some effort on your part to get it all sold. With twenty-five hives, you're going to be bringing in around a minimum of a thousand pounds of honey (if you lived here in southeast Missouri).

That thousand pound "guesstimate" is a very conservative estimate of forty pounds per hive. That's a little more than one medium super full of honey. And keep two things in mind. First, this is an average as some hives will really produce and some will not. Second, it's not likely you will get this kind of production your first year when you move up to twenty-five hives. But don't discount the option that you might! Once you reach twenty-five hives, and if you can average forty pounds of honey per hive, that's a thousand pounds of honey to market.

A thousand pounds is roughly 330 quarts jars, or seventeen 5-gallon buckets. Since the harvest happens over a short period of time, do you have seventeen 5-gallon buckets ready to store your honey? (Visit your local bakery or the deli section in an upscale grocery store and you can pick them up for around a buck for a bucket).

With twenty-five hives, we're moving into some sizeable quantities of honey. So we need to start thinking about a marketing plan or you're going to have to get more relatives so you can give away more honey at Christmas time!

Most beekeepers, as they move up to twenty-five hives, will have an abundance of honey waiting to be marketed. I have no doubt that you will have more honey your first years then you will have customers.

Your markets will need to be developed, which I am thinking will start out slow and grow with time (and the energy you put into marketing your honey).

But don't despise small beginnings, even if you have to give away your honey initially. Give smaller jars away as "samples." Markets for honey grow. It still amazes me how people possess ignorant perceptions of honey. They know what it is but they have no idea how good it is for them. As I sell at seasonal farmer's markets, I bump into people who say, "Oh, we still have that jar of honey from three years ago." (That's usually a cheap jar of the foreign, store-brand honey we presume is possibly adulterated with corn syrup.)

That honey they are referring to is that generic store-bought honey, blended from cheap imports and cooked to insure a long shelf-life. Once they taste my honey, they know there is a difference. But breaking down that stereotype is a huge problem. Don't be so cheap that you are not willing to give some honey away today in order to make a sale tomorrow and retain a customer for the future. Price your honey for what it's worth.

So we start with the end: how are you going to get rid of that much honey? The good news is your options are numerous. But the question becomes, should you develop a market for your honey, then get the bees producing honey to meet that market demand? Or should you get the bees producing all they can produce and then develop your markets?

I like to think of markets and production as growing together, hand in hand. That's how it worked best for me.

My initial jump into beekeeping, so many years ago when I was first out of college, was based on production goals. I was set up with twenty-hives. I was going to keep bees and produce honey. Lesson number one is don't count your chickens before they hatch and don't anticipate your honey crop before you extract it. But being young and naïve, I was anticipating a large crop of honey. I was going to be filthy rich.

What I was going to do with all that mythical honey was not even on the horizon, let alone on my radar screen. Basically I was hoping and praying the markets would somehow magically develop when all of this honey was harvested. However, most of my "hope" was more like irresponsible, wishful thinking, believing that somehow, people would flock to my farm and buy honey. But I set out to produce the honey first, then once I had honey to sell, to find the markets.

My first honey harvest was ten, five-gallon buckets (a GREAT first year harvest) which I promptly set aside awaiting the crush of customers. I also figured that since my beehives sat in the front yard, everyone knew I had bees (or knew what those white boxes were) and they'd beat a path to my door and I'd be rich.

But this was not the case. I had good bees and good first-year production levels, but I had lots of honey sitting around in 5-gallon buckets. And then it crystallized on me and I had no way to gently re-warm the honey to liquefy it. Actually, I had no idea honey granulated like it did, or as fast as it did.

And I really wasn't set up to package my honey for the retail trade. I simply had not thought far enough ahead to buy the smaller jars, develop a label, show it to people and give them a sample.

So in the meantime of trying to make a label (this in the days before computers and desktop publishing) I tried to sell five-gallon buckets to the bakery. To my frustration, they didn't use a lot of honey, and the honey they bought from a wholesaler was about half the price of what I wanted for my honey (the quality of that wholesale honey was about half of mine as well). I gave some honey away, but I was still looking for the mountainous financial return. I was looking to get rich overnight.

Unfortunately, I was too impatient to turn a dollar on that honey. That first year of production I ended up getting a "CCC" loan from the Commodity Credit Corporation of the USDA. Then to pay the loan, I forfeited the honey and we called it even. This was the easiest, and laziest, way to dispose of my honey and collect some money. What I should have done was set my honey aside, package it in smaller jars or bottles, then gone to the stores and my friends to sell it face-to-face. And it's not nearly as hard as you may think, but it takes more energy than simply forfeiting the honey on a CCC loan.

I know of several beekeepers who have a buddy who owns a gas station, or a convenience store, or a restaurant. The beekeeper sets up a small table or takes up a little space by the cash register. The store owner gives them a little shelf space, and in most of these cases, the store owner turns over all the money that comes in from the sale of the honey. There is even a barber shop where a beekeeper set up a narrow card table with a display of pint jars. He set a coffee can along side with a sign that simply reads, "Honey, $5."

Note the simplicity of this arrangement. He has one size and charges one price. Almost everyone has a $5 dollar bill and the nice gleam of the honey is very attractive. The barber doesn't have to do anything but point his customers to the table and maybe make some change for those who only have a ten dollar bill.

And while this particular beekeeper is not a large volume producer, he sells out every year from marketing his honey through the barbershop, packing his honey in common canning jars that he buys at the local garden shop.

Marketing is not necessarily difficult. But it does take energy, and a healthy imagination helps. My first year I got lazy and sold my honey too cheap. Basically, I put my honey into the government loan program and defaulted on my loan (which is legal) but you forfeit your honey which was put up for collateral in lieu of paying back the loan. It's really a nifty program, especially for grain farmers, and the government has this program available for all kinds of agricultural commodities.

So my first year, I simply lacked imagination and patience. If I had put in more work, I would have brought in more money. The next year I started selling my honey face-to-face. It's hard because selling also involves rejection. Too many people would rather give their honey away then face the rejection or the insulting notion that you're charging too much for your honey. My plan was to carry small jars, and if they balked at my asking price for larger jars, I would simply give them a small jar so they could taste the quality.

At this point, I was recycling baby food jars for my smaller quantity give-aways. This is not appropriate from a health standard, and it also lacks professionalism. Check any of the supply catalogs or visit your local hardware store for small "jelly" jars. Put a nice label on it. The price of the jar will be about the same price as the honey. Sometimes you need to give people a sample in the name of consumer education.

And while this method of face-to-face marketing takes more time and more energy, I kept having this horrible feeling like I wasn't making any money. The volume of honey I was selling was still small. I wasn't getting rich over night!

What I forgot was how making a customer today makes for a repeat sale tomorrow that I don't have to work as hard for. Marketing is about building a customer base. And little by little, I sold my honey. It took some patience on my part.

But that was my first couple of years. Then my plans changed and I let my bees die as I put my hives in storage. I went on to continue my education. Then I met a young lady, we married, and before we knew it, children came along. No time for bees! But my heart was still fixed on getting bees some day.

Later on in life, when I re-established my hobby and only had four hives, I had just enough honey to give away to my family and friends. I felt I had to give it away because I didn't have any markets yet developed in this new location, and I was short on time to try and develop them.

For me, bees were just a hobby, and a hobby that was fun (which meant that I did things when I wanted to do them, not necessarily when they needed to be done to maximize production). And as long as your bees are a hobby, a mental diversion, or just fun, then the financial costs of keeping this hobby is probably cheaper than playing golf every weekend (not that there's anything wrong with golf). My return on the investment of my time and energy was the joy of sharing my honey. I subsidized all my costs with my real job.

Word got around that I had honey, but I still was considered a hobby beekeeper, kind of like those guys that grow monstrous pumpkins for the county fair. They do it for fun and people thought what I did for fun was keep bees, and keeping bees for fun meant I had no financial motive. And since the bees are the ones who are "really doing the work," then asking for a free jar of honey was no big deal to my friends and family.

But things do change. As more people asked for honey, and they noticed I was buying canning jars, they were now willing to pay me a little to "cover the expense of the jar." So at this stage, I rather apologetically shuffled my feet and said, "Oh, just give me a couple of bucks and it will be okay."

At this point, I still gave my honey away and basically accepted a "free-will donation." Then a few well-intentioned people brought me a dusty old box of canning jars from their garage to "trade" for a free jar of honey. My wife was not too happy about this arrangement as boxes of old jars (some of which were not real canning jars but old peanut butter jars without lids) don't pay for beekeeping equipment. And she didn't like the idea of running those dusty jars through her kitchen dishwasher!

And as it would turn out, some of those jars were so nasty they never came clean.

Let me at this point just say that accepting used jars is okay, but it will take you more effort to clean them than you think. Even after running them through the dishwasher twice, many of these jars are stained with rust, calcium deposits, nicks and chips around the rim, plus, you still have to buy new lids. And some of those jars people brought me were not standard-sized canning jars but rather odd-sized jelly jars, apple butter jars, pickle jars, etc.

At the writing of this manuscript, a case of quarts (twelve) will cost me around $8 to $10, depending on where I buy them and if they have them in stock (lots of places stock canning jars only as a summer seasonal item). These cases of jars come with the lids.

A case of lids (twelve) will run $2 to $3, again depending on where I buy them. So basically, when people give me old dusty jars, I save $6 to $7 per case of twelve jars, or about 50 cents per jar. Because the lids by themselves are so expensive, it really isn't very cost effective to buy lids to fit those free jars everyone wants to give me. And even at yard sales and auctions, a box of canning jars will go for $1 to $2, which after buying the lids, I'm only ahead by a couple of bucks.

Some of these used jars are filthy and I easily spend more than 50 cents of my labor washing them. Some of the calcium-laden jars I soaked in vinegar, with some satisfaction. Some of the older jars turned a milky-opaque in the dishwasher. I didn't feel right putting honey in them. So after all my cleaning and scrubbing, I took them to the recycle center.

So much for these jars being "free." So what would you do?

My advice is to go ahead and take the donations of dusty old jars. By taking the donation and saying, "thanks," you at least honor their generosity. I also have an old man who thinks that if he brings me his empty honey jars he should be entitled to a 50 cent discount on his next jar of honey. Since this was a new jar to start with, I agree. I give him a 50 cent discount on a jar that would easily cost me 50 cents to replace.

After soaking off the label and running this jar through the dishwasher, I'm probably breaking even. Ecologically speaking, I'm recycling, hopefully doing my part to slow global warming. From a consumer standpoint, I'm retaining a customer. He buys about one quart jar every month. But this is something under the category of "personalized customer service" that the big packers cannot handle.

At one point I knew a man in Illinois who was famous for his apple butter. He provided apple butter by the case to Amish restaurants. Being frugal people, they gave him back his jars, with the lids, sent back in their original cases. And the jars were washed! For whatever reason, he would not reuse them for apple butter, but rather sold the case of used jars for $2.00 to anyone who wanted them.

I bought several cases, but they all required new lids. Again, after all the dust settled and after I rewashed the jars to my satisfaction, I was probably just breaking even financially.

There are deals out there, but every deal has a cost that is not always measured in dollars and cents. But if you have more time than money, there are ways to make your marketing more profitable.

As time went on, I added more hives by catching more swarms. I was still making most of my own hives but I started to buy more frames and foundation. I needed more financial backing, which for me came from my "real" job. My hobby was taking more money than I wanted, but I kept on making money as people were now more willing to give me "a couple of bucks" for a jar of honey. But I also found that my costs were still running ahead of my income with my purchased equipment. I was now starting to look for a greater financial return. My hobby was being subsidized by my real job and I wanted it to begin to stand alone. It was time to graduate to asking for a real market value for my honey.

Somewhere in your venture you too, will also come to that point where you want to get more money out of your bees, or at least make them pay their way. Do not feel any need to apologize. Your hobby is now becoming more of a business. If you have a good product, then ask a price for what it is worth. Initially people will balk, especially those loyal customers who got used to you giving your honey away. You may have to continue to give your honey to these customers.

With more bees, and a greater investment in my bee equipment, I also began to have more honey. More honey means more money, but only if you can sell it. With more honey, I began to explore more markets. With more honey you'll have to figure out new places to sell your honey. After all, you only have so many friends who will only eat a certain amount of honey.

But with more honey to sell, you have more confidence in approaching other potential markets to sell your honey.

The first market I approached was the local health food store. It seemed like a logical approach. People who like honey shop at these kinds of stores, don't they?

The owner was pleasant and encouraging, however, he said he required me to be insured, specifically with liability insurance, which I did not have. While honey is a very low risk of causing any liabilities, I could see his point in this overly litigious society. People will sue you at the drop of a hat. Remember the human finger that was "found" in a bowl of chili at a national chain of fast-food restaurants? The customer immediately launched a lawsuit. Then it was found she tried similar stunts at other restaurants with different ploys purely for the idea of suing them.

It pays to be insured. Someday a diabetic is going to load up on honey, get sick and sue some beekeeper. It's nonsense. But at this point, insurance was not easily found nor did any insurance agent rush up to me to sell me a policy. Bees have a bad perception to someone who wants to insure you. They have a worse reputation to someone who sells insurance. So I put the health food store on hold until I could figure out my insurance plan (and at this point, with insurance costing money, I was not ready to pursue this avenue).

So I approached the manager at the local grocery store, and unless I could supply a consistent supply, year round, he wasn't interested in my honey. And, as a small supplier, it was next to impossible to find out how to get those fancy UPC bar codes to sell to larger warehouses. Further, I could probably supply enough honey to the grocery store if I stopped selling to my friends and family, and those people I would call "casual" customers. At this point, it seemed to be another "make or break" situation. I could either sell to my casual customers or I begin to break into the commercial markets (grocery stores and commercial retail). But I also needed to think seriously about getting insured. While the grocery store owner didn't say anything about being insured, it doesn't take much thought to conclude this may be a good idea.

This is the point that will either make you or break you. Either you make the commitment to get bigger and enter these kinds of commercial markets, or you back down and stay at the hobby level and sell to your friends and family. Or you wait until you have the production to satisfy both. I found it hard to start down the commercial market route because I did not want to disappoint my loyal casual customers. I needed to expand and produce more honey.

I believe, especially as I look back with 20/20 hindsight, that the financial commitment to enter these commercial markets is worth the risk. But it takes a firm COMMITMENT. I would not enter them without insuring I can continue to supply my loyal customers. It will take more money to expand, and on each pound of honey you sell to a commercial account, you will earn less money on each jar because you wholesale it rather than retail it, but these markets will open the door to selling more total honey, and in the long run will bring more money.

And in the end, the name of the game is marketing your honey. This is the end at which we must really start as you contemplate moving up to twenty-five hives. This is the end that I failed to grasp when I started my initial beekeeping venture with twenty hives right out of college. I simply presumed that people would want my honey. Isn't that how it works?

Yeah, right.

So at this point in my story, as I was still too small to really crack open the markets that seemed to be the easiest (the commercial grocery markets), I set out to sell my extra honey (over and above what I sold to my loyal, casual customers) the old fashioned way: I set up a table in my driveway with different jars of honey, and with a coffee can for the money. I even left some money in the coffee can so people could make change. Since I live on a major highway, the traffic is pretty good past my house. I painted a yellow sign for the road-side ditch that simply said, "Honey For Sale."

Much to my surprise, quite a few people stopped by my house. Total strangers who said they were driving down the road and saw my sign and they stopped in to get a jar of local honey. It was the most effortless marketing venture I ever thought of, and thankfully, I live on a well-traveled road. There is something to those three factors that determine success of "location, location and location."

I bought old-fashioned canning jars from the farm supply store. I made simple labels on my computer with Microsoft Publisher and the Avery labels I picked up from any office supply store. I made sure people knew my honey was locally produced and "raw." I also made sure I followed the right labeling laws such as weight, what it is (honey), my name and address as the law requires. It was fun. At this point I assessed the legitimate, retail market value for my honey. I made up labels with prices to go on the top of the jar.

Much to the surprise of my customers, they could not believe I trusted people to leave the money when they purchased my honey. And most of the time, there's enough money in the can to cover the jars of honey that disappear from the table.

Most of the time.

Not all the time, but most of the time. And there are times I go out to check on my money, not wanting to leave too much out there on the table........and it's all gone. Someone swings in and takes all my money.

So much for the honor system.

Events like this disappoint me, not so much in the lost money but in the lost trust. I simply chalk it up to experience and vow to not leave too much money sitting in the coffee can at any one time. And there are times I can tell people have only left a $10 bill for that $12.00 quart of honey.

Then I moved to a locking mail box for my money. The mail box was purchased at Lowe's for $60 bucks, but I discovered it paid for itself.

Oh well. At least this is not my real job.

So at this point I have a local following of casual customers and a table in my driveway with a mail box. Life is pretty good, but I'm still keeping my eye on the commercial grocery avenue. To sell commercially will allow me to market more honey, and make more money. But the commercial avenue takes more of a commitment than I was ready to accept at that time. But then it dawned on me that there are many more commercial markets to sell honey than the health food store and the grocery store.

As more and more people knew I was selling honey, I thought I might look into a farmer's market. Much to my chagrin, the only local farmer's market was a "member's only" club, most of the members living from out of the state, namely Illinois. To sell at this respective farmer's market, you had to attend the annual meeting in March, present your situation and tell them about your product, then accept the vote of the other members if you could join their club.

Well, there was already a honey seller in the club, a gentleman who came from 90 miles away to sell his honey. He didn't want to share the honey sales, and because membership provides a certain degree of control over who sells what at the market, I was not voted in. It also cost $175 to join this club, but that fee paid for advertising, insurance and parking lot rent. And if you are a member, you receive a certain degree of "protection" for marketing your product. Conceivably, the market could become an organized monopoly.

So they would not vote me in as a member. I felt discouraged and it must have showed. As I left, some of the other members at this meeting pulled me aside and suggested I come to the market anyway. I could ask to sell as a "daily" vendor.

This market had a clause that if this particular vendor selling a particular product was not present, I could ask the market manager to sell for that day only and pay a $15 fee. I did this a couple of times that first year, and I had good success. The second year this other honey vendor told the market manager that I was not welcome, that he was to be the sole honey vendor, and as a paid member, he felt he had a right to demand protection for his product. I was asked that I not return to this farmer's market as a daily vendor.

And so it goes. You win some, you lose some. Each market has their own set of rules, and quite frankly, if I was in his shoes, I probably would want my interests protected as a paid member as well.

The long and short of this story is that several other Missouri vendors were not voted in as members. The market was controlled by Illinois vendors and they did not want anyone else coming in.

So the Missouri vendors got together and set up an alternative market, one that required no vote but stipulated you had to be from Missouri. This market really got my foot in the door. This was a Wednesday morning market. I introduced my honey to several people, many of them new customers who were looking for locally grown produce.

Then I began putting up a tent at several of the annual fall "harvest" festivals. And another farmer's market opened up on Saturday mornings in a neighboring town.

As my production increased, I was approached by two locally owned supermarkets. Each one asked me to sell them honey at a 25% discount from the retail price (that was how they calculated their wholesale price). After careful thought, I agreed. Then another supermarket in a neighboring town asked to carry my honey. That's when I decided maybe I better get liability insurance. Liability insurance for "product and premises" cost me around $400 for the year, but it also gave me an open door to talk to the health food store owner again.

All along the way, production crept up to keep pace with the market demand. But then one year I ran out of honey. My experience then said, "Oh, this is no big deal, I'll just tell everyone to wait for the next season and when I get my honey harvested, they can buy again."

Well, the people who wanted my locally grown, raw honey were understanding, but they also started calling in early spring wanting to know if I had any honey. They had no knowledge of seasonal production of honey. They thought that if their yard was in bloom, I ought to have honey ready. But I kept apologizing and telling them it was not yet time for the new crop of honey.

Then a funny thing happened when I finally got my honey crop harvested in July. I had more honey than I knew what to do with. It was a great year for honey. But when I went to my regular customers, they were less than enthusiastic. All of the demand for my honey was either lost or it was replaced by something else. It took me a year to gain back those customers.

Today, as I continue to expand my markets to meet the honey production, I focus on the demand first. I educate, give away samples, put on programs at schools and service clubs. I carry around my observation hive to various functions so people can see the bees close up. I continually preach the benefits of locally grown, raw honey. Demand for good honey is out there, but sometimes you need to remind people you have honey and how good it is for them.

Marketing will probably be your greatest challenge with twenty-five hives. It becomes a "chicken and egg" argument. Which should come first? Should you have customers asking for honey or should you have ample production of honey to meet the customers as they come?

I think you need both simultaneously.

And lest you think I'm talking out of both sides of my mouth, I am. I keep increasing my production each year, through more hives and through more swarms. I also keep increasing my marketing opportunities and look for new outlets for my honey.

The two go together. If I had to choose which one is better to have, definitely the production of honey is best. You cannot sell what you do not have. And people don't have the patience to wait for the product. I will always strive to keep honey on hand to meet the demand. When demand is hot and you're out of honey, demand quickly cools. Then you are out of luck. And remember how luck is nothing more than experience and preparation meeting opportunity. When opportunity knocks, you have to be prepared with the honey. If you're out of honey, you're out of luck.

Do not ignore demand. You can't sell honey if no one knows you have it for sale. My advertisement is by word of mouth. I frequent the farmer's markets. I sell from the table in my driveway. I do programs for schools and service clubs. I'm now selling in retail supermarkets. You have to keep stimulating demand, though stimulating this demand is not hard. But do not let demand go unfulfilled. If people know you do not have honey left, they seem to go somewhere else or buy something else.

My encouragement in this chapter is to make sure you have a place to sell your honey. If nothing else, you can give it away, but with twenty-five hives, you can only give away so much. People who appreciate locally grown, raw honey are out there, but you have to find them, and at times, educate them. Markets that will sell your honey for you (supermarkets and health food stores) are not interested until you can guarantee some level of consistent supply.

And then there is another point to bring up. Producing good honey is one aspect of having twenty-five hives. It takes a lot of time and energy. Marketing the honey you produce is another aspect. It also takes a lot of time and energy. At times you will find yourself conflicted by the things that need to be done in the bee yard and the time and energy it takes to create markets for the honey you produce.

I've also been trying to get my children involved in the marketing which would give me more time to produce the honey and tend the bees. That is still a work in process.

Production, at times, seems to work against my plans for marketing. And there are times I wish I could devote more time to one or the other.

Marketing honey is frustrating at first. It seems hard, but once this train leaves the station, you'll find it rolls along the tracks remarkably well.

I put this chapter together because somewhere in the process of keeping twenty-five hives of bees, you're going to have honey that needs to be disposed of, preferably for money. For me, keeping the bees is the fun part of beekeeping, but marketing is the necessary chore that allows me to keep the bees.

Marketing is the end. And all good ventures start with the end in mind. When you have an idea of where your honey can be disposed of (whether commercially or casually), it will give you more confidence to produce the sizable amount of honey that will come from twenty-five hives.

Two other thoughts to add to this chapter on marketing. I am presently selling honey on a wholesale volume to the local health food store. He insisted I have insurance. I purchased a simple "product and premises" policy. I didn't need flood, tornado or terrorism insurance, but you may.

Secondly, as I put this chapter together, I am expanding into the "gift" store market. This market involves putting small amounts of honey in smaller, fancier, "designer" bottles. The bottles are decorative and very expensive. I am required by the store owner (a local person) to put a "shrink wrap" protection around the lid. Most beekeeping supply catalogs carry these products. And this will add a few pennies to your cost.

Again, the time and energy to market honey in these kinds of jars through a gift store is higher, but the prices I can charge them, which they will, in turn, pass along to the customer, are well worth it. Knowing your customers, what size they want and what price they are willing to pay, is critical to any marketing plan.

Marketing is nothing more than creative energy. The more energy you put into promoting and marketing your honey, the more money you will make. And always remember a satisfied customer is really the end that matters, not the amount of money you bring in.

Beekeeping with Twenty-Five Hives

Chapter Three

Time management

As I suggested at the beginning of this manuscript, time and energy will be one of the biggest concerns for you as you ascend to the level of maintaining twenty-five hives.

Or if you presently have twenty-five or more hives, you have likely come to realize that twenty-five hives of bees takes a considerable amount of time. This is not your weekend hobby anymore.

Again, let me make this perfectly clear: ***beekeeping with twenty-five hives is not for***

procrastinators. Personally, irrespective of how many hives you run, even if you only have four hives, I firmly believe procrastination will only work against you, never for you, if you are a beekeeper. You just cannot fool around with twenty-five hives and do what needs to be done when you feel like it, or "when I find time," or "when the weather is suitable." You will always seem to find time when it's rainy outside, but when the sun shines, there will always be another competing demand upon your time. It just doesn't pay to procrastinate.

Alternatively, you cannot justify the lame excuse of, "I'm letting the bees do what comes naturally," as your rationale for procrastinating. However, the more you tend your bees, the more productive they will be. Productive beekeepers give their bees what they need and when they need it. Most beekeepers balk at the cost of the inputs to keep the bees healthy and productive, which is itself a form of procrastination.

The only advantage to the procrastinator with four hives is that the consequences are not too damaging if you mess up. Procrastinate with four hives and you'll live and keep bees another day. If you harvest no honey, keep an old, unproductive queen, have no production of brood or if the bees all died out from your lack of mite control, you can always buy more packages the next spring. It's just not that big of a deal, relatively speaking.

Procrastinate with twenty-five hives and the stakes are significantly higher. If all twenty-five of your hives swarm you may be out of business. This is especially true if you have developed markets where you have promised honey. Once a market is lost, it is really difficult to get it back. Most commercial outlets want a consistent supply of honey.

The costs are also higher, proportionately with twenty-five hives. Your mistakes become magnified as well. The consequences are greater. You just don't have the luxury of procrastinating with twenty-five hives as you do with four hives, but even with four hives, there really is no place for procrastination either. It's just that the costs of procrastinating don't hurt as bad.

A second axiom to keep in mind if you are moving up to twenty-five hives is this: ***beekeeping with twenty-five hives is not for wimps.***

Don't tell me how you have a couple of "hot" hives and how you just cannot bring yourself to get "motivated" to requeen them. Don't complain to me about how you can't find the old queen to "dequeen" her before you attempt to introduce a new queen. Don't complain to me of how you're so busy you didn't get a chance to work your bees, or how hot you get when you wear your bee suit in the humidity of July. Don't look out the window at a coming storm front and fret about how the bees might be a little "testy" today. Set your wimpiness aside and fire up the smoker and go work your bees. When time is short, there will be days you absolutely have to work your bees so you might as well bite the bullet and do it.

And yes, I know you're busy. We're all busy and we make time for what we _want_ to do, which is not always what we _need_ to do. If anything, the greatest temptation is to take the path of least _resistance_, or in fact, the path of least _persistence_ when you have twenty-five hives.

It takes a certain passion to be a beekeeper. Amid all the troubles and frustrations, it takes a certain "hunger" factor that drives you to want to do what most normal people consider to be an insane hobby. It takes discipline to set aside those days you'd rather be fishing.

Or if you have family obligations, you have to fit your beekeeping around something that is more important, and family should always come before the bees. So it becomes your responsibility to take care of the bees during a time that does not conflict with your family obligations.

When it comes time to perform a certain management item in your bee yards, there are few options. The work has to be done. Putting it off because you don't like the weather and you think the bees will be a little ornery just will not do. Suit up and get to it. If you know you need to get out and reverse the hive bodies to prevent swarming, make your plans around the weather. Be proactive and not reactive.

With today's computers and computerized weather forecasts on the news, making the time to work the bees is not a problem. Within certain parameters, you can work around the weather and adjust your plans accordingly. Making time is not the problem. Taking time is another issue. If you're busy like all the rest of us, life is not about **making** the time but **taking** the time. You have to do what needs to be done, when it needs to be done.

If motivation and energy are lacking, then maybe beekeeping with twenty-five hives is not for you. Maybe you're better off sticking with four hives. But only you can really make that decision, and sometimes it seems we need to stretch our goals and suffer a setback before we really get motivated to do what needs to be done.

I can tell you from my own experience how I thought keeping twenty-five hives was just like keeping twelve hives, only that it would take twice as long. My expansion brought with it frustrations because everything seemed to compete with my schedule, and of course, the bees, since they were still just a hobby for me, came in last.

Then winter set in and I lost some hives. So I bought a few more packages. Then spring came and the hives that survived the winter swarmed. All of my hives failed to produce any substantial amounts of honey that year. And this came at a time when my markets were really starting to develop for local honey.

But I learned my lessons from my mistakes. I readjusted my goals and expectations. I organized my priorities and disciplined my procrastination. I made better use of my time. I started to keep better records. Failure is just finding out ways that some things don't work. It's not the falling down that matters, it's the will to get up after you fall down that really counts.

In this chapter, I present three ideas on time management that have helped me get done all there is to get done. And what you'll find is you never really get all your work done. There is always something else that pops up immediately when you think you've finally caught up. You move from one season right into the next season. Even when there is snow on the ground and the bees are safely nestled in their hives for the winter, there are the indoor jobs of nailing frames together and cutting out bottom boards. The work really never ends, even for someone with only four hives.

On one hand, expanding to twenty-five hives is harder because there is more work to do, and more works simply takes more time. Yet on the other hand, the more you work with bees the more your efficiency increases. In the long run, you get better at what you do and you will be able to handle more hives in less time.

I can remember my early days of opening hives so slowly and carefully. Inexperience told me to go slow, don't squish the queen, and if a few bees started buzzing my veil, I got nervous and fearful. Then I felt like I had to personally escort all those buzzing bees back in the hive before I closed up. Leaving a hive open for too long is also an invitation to initiate robbing. When the robbing starts, I would feel demoralized and feel like I had to come back after things settled down and when I had more time. Can you guess how hard it is to find "more time?"

Today, I go much faster with my hive inspections, my observations are more adept, my handling of the frames is more confident. I know to open the hive with efficiency and I know what to look for. However, if there is a downside to beekeeping with twenty-five hives, it is the fact that I cannot spend my time leisurely handling every frame in every box. But the upside is your efficiency increases and you can work more hives.

In terms of time management, I present three ideas to help increase your efficiency.

The first idea is to block off single, uninterrupted blocks of time. This allows you to get into a bee yard and do all that you need to do. Make sure, as you set up these blocks of time, that you find as large a block as possible, certainly as large as the chores require. Include travel time and then a little cushion for when Mr. Murphy comes to visit. Murphy, of "Murphy's Law," comes to see me every time I venture into a bee yard. It makes me wonder how he knows my schedule so well!

I cannot tell you how frustrating it was when I once tried to go out and take care of one bee yard with a free hour during lunch or in the early afternoon, only to find the chore took more time than I could devote to it. Or I wasn't organized enough to collect and load the resources (tools and equipment) I needed to work the yard. Or I would come home and check my e-mail first before going out to the bee yard (and remember what I said about procrastination?).

Then, once I got out and began working the bees, I would get a call on my cell phone and I had to leave to tend to some "real" work or pick up my children from school or something else. Then I hoped I had time to return and finish what I started. Then I also had to keep notes on which hives were worked, which hives yet needed to be worked, and which hives needed some kind of remedial treatment or manipulation, and what resources I needed the second time that I forgot the first time out.

Simply put, I need large blocks of interrupted time. I need a couple of hours, and I also need a reasonable estimate of what I can accomplish in those couple of hours, and this block of time also includes transportation time from work, to home, then out to the bee yard. And the best time to work the bees is also the best time for just about everything else. Time is always in short supply because it's in the highest demand.

I also find I need to schedule these blocks of times. I need to make an appointment with myself. There are always a hundred different priorities competing for my time every day. There are times of year I simply need to make certain that specific tasks in the bee yard remain a top priority. Swarm prevention and supering are key times when the work absolutely has to get done. I need to make my bees a priority during these key times. Then I need to schedule an "appointment" with myself to insure I keep that schedule as a priority.

I like larger blocks of time (like entire afternoons) so I can swing into the bee yard and do the same thing to all the hives. In early April, I start my hive inspections and I like to block out the time and go in and look at all the hives, all on that same day in that respective bee yard. Later, as I start reversing brood boxes, I like to go in and manipulate all the boxes that need reversing. And how do I know which ones need reversing? I keep records. More on that in another chapter.

For me, trying to do a little bit here, then a little bit later just didn't work. It was more stressful to do some of the work a little at a time, only to have to return to continue the work again at a later time. I felt like I was accomplishing more when I could go out for three solid hours in one afternoon rather than work one lunch hour for three afternoons. The drive to the bee yard would take more time than the time I spent with the bees. Just getting organized to get out there is a huge hurdle. Once I make it to the bee yard, I'm good to go.

So for me, blocking off a large block of time and doing everything that needs to be done is the first key to my time management.

This brings up my second idea: group the chores and do them all at once to all the hives. As an example, I'll go to the bee yard and do **two things** to all the hives. Then I'll come back the next week and do **four different things** to all the hives. I found this easier than opening up a hive and doing **all six things**, but only working half of the hives in the yard. Then I have to come back on another day and work the other half of the hives. But often the weather provides me with alternative plans!

What this does is force me to think about my hives and what needs to be done first. I prioritize my to-do list and think about what chores really need to be done right now and which chores can wait. For me, swarm prevention is a big issue. Queen quality is a secondary issue. Spring mite control is third. Once these issues get settled, then I look to supering.

But in my early days, when I would open a few hives today and do all those things, then a week later I would work a couple of more hives as time allowed, then a week later I'd come to those other hives I meant to get to on the first trip. But then I'd start finding swarm cells in that third group. By the time you find swarm cells, you're about two weeks behind schedule. If you like to cut out swarm cells, plan on doing it again in nine days. Your neglect, even if it's justifiable due to a busy schedule, sets the stage to trigger the bees to start swarm preparations. Bees don't suddenly decide to swarm. The impulse to swarm is triggered at least two weeks before they start building swarm cells.

Working with twenty-five hives can be stressful, especially if you want to do it right, especially if you're trying to "shoe-horn" beekeeping into an already too-full schedule of work and family responsibilities.

My first suggestion is to block off enough time so you can do what needs to be done. When you get to the bee yard, decide ahead of time what tasks are more important, or what single task is most important, then do it to all your hives. In this way, all your hives are kept on a schedule, they are kept relatively even in their management, and important tasks are done in a timely manner and no hive falls behind and swarms on you.

My second thought on time management is to prioritize what needs to be done and when I'm going to do it, then do that task to all the hives in the bee yard. It will give you a subtle feeling of accomplishment.

This brings me to my third thought on time management: record keeping. Record keeping is an entirely separate chapter so I'll be brief as it portends to time management. Keep a system where you know what you did, and when you did it, and to what hives it was done.

My current record system is basically two spiral notebooks. The first spiral notebook is the one that I carry in the bee yards. I call it my field notebook. As my hands get coated in propolis and honey, it becomes a sticky mess. But this is not my main concern at this point. My field notebook serves the purpose of noting what was done to which hive on that particular visit to the bee yard.

For each hive, I simply note the hive number, how it looks (poor-fair-good-great) and what it needs (mite treatment, super, requeening) or what was done. Let me remind you that every hive I have has a number. In this notebook, on the first page that is available, I write down the designated number not becoming concerned with keeping things in the right order. Then I jot down what I did and what that hive needs for the next visit to the bee yard.

But later, as I clean up at home, I take those field notes and put them in a second spiral notebook, one that I call my "log" book. I created a simple notebook with a numbered page that corresponds to a numbered hive. These pages have the hive numbers in their numerical sequence. All my hives are given a number so I'm sure which hive I've worked. Additionally, when I know there is something that needs to be done to a specific hive, the number on the hive is a whole lot simpler than trying to remember, "old hive on north side of locust tree next to strong hive that came from the swarm at the old school house."

Find some way to designate and distinguish your hives from one another.

Each hive has a numbered page in my log book corresponding to that respective hive. On these pages, with clean hands free of propolis and honey, I copy down what I observed in the bee yard and wrote in my field notebook.

After I copy, translate and interpret my field notes, I tear those sticky pages out of my field notebook and throw them away. They have no further purpose for me.

From my second notebook, my log book, I make a to-do list on a clean page in my field notebook. As I schedule my next trip out to the bee yard, I open my field notebook and make a note of what needs to be done to which hives, and what equipment I need to do it (supers, queen excluders, etc.)

One of the most frustrating feelings is when I get out to a bee yard and then I remember that I need to tend to a couple of hives with a chore left from my last trip. Even more frustrating is my remembrance of something I needed to do but I failed to bring out the right things like supers, extra dividers, etc.

There have been times I thought to myself, "Well, this is no problem. I'll bring out that item the next time I drive by."

By the next time I come to that bee yard to do my normal inspections, I find the bees have continued their normal quest without my permission, and generally have made the situation worse (thanks in part to my neglect).

Here's an axiom you can take to the bank: ***a long list is better than a short memory.***

Also: Nothing really happens until you write it down.

I've known beekeepers who use the "brick" method of hive analysis and record keeping. They weigh down the hive cover with a brick, and if the brick is on the front edge of the cover, things are good. If the brick is on the back side of the cover, it needs a super. If the brick is in the middle, it needs requeening. If the brick is standing up the hive is in need of something else. If the brick is wet it's probably raining and you should go home.

The brick method works well if you can remember what each configuration means, but it only benefits you when you are standing in front of the hive. I need, since I have remote hives located all around the county, a record keeping system that gently reminds me of what I need to bring along with me before I get there. Many of these bee yards are too far away for me to make a return trip back home for a single super, etc.

Along these lines, there are some essential items I need every time I go out to the bee yard. These include my veil, my smoker, an assortment of hive tools, my queen catcher, queen marking stuff, a bottle of rubbing alcohol to clean the propolis off my fingers, extra hive tools if I drop one in the grass. I want all these things available so if I decide on a moment's notice that my schedule is free for the afternoon, I can swing home, change my clothes, pick up my essentials and head on out to the bee yard.

Right now I keep my smoker in an old munitions can. I have a bucket of wood chips and newspapers to light my smoker. I have a plastic tub for my veil and gloves. I also have an old milk crate to hold my hive tools, matches, markers, queen catcher, alcohol bottle, etc. When I'm on the run and I want to go work my hives, it becomes quite easy to simply pull into the house, pick up my munitions canister, the plastic bucket, the plastic tub and my milk crate and I'm good to go. I have everything I need. This saves time from looking around the garage trying to find my veil, smoker, etc. I have it all boxed up and ready to go. Additionally, I usually keep these things with me anyway, especially during the early spring.

To reiterate how I manage twenty-five hives, there are three things I do that will help. **First**, I try and block off enough uninterrupted time to do what needs to be done. And you might even make a little cushion in this block as time has a habit of expiring before everything you need to do gets done. **Second**, try and organize your management tasks to get the same treatment done to all the hives in that bee yard, all at once on this one trip. **Third**, keep records, or at least a "to-do" list of what you want to do so you know what tools or items you need to bring.

And then as a **fourth** thing, have your necessary and essential equipment ready to go at a moment's notice so you don't waste time hunting for it. My equipment is packed such that I carry it around with me in the car all the time during the normal bee season. If not, I have it contained and organized in the garage that I can simply load and go.

One last thought: I think keeping twenty-five hives in one place is just fine. Sooner or later, if you keep adding hives, you may be looking at several locations. If you wonder about how you can manage multiple locations, start out with just a couple of hives in different places. See how it works to come into a bee yard, work the hives, then pack up and move to the next bee yard and work those hives. Sometimes the hardest time management obstacle, other than your own procrastination, is the drive between the different yards where you keep your bees. Once you reach your destination, the work becomes easier.

When it comes to managing twenty-five hives, time management plays a huge roll in your success. The better organized you are, the more efficient your time management will become. At first, it will seem impossible, but as time moves along, your time management skills improve.

And if you are still struggling to work ten hives in one afternoon, relax. The more you work your bees, the better at it you will get.

Beekeeping with Twenty-Five Hives

Chapter Four

Mentoring and Being Mentored

I am a firm believer in mentoring. I think it is the best way to teach someone, especially yourself. Mentoring is a two-way street. It's about a relationship. And further, if you need to learn a few things, the best way to learn things yourself is to prepare the lesson and teach someone else. You'd be surprised at how much you learn when you prepare to teach someone else.

I'm also a firm believer in the principles of showing a person how things are done, then doing it with them, then having them do it as you watch. There used to be an old mantra (which I cannot recall perfectly) but it went something like this:

Be One - Do One - Show One

This pattern of "show and share" is what I believe is at the heart mentoring. Mentoring is also about a relationship, the two-way street of give-and-take. It's about sharing ideals while still respecting opinions. If there is one thing to glean from this chapter it is the ideal that we benefit from relationships focused around a common goal. In this case, it is beekeeping.

But here is a caveat: I've never met a beekeeper who wasn't also very opinionated. And don't get me wrong. Opinions are fine. But beekeepers seem to become almost entrenched in their opinions.

Thankfully, there are more ways to keep bees than we realize. We need to "live and let live," and follow the admonition, "to each their own." So in our zeal to help someone, let us remember our own need for help and our own need for learning. In our enthusiasm to teach, let us remember that we also need to be taught. Mentoring is a shared partnership.

It is also my hope that you would contribute to the world of beekeeping by helping someone else, and conversely, you'd recognize the benefits that come as you seek and find another beekeeper to become your mentor. My advice is to develop relationships where you give and where you receive.

It's a lot like the counseling profession. Counselors open their doors to help people, but they also submit themselves to a colleague for accountability and supervision. They give help and they receive help, they render advice and they accept advice, they share their thoughts and they listen to their peers. This is how they grow in their profession. And they learn a lot about themselves as they help people with personal problems. And so it is with beekeeping.

In my early years of keeping bees, I was blessed to have a couple of older gentlemen who acted as my mentors. While we didn't have a specific relationship of teacher-student or leader-pupil, these old men were my "go-to" guys. When I had a problem or a question, I would go to these guys.

In reflection, they had a TON of patience with me. I was young, idealistic, energetic, full of enthusiasm and passion. I also had some wild-hair ideas. I also thought

I knew it all. When I'd bounce an opinion or a new idea off of these old boys, they'd usually respond with a respectful, "Well, that's one way to do it." Sometimes they'd say, "Seems like a lot of extra work to me, but if that's what you want to do, then do it."

What made our relationship difficult is that they were retired and small. I was full of energy, idealism and I wanted to become big, no, not big, HUGE. They were content with their level of beekeeping and I was itching for things bigger and better (or so I thought). I am continually reminding myself that we're all on a different journey. Further, it's not the destination that's important but the joy of walking along the journey as partners and friends. That is the joy of mentoring.

And even though we had different aspirations when it came to our respective bees, there are problems shared by all beekeepers. Every one of us will have a colony go queenless or swarm excessively. We all welcome some advice on how to chase bees from the super you want to take home. This is where a shared partnership works. In the end, they were content and I was itching for more.

But the point is I had someone to talk to, to bounce ideas off of, to gather advice and experience.

What was lacking in my youthful zeal was someone to share my ideals with, someone else who needed help that I could offer. You have to give as much as you receive. And it doesn't matter if you are a rookie, a newbee or a wannabee. Help someone else and don't worry about what you don't know. Mentoring is a learning process and you'll learn some things along the way as you wrap yourself up in the teaching.

There is an analogy to the Dead Sea in the Holy Land. The Dead Sea has an extremely high salt content, due in part to the fact that the waters of that area flow into it. Unfortunately, there is no outlet, and with the evaporation process, the water in this body of water increased in its salinity with every passing year. Finally, it got to the point where it could no longer support life and everything within it died. It is a dead sea so they named it, the Dead Sea.

And so it is with humans. You cannot live your life continually taking without doing some kind of giving, some kind of sharing. We all need help. We all have questions. We all have some goofy ideas and so we are always asking questions and seeking advice. My advice is to find someone with which you can share, someone with which you can contribute your help.

Even if you don't know too much about beekeeping, at least share your enthusiasm and your encouragement. Life is about giving. And did you know that people who donate blood to the Red Cross live longer? It is true, especially for men. And yet it seems like a paradox: give blood and live longer. Giving to others helps, and mentoring is really about a giving relationship.

As you come to the level of keeping twenty-five hives of bees, my advice is to seek out someone to help you with your problems and questions, but also do your best to continue to help others. We were all beginners once. And everybody has a first day on the job. They may even test your patience, but find someone to help get started in bees.

I was blessed in my early years with those good old boys who had been around a long time and seen a lot with their bees. Thankfully, no matter how crazy my ideas, they were gentle and kind, and in retrospect, many of my ideas were, well, just down right crazy.

What I've learned over the years is that we all will develop certain ways on how we like to do things. We also have different ways we learn how to do things. We also have some strong ideas on what we do not want to do. And we all have the same resistance to change.

Over my years, especially as I watch my children grow, there are different ways and styles of learning. Some people can read a book and instantly translate the knowledge into application. There are some people who read, but they cannot make the transition of the key ideas into the actual learning process. We call them "visual learners." Instead of reading, they have to be shown. They need a demonstration. And you will also find people who consistently make errors of common sense, but if you correct them, they become horribly insecure. They'll get defensive, call you "arrogant," and they'll begin to belittle your beekeeping practice behind your back. What you may think is "constructive criticism" will be nothing but "tearing them down" in their defensive opinion.

Don't worry about them. We're all human. Take a deep breath. Don't let their problems become your problems. Some people just need more love and encouragement. One of my pastor friends refers to these kinds of people as "E.G.R." people. E.G.R. stands for "Extra Grace Required."

I think everyone ought to have a mentor, and everyone ought to mentor someone else. And this may be the same person from which you take as you give. Even if you feel you don't have the education or the experience, you can still be a listening ear, you can be a non-judgmental associate to present a balanced objective (which is not the classical "devil's advocate"—I don't think the devil ever needs advocates!). In short, everyone needs a friend in the beekeeping profession, even if you're only doing it as a hobby, and even if you don't know too much.

As a mentor, and as I've been mentored, I've learned the hard way, on both the giving and the receiving ends, that the last thing you need to say is, "Well, if I was you..." as you proceed to tell someone how they need to do it (as if there was only one right way to do things). Remember what I said about beekeepers having lofty opinions of their own personal methods.

If you find yourself saying, "Well, if I was you..."

Stop.

You are not them. And we have to remember that all of us are going to do things differently for different reasons. We all learn differently. We have different purposes, and maybe you ought to find out what their purpose is in beekeeping. Then you can adjust your teaching process to their learning ability. Maybe they don't have your lofty goals. Maybe they don't want to work as hard as you do. Maybe they just want to have fun and if their colonies swarm it's no big deal to them.

(I, by the way, think anyone who lets their bees swarm is not taking care of their bees, but that's just my opinion).

We're all on the same journey in beekeeping, but others will want to go at a slower pace or others may want to take a side trip. Some have specific destinations and some are just along for the ride. We're all different, and mentoring respects those differences.

I'll say that again with emphasis: **Mentoring respects those differences.**

I find it helpful in the mentoring process to start by saying, "Well, if this beehive were in my yard, then I would..."

And then I offer the upside of my methods, and then balance my suggestion with the downside. Every solution has a benefit but also a cost. There are advantages and disadvantages to the same solution.

Then I offer, "And there are other ways to address this problem." I might also share what my purpose is in keeping bees, then explain why my solutions would be my choice. Then I'd ask them what their purpose in keeping bees is and what possible solutions might fulfill their purpose.

Then I let them decide. There's no use advocating any one solution, even if it's the one you would do personally, even if you know it's the only real solution to the problem. Sometimes people have to learn by failing or making mistakes on their own. And don't be offended if they choose another way other than the one you've offered them, even if it appears they are headed for disaster.

As it has been said,

"Life is a great teacher,
but her tuition is mighty expensive.

Sometimes people will come to me and they'll say, "I'm thinking of doing XYZ. What do you think? Is this the right thing to do?"

It may be the right thing for them, but not for me. Or I might be able to tell it is way too ambitious for their skill level. So do I beat them up and ridicule their ideas as ignorant and stupid?

Only if I want to lose a friend.

You can be right, or you can be in a relationship. But often you cannot be both.

Many times people offer ideas looking for validation. Sometimes they just want their opinion heard. Sometimes they want to show you how they, too, know a few things about keeping bees. That's okay. Validate them as people, as beekeepers, even if you'd never in a million years do what they propose.

I remember one of my college professors, when asked a question about a certain treatment or experimental theory, would answer, "Well, with all things being equal..." Then he'd give his response. Then he'd remind us that all things have to be equal.

However, in real life, few things are seldom equal. What he was saying is that there are answers that work in one situation, and they won't necessarily give the same results in another situation. It's like how two cooks can take the same recipe and turn out two different results.

There have been times when someone asked me about trying certain practices, expecting specific results. My response has usually been, "Well it's been my experience…"

This response doesn't tell them they're wrong, nor does it tell them it won't work. What it does is respect their opinion (or perceived hopes), suggest the possibility that results may vary (because there a host of unintentional variables, hence, my college professor's caveat that "all things being equal,"). And it also alerts them to the possibility that you may have tried the same thing and found different results than they are expecting. It gives them the latitude to try it, but not to get bashed with the old fashioned, "Well, I told you so," when it didn't reach their expectations.

And what do you do with the person who rejects every idea you offer but continue to ask what you'd do with their problem? In almost every profession, from pastors to trapshooters to golfers to the Master Gardeners, there are people who ask you a question as they present you with a problem, then with every solution you offer, they find fault and come up with a million reasons why your ideas won't work. Or why they can't make it work. Or why they don't want to accept your solution.

Or they take your advice, screw it up by taking a short cut or avoiding all semblance of hard work by cutting corners or leaving out the main ingredient, only to find out it wouldn't work. And they're genuinely surprised that it didn't work! You know who is going to get blamed for their mistake, don't you?

So what do you do? You could continue to offer solutions to their problems, only to be shot down time and time again. But remember that Jesus said there was something simply wrong about tossing out pearls before swine. So what do you do?

I get them talking. Since they won't listen to me, I try and get them to listen to themselves. There's another barnyard analogy about leading a horse to water, and how you can't necessarily make it drink. However, if it won't drink, you feed it salt. You make it thirsty.

If a person won't listen to me and only comes up with excuses why my solutions won't work, or why they won't even try it, I get them talking. I try and get them to listen to themselves. So I start asking a variety of questions, some questions being rhetorical, some open-ended, some just plain obvious. My goal is to get them to come up with their own solution. So I ask them questions. I make them thirsty. Sometimes they don't realize they're thirsty so this may take a little more time than you have patience.

My first questions are pretty broad. Then I narrow the questions down to their specific problem. I ask what they want from their bees, where they want to go with this hive, then how they think they can get there. I ask them how much money they want to spend, or how quick they want to solve their dilemma. I ask them what ends (or goals, objectives) they hope to accomplish, then what they think they have to do to achieve those ends.

Sometimes the questioning starts out with the question, "So what do you want?" What is the end they have in mind? What does success look like to them?

The next question is, "So what will it take to get there?" What tools, resources and equipment will they need? How much will it cost?

Then I follow up with, "So what is the obstacle that is keeping you from what it takes to get there?" That leads us to the real crux of the matter, namely, what do you have to do in order to overcome the obstacles? Sometimes what they need is more time, more energy or more money. Sometimes it's just a simple little device they didn't know they needed.

That's where the real work begins. It's not where you want to go, not what you need, but what you must overcome to get there. But you have to start with some kind of "end in mind." This is what I suggested in an earlier chapter.

Think about your own beekeeping plans. I raised this question early in this manuscript. What do you want? Where to you want to go? What are your hopes, your dreams, your aspirations?

When you can name this place, or when you can identify what this level of beekeeping looks like, you've answered the first question.

But then you need to ask, "So what will it take to get there?" In other words, what do you have to do first? What are the natural stepping stones that follow? How will you work on moving toward that goal and what needs to be done each day to move you along the path to that goal?

And thirdly, what are the obstacles to keeping you from getting there? And then the fourth aspect is to ask, "So what do you need to do to overcome those obstacles?"

As an example, I had a conversation quite a while ago with a person who didn't keep bees yet, but wanted to get started. He even had a spot picked out in the yard to place the hives. So I suggested he order a couple of hives, and during the winter, assemble and paint the boxes, put the frames together. Then in the spring, get his bees. This sounded fine to him.

So far so good, I thought.

With my initial questions, he identified the first answer of the four questions by identifying where he wanted to go. He wanted to get started with two hives. And that's far enough for the first year. Once he got his feet wet, he could revise that goal and expand the numbers or redirect his energy to marketing his honey. But he needed to identify where he wanted to go his first year. He needed a starting line.

So my next question was, "Okay, you know where you want to go. What will it take to get there?" He said he'd need to find the extra money to buy the hives. As a young man, newly married, he didn't have a lot of extra money. His personal budget was tight, but he had this dream of keeping honeybees. I had given him a couple of catalogs and he found out it would take about $325 to get two hives started. But he didn't have $325 to spend. And then he needed about another $70 to acquire two packages of bees. He didn't have that money either.

Now he identified his real obstacle. He needed some extra money freed up from his personal budget. Then he found a second obstacle: his wife's objection to spending money on bees when their personal budget was simply too tight to allow such a luxury.

So what did he do? He identified his real need as more money to overcome the financial obstacle, so his solution to was take on some weekend work during winter. This would give him the opportunity to earn the extra money without hurting his personal budget. With the extra money obstacle solved, his wife relented and agreed to allow him to get the bees.

Now his four-fold mission was complete: (a) identifying where he wanted to go, (b) listing what he needed to do to get there, (c) naming the obstacles that prevented him from getting there, and (d) and then identifying what he really needed to do to overcome the obstacles.

When you mentor somebody, it is the obstacles that really prevent that person from moving forward. Often the obstacles become excuses, and when you can get them talking through their hopes and dreams by asking questions, you get them listening to themselves. And sometimes you have to say, "Is that excuse really holding you back?" Or, "Are you going to let that excuse keep you from attaining your dreams?"

Or to borrow a question from Dr. Phil, the television counselor, "So how's that working for you?" This question implies the obstacle needs to be addressed by some form of action. We cannot allow the obstacles to hold us back, and in truth, the obstacles will be the thing that holds us back. So we don't work on the main goal; we work on the obstacle.

Here's another example. A young lady from my church mentioned, somewhat casually, that she wanted to lose weight. So I asked her where she wanted to go. She identified a measurable goal of getting into a size 8 dress. (That meant nothing to me but it did to her. It gave her a destination.) This is step one, naming or identifying where she wanted to go.

So I asked her what she needed to do to get to a size 8. She responded by saying she really needed to start eating healthier and she needed to exercise. This is step two, identifying what it will take to reach that goal.

I asked her to identify the obstacles to eating healthier and what prevented her from exercising. After all, if this is what it would take to fit into a size 8 dress, then why not just do it? Why not just start exercising and eating healthier?

She laughed. She said she has no time for breakfast, and at lunchtime, all her friends go to any one of the hundred fast food (high fat, unhealthy) restaurants in the area. By lunchtime she's practically starving because she missed breakfast so she eats way too much at lunch. Her work is over at five, and she needs to pick up her child from the daycare and go home to fix dinner, dinner usually being a take-out pizza or fast-food drive-through. By dinner time, she's so tired she flops on the couch and watches television until bedtime. She has no social life because she can't find, or afford, a babysitter. Then the next day is played out just the same. This is step three, identifying the obstacles.

And in her case, those are some pretty strong obstacles. My next question brought her to the real problem: how does she overcome these obstacles? This is step four, identifying what you really need to do to overcome the obstacles.

She had no idea. To her, the situation was hopeless and she was helpless. But still she had this elusive dream of fitting into a size 8. Here's an important part of mentoring:

It's not really where you want to go, it's the obstacles that prevent you from getting there.

So I suggested, with a "what if" type question, that perhaps she get up a little earlier each morning and eat a balanced breakfast. This would keep her from getting so hungry around lunch time. Then, instead of going with her co-workers to eat fast food, she takes that noon-time lunch hour to hit the gym at the health club and put in an hour's worth of exercise. Then she goes back to work, picks up her child at five, and goes home to fix a decent dinner.

This way she finds time in her day to get the exercise she needs, during a portion of the day when she has arrangements for childcare. She replaces the unhealthy eating pattern with exercise, and she gets the exercise before she gets too tired at the end of the day. I suggested she make some meal plans, once a week, and do some sensible grocery shopping as she plans ahead. I laid this out as a suggestion, then let her decide.

But she said she had no money for the membership at the health club. Here, she identified another obstacle. She claimed she could not afford the membership. So what does she need to do in order to find the money for a gym membership? I asked her how much she was spending on her lunches. She had no idea. Her ignorance of how much she was spending for lunch with her coworkers was another obstacle. I called it the obstacle of ignorance.

So we tracked her expenses for one week as a means of eliminating this obstacle of ignorance. The amount of money she was spending on lunches was staggering. If she skipped lunch, she would save more than enough money in one week to pay for a month of her gym membership, plus she would have extra money left over to pay off her car loan earlier than expected.

As I look at her decisions, she had a goal of fitting into a size 8 dress. That was her goal. This is step one.

She identified exercise as her means to get there. This is step two. But then she quickly identified the real issues, the obstacles to a gym membership were a lack of time and money. This is step three.

She then went to work on the obstacles. By rearranging her time and adjusting her eating habits, she was able to find the time and the money to afford the gym. This is step four.

Because we identified the obstacles (the real problem) first, she was open to accepting my suggestions. Upon accepting my suggestions, she took ownership of the ideas as her own. And a lot of these ideas I simply posed as, "So what about....?" and, "What if...?"

It's marvelous stuff.

And she did it. She lost the weight and found herself wearing a size 8, not because I said she should, but because I laid the situation out with possible methods of overcoming the obstacles. I'm sure if I said, that to lose the weight, she needed to join the gym and cut out the fast food, she would have a host of excuses why that wasn't possible. I didn't tell her to reach her goal, I helped her overcome the obstacles.

This line of questioning, a form of mentoring, moves a person from a seemingly impossible goal to overcoming the obstacles to that goal. When you can overcome the obstacles, you can reach the goal. Shoot for the goal and you'll encounter the obstacles. It is the obstacles that need to be addressed. Often times we're trying to reach a goal when in fact it is the obstacles that need to be addressed and conquered. It's like looking at the mountain peak and we need to find a way to cross the river at the base of the mountain first.

And here is the real key. If you won't work at tackling the obstacles, then I doubt if you're very serious about reaching your goal. Your goal might be something that you're aiming for because everyone else thinks it's a good idea. We like to talk a good talk about goals, but the real work (and the real progress) is found in tackling the obstacles.

Let's take a look at a beekeeping example. An older gentleman with five hives came to me complaining how he wasn't getting any honey, and hadn't for the past few seasons. I asked him what he thought the problem might be. He didn't know. So we went out to his bee yard, and all five of his hives were set up with a single brood box and a honey super. In most cases, as we opened the lid, the honey super had quite a bit of capped brood in it, and a few frames of uncapped honey.

The first thing I noticed is that there were very few bees in his hives. This was odd. For all the capped brood present, I expected to find more adult bees in the hive. As we lifted off the super and tore apart his brood box, I found out why. I found frame after frame with old swarm cells attached to the bottom of the frame, surrounded by frames of capped brood and sealed honey (it was very dark and appeared to be last year's honey). There were also several frames solid with pollen.

I tried to explain that every frame of solid honey or pollen was like a brick wall. It was of no use to the queen to lay eggs in, and it provided no room for incoming nectar. Basically this beekeeper had a five-frame nuc. All the other frames were filled with honey rendering them unavailable to the queen. No wonder the colony swarmed. I also tried to explain that all of this sealed brood, by the time the bees emerge and mature and become foragers, the honey flow would likely be way beyond its potential. The bees would be lucky to bring in enough nectar to make enough honey for their winter stores.

But I did point out a key advantage. He now had a colony that was run by a brand-new queen. She would have the youth and the vigor to produce a goodly amount of bees for the next year. But if he didn't add more room, then that vigorous queen would tie up a lot of cells with her eggs which would trigger swarming. And it appeared this was his annual problem.

Upon this inspection, it was obvious his problem was congestion which triggered swarming. Congestion is the competition between eggs and nectar for the open cell space. As this was an older colony, pollen was also plugging up a lot of the cell space.

I said, "Your problem is that this colony has swarmed. It's too weak to produce any surplus honey this year, and it's been doing this every year. Now all you can do is plan for next year, and if you want honey, you need to make sure your bees don't swarm. When they swarm they leave with the work force of foragers that's the backbone of the nectar gathering."

He responded by saying, "So what do I need to do?"

I said, "You'll need to buy another brood box for each hive, and probably buy a couple of more supers for each hive. And, of course, you'll also need the frames and the foundation for all those boxes."

"How much will that cost me?" he asked.

I did some quick math. He needed five brood boxes at $10 each, ten supers at $8 each, plus 150 frames (ten brood and twenty medium for each hive) that run about $1 apiece with the foundation. So I gave him a conservative, ballpark figure of $300 when you figure in shipping."

He gasped, "Three-hundred dollars?"

"Well," I said calmly, trying to calm him down. "You said you wanted honey. If you want to keep your bees from swarming, you need to give them more room."

"But not for three-hundred dollars," he interrupted.

Taking the conversation another direction, I asked, "So what do you really want?"

He thought for a moment, then said, "I'll tell you what I don't want. I don't want to spend no three-hundred dollars to get some honey."

"So what you really want is to keep bees but you don't want to spend any money on them. You don't want to spend money to give them enough room to store surplus honey." I tried to say this without sounding judgmental or overly critical.

"Well, yeah, but I want some honey."

I said, "But you can't have it both ways. What do you really want? You either take the little honey they'll produce, if any, or you give them more room so they won't swarm."

"But if I give them all that room," he began to protest, "what am I going to do with all that honey?"

"I thought you wanted to harvest some honey," I replied.

"Well, yeah, but not that much," he countered.

"So what do you really want?" I asked.

He was silent for a while, then he finally said, "I guess I want the bees to work it out on their own. I don't want to spend any more money on them. Maybe I'll buy my honey from you if I don't get any this year."

Now we know what he really wanted. He didn't really want honey. He wanted the bees to make due with what they had. We put the hives back together without saying too much, then I went home. I never heard from that man again. I don't know if he still is keeping bees or if he sold his equipment. It really doesn't matter. He never did come and buy a jar of honey from me.

People are funny in that they say they want one thing but in reality, they want something else. Sometimes they don't know what they want but they will tell you what they don't want. Or they'll tell you what you want them to hear. Asking questions clarifies what they want.

Asking good questions also helps them to reveal the obstacles. We often speak in the language of goals, but it is the unspoken obstacles that prevent us from moving forward and eventually reaching our goals.

Then there are also some people who will clearly identify what they want, but when you explore the obstacles, they don't want to work through the obstacles. And if they are not willing to work through the obstacles, then they have to be satisfied with what they presently have: an unmet goal.

In counseling, I frequently find people who have problems, but they don't really want to work on them. Working on problems takes work. But living with the problems is painful. The question I often pose to the person seeking counseling is this: Is living with the pain of the problem greater than the work it takes to fix it? If the work to fix it is greater, they will usually learn to accept their problem and live with it. Only when the pain of the problem is greater than the work will they choose to find a solution to their problem.

In a nutshell, until the pain of the problem is greater than the work it takes to fix it, most people are unwilling to work on their problems.

And so it is in beekeeping. For this gentleman in the last example, buying three-hundred dollars worth of new equipment was the solution. But the cost of the solution was greater than the pain of the annual swarming and the lack of any harvestable honey. Until he decided that he wanted honey, he chose (by default) to keep doing what he was doing. The only problem was he was going to keep doing what he was doing only he was looking and hoping for different results.

Here's another lesson from the Book of Grant: If you keep doing what you've been doing, you'll keep getting what you've been getting. Anytime you think you're going to get different results when you keep doing what you've always been doing is the **definition of insanity**.

Here's the **definition of wisdom**: To look objectively at life and change the things that can be changed and accept that which cannot be changed.

But you know how resistant we all are to change. So often in the church I hear one of two things. I hear, "But we've **never** done it that way before," or I hear, "But we've **always** done it this way before."

Both statements are recipes for frustration. They both convey the idea that things will not change, nor will they be changed.

And that's too bad.

You can lead a horse to water, but you can't make him drink. There are some people who claim they are thirsty. They say they want this water. They boldly say that they'll do anything to get this water, but even if led to it, they won't drink. You, as a mentor, need to remind them they are thirsty. You do this by asking questions that guide them through their situation to clarify what they really want.

And what you may find, instead, is their confession of what they really don't want or that which they are truly unwilling to do. And by default, if they are unwilling to change, they have made their choice in what they really want to do. Actions will always speak louder than words. Don't tell me what you think you want, show me by your actions.

Mentoring is a lot of fun, but it can be frustrating because you know people say one thing and yet settle for something completely different. So watch how this works. Ask some questions. Pretty soon a light goes on in their head and they blink wildly for a few minutes. They start to "get it," but they fail to realize you guided them to come up with their own solution.

And it's funny how if you had said the very same thing, or offered the very same solution they came up with, you'd be rejected along with your lame ideas. Yet when they come up with the solution, they like it. That's the trick I've learned in many different contexts: people like ideas when they think they came up with them, and in a technical sense, they did. You just guided them through the decision making process. You made them thirsty.

It's like that old bit of advice: Ideas are like children; you own are always the best. You just have to guide them to find those ideas that are their own.

And if you really want to improve your own beekeeping operation, ask yourself those same questions you ask in the mentoring process. Be a mentor to yourself. Challenge yourself to overcome the obstacles. Ask yourself these four critical questions:

1) What do I really want with my beekeeping hobby, where do I want to go?

2) What is it going to take, what do I need to get me to that level?

3) What are the obstacles that prevent me from getting what I need?

4) What do I need to do to overcome the obstacles?

And in a nutshell, you have mentored yourself.

Sometimes a good mentor does nothing but guide a person through the myriad of choices and objectives with a projection of the possible outcomes. In the end, we all need to decide what to do, and in the end, we're all responsible for our own actions, even the ones when we followed someone else's ideas.

And when a person says, "Oh, I think I'll just keep doing what I've been doing," remember that when they decide not to do something, they have made a decision. Even indecision is a decision.

The point of this chapter is to have you thinking about being a mentor to someone else, but also to be in a mentoring relationship. You'd be surprised how much you learn about keeping bees (and about yourself) when you seek to help someone else. But don't think you are beyond being taught something new. Even old dogs, even old, stubborn, obstinate know-it-all dogs can be taught new tricks. My advice is to find a mentor who will help you as you seek to help others.

One of the most eye-opening moments for me came when I took a person under my wing to mentor. I had all the grandiose designs how I was going to change this person, how I was going to make them into the Prince Charming of the local beekeepers.

Well, he didn't change. In fact, after a couple of seasons, he quit keeping bees and he gave me his equipment. At first, I considered all my work with this beekeeper to be a failure as it amounted to nothing. But looking back, trying to figure out where I went wrong, I began to see how I grew in my beekeeping expertise. I began to appreciate how teaching this new beekeeper helped me to learn a few things myself.

That's the value of mentoring. It's not a one-way, top-down dissemination of information. It's a two-way street of mutual sharing and mutual growth. So my strong advice, especially if you are seeking to move up and expand, is to find someone to mentor, and secondly, to find someone who will mentor you.

And there are times when you may be the only beekeeper in the county, or you may be the only one who has attained a certain level of accomplishment. Where do you find mentors? Where do you find others who share your aspirations to attain the level of twenty-five hives?

First, find good books. Read widely. Find some of the old classics and keep up to speed on the new books. I find a lot of the older books available from the public library. They're good, and a lot of things with bees have not changed, but they are old and some things have changed. Many of the old library books have absolutely nothing on the contemporary problems of mites, Africanized bees, small hive beetles, hygienic behavior, screen bottom boards, etc. But bee biology is still the same. The bee space is the same. The way nectar is processed is still the same.

You can also find some of the old classics on www.ebay.com and they are fun to read. But to find the newest, latest books on bees, my advice is to go to www.amazon.com and try a search for beekeeping or some other related topic. Save yourself a trip to the local, big-box retailing book store. The demand for beekeeping books is so small they won't have anything at all. But if you still want an enjoyable day at the bookstore sipping a cup of over-priced coffee, then by all means, go. Just don't have the high hope of finding any books on beekeeping.

Read widely. Read alternative books on beekeeping you might not normally find interesting. There are a couple of novels (Sue Monk Kidd's, *The Secret Life of Bees*) with beekeeping as their center piece. Watch the video of "Ulee's Gold." Pick up books on "Top Bar Hives" (popular in Kenya, Africa) or comb honey production or raising your own queens. While you may not want to do this kind of beekeeping, it will stimulate new ideas and creative thinking.

And remember, the person who doesn't read books is no better than the person who cannot read. And the person who can read, but doesn't, and thinks that it doesn't matter, is even worse. Expand your horizons by reading.

Second, subscribe to the leading magazines, *Bee Culture* (www.beeculture.com) and *The American Bee*

Journal (www.dadant.com/journal/). These will keep you up to speed on the latest trends. The advertisements in the back give you a good idea of what is driving the beekeeping market and what it costs to keep bees.

Third, join a local beekeeping group. In my area there are two groups. One is an hour and fifteen minute drive from my house. It is run in the classic sense of having officers, reading the minutes from the last meeting, accepting the treasurer's report, etc. It organizes committees for the country fair, the new beekeeper's classes, the fall festival, and other events. They charge dues and have a specific membership program. They are a great bunch of people and are very patient with beginning beekeepers. They even teach a beginning beekeeper's course every spring.

I attended this meeting for a couple of years then the travel time, gas expense and getting home really late wore me down. We had no local group so I started one. The new beekeeping group in my area is one I founded. If you want to read our mission statement, our statement of "purpose," go to

http://www.beeclub.homestead.com.

We are not a formal club or an organization in a classic sense, but in reality we are a self-mentoring, "mentors" group. We have no officers, no minutes, no committees. We gather at 7:00 p.m. on the fourth Tuesday of the month, and when it seems most of us have gathered (or even before some get there), someone says, "Should I be seeing larvae yet?" And we all render our opinion on what's happening in our hives.

Then the topic changes, and someone else asks about buying some more equipment, and if anyone wants to share the shipping charges on a larger order. Then someone asks about another beekeeper who didn't make the meeting and how they are doing with their new polystyrene hives.

It may appear to the outside observer that our meeting is nothing but an unfettered stream of collective consciousness. But we gather to talk bees and beekeeping. We share rather openly about what we hope to do. We have a couple of beekeepers with two hives. We have one that has over four-hundred hives. We're all in this together. I founded this group as a loosely-knit group that was designed to meet my needs. The other group was just too far away to participate fully in their special events. I was looking more for fellowship than for special events and committees.

Then I also joined the state beekeepers group, the Missouri State Beekeepers Association.

http://www.mostatebeekeepers.org

They offer more organized agendas and specific events. They are also a larger group. They have two meetings a year, and in most cases, the meetings are in another corner of the state and too far to reach with my work schedule. They have deeply embedded by-laws and an immensely organized hierarchy. And don't get me wrong, this is not a bad thing. Structure serves the purpose of the group. Each level has a specific agenda. And the people on the state level are also a really great bunch of beekeepers.

And then I've also joined a national group, The American Beekeeping Federation (ABF), that focuses on the special interests of commercial beekeepers and the national trends of honey promotion.

http://www.abfnet.org

Joining each group helps me understand beekeeping on different levels, but each group has a specific purpose and a different agenda. The point of my involvement, or at minimum, my attendance at these events, is to help me become a better beekeeper.

Last year I let my dues lapse in the national organization. It just wasn't meeting my needs.

Are there groups in your area? The first place to check is with your local extension office. They might know, but if there are no beekeepers in your area, then they probably don't. If you are interested in forming a group all you need is a meeting place and an idea. We meet at my church. You could pick the corner table at the local fast-food restaurant or the public library. The point is this: there is no real model that you have to follow. Change the group to fit the needs, design your own ideals and guidelines, define yourselves as you see fit.

Fourth, if you can't find a local bee group, join one of the groups on the Internet. There are two main groups that you can join (with a log-in name and a password of your choosing). You'll find one at www.bee-l.com and www.beesource.com. Type in the URL's and follow the advice on how to get started. If you don't want to log-in with any personal information, you can still read the posts. Those who look from the outside without joining are called "lurkers." Lurkers are welcome!

But my advice is to log-in and ask questions. And of course, you'll need a computer and some rudimentary computer skills, but even if you don't have a computer, you can go down to the public library and use their computers (during normal business hours, of course).

The beauty of these Internet groups is that you can be anonymous. You can log-in with a fake name or false I.D., One of the recent names on one of the group's list was "Moth Breeder," a name facetiously and humorously chosen because this particular beekeeper had a problem with wax moths.

There are many different ways to connect with other beekeepers. For some people, face-to-face contact is the best. They want a highly personal exchange. For others, they like the anonymous flow of consciousness and freedom of the computer screen.

But give consideration to finding someone you can help. In helping them, you will learn a lot about yourself, and in teaching someone else, you will learn a lot about bees. But don't feel you are above learning something yourself. Be willing to engage someone with your questions, even if it is someone with less experience, they may provide you with insights that you've overlooked.

And as you expand to twenty-five hives, or as you seek to maintain twenty-five hives, you'll need all the help you can get. Even to this day, I still need help!

And best of all, mentoring is free.

Lastly, remember we are all different. When you mentor someone it is not to try and persuade them to your point of view or your style of beekeeping. And if you disagree with a person, it's no reason to break fellowship with them.

There are more than a few ways to keep bees. You can always share with a person what works for you, but there is no need to proselytize or brain wash them. Respect is the cornerstone to keeping bees and to mentoring another beekeeper. We all have different purposes, and different ways to get there.

When I engage another beekeeper, I remember what one old boy said. When he was young, he asked his mentor (who was an old man himself at the time) why there were so many different beekeepers and so many different ways to keep bees.

The old man replied, "Every time God makes a new beekeeper, he breaks the mold. That's why we're all so different."

Beekeeping with Twenty-Five Hives

Chapter Five

Fix and Repair

When it comes to twenty-five hives, you're going to have to deal with two things. The **first** thing you'll need is a place to organize your equipment, and your storage shed ought to be large enough to sort as well as store your burgeoning overflow of stuff. With twenty-five hives, you'll notice a growing and sizable pile of equipment, none of which easily breaks down for convenient storage. If you are presently using your basement, garage or one of those portable storage buildings, plan on definitely needing more room. You can never have enough room for beekeeping equipment.

The **second** thing you'll need is a place to fix things. Which also means you're going to need a **third** place, a place to put the things that need fixing until you find the time to fix them. Ideally, this third place is somewhere you can drop things off, a "dump" stack, so they are out of your way, additionally, it should be large enough for you to sort through this stack and pick out the neediest cases requiring repair.

In the ideal world (and I'm not there yet myself) I would envision a large storage building with an overhead door that allows you to drive a vehicle inside. I envision lots of open space to store stacks of hive bodies and honey supers on pallets. In addition, I like to have a "dump" stack, where I bring items that need sorting or cleaning before they go to their designated spot in the storage section, plus a pallet where I neatly stack all my "need some fixin' up" items until I find that elusive time on rainy days to fix up those broken items. Then off to one side I would have my enclosed workshop to saw and paint during the winter months. Preferably this would be a modest section of this larger building that could be heated or air-conditioned.

To push this ideal fantasy further, it would be great to have yet another small section of this large building to be a smaller, bee-tight room, air-conditioned with sinks for washing, where I could extract honey. It ought to be a two-part room where you can store loaded supers in a warm room to remove excess moisture from the honey. And then (again in the ideal fantasy world) you would be able to bring your truck or trailer into the storage area, unload the supers, move them to the extracting room, extract, then move them to the storage area after the wet supers were cleaned up by the bees.

And this storage area would also be big enough to store your buckets or drums of honey. Then you could use the extracting room to bottle your honey. It would all be done in one area. And, if possible, the front corner of this building could be sectioned off to be a little store to market my honey, maybe even a nice customer relations office with a nice observation hive next to one of the windows.

I don't ask for much, do I?

And maybe someday I'll have enough land and money to build such a building. Until then, I'll just have to make do with what I have. This is where a lot of beekeepers, both large and small, find themselves. They find their storage and work spaces stretched, or combined, or even compromised with other demands. My garage is my temporary storage and fix-it-up shop, a hive body factory and paint shop. Unfortunately, it is not heated so my work in there is seasonal, but it also becomes the dumping station for things that need fixing and await a warm day. There are months during the early spring and summer in which our vehicles must stay outside. (Warning: this will tend to test your spouse's patience).

And as you increase the number of your hives to twenty-five and higher, you will always remind yourself how time is always in short supply. But storage is a quick second on your list of shortages. Finding a dedicated area to saw, set out pieces awaiting assembly, paint and dry is difficult. And bee hives take a lot of room.

Further, if you tend to collect a host of odd-sized, orphaned, used equipment, as I have, or if you are trying to expand through acquiring used equipment from a retiring beekeeper, you will also find a lot of mouse-gnawed, moth-infested, dry-rotted items. Some of these items will be home-made where someone tried to re-invent the wheel (like I tried). They're okay, and they will work, the only problem is they don't always fit the standard conventions of the Langstroth hive. Which may mean you need to have home-made tops that fit these home-made hives. You end up with some hives of different sizes, which is no big deal, but you still need somewhere to sort and repair the different sized items.

In the long run, I prefer to keep everything to the standard sizes that fit the conventions of the hives designed by Rev. Langstroth.

Even as you have all Langstroth-sized items, you have brood-sized boxes, medium supers and shallow supers, plus comb supers, in addition to tops, bottoms, inner covers, queen excluders. I have also run across some 8-frame equipment, the standard 10-frame equipment, and a few pieces that fit a long-retired line of 12-frame equipment. You will need enough space to set up different size-specific stacks.

There is nothing I find more annoying than to have to dig through a pile of supers to get to that bottom brood box that I need for the swarm I just caught. I've also had problems with storage of empty supers, supers with plain foundation and supers with drawn comb.

I never seem to have enough room. My wife doesn't think I have enough room, either.

Or you could do the same thing like that beekeeper from Iowa. He had a very small storage shed. After the honey harvest, he would set up a pallet in his yard with a bottom board. He would then stack the honey supers and extra hive bodies on top of the bottom board. Some hive bodies had frames and some were empty. When the stack reached six feet, he would then top off this small stack with an outer cover.

If someone were passing by, the arrangement looked like a regular, though very tall, bee hive! He would make sure and protect it from mice, but to the untrained eye, it was an outdoor warehouse as he stored his extra equipment outside. For the most part, it was protected from the weather like a normal bee hive. And since they were level and neat, it didn't create an eye-sore for the neighbors.

Though I have an assortment of home-made, off-spec, odd-sized equipment, it has been my experience, that it is better to stick with Langstroth conventions, or if you want to make all your own equipment a certain size (and I have no problem with this idea) that you stick with a master plan of consistent dimensions. I've tried other designs, and as long as everything was consistent and interchangeable, I had no problem. But the only way things really work is when everything is interchangeable.

In my years of beekeeping I have made eight-frame equipment, twelve-frame equipment, only to go back to the standardized, conventional ten-frame Langstroth hive. But if you're going to try something different, then by all means keep all the same measurements for all your equipment so all of your equipment is interchangeable. It doesn't pay to have eight-frame tops when you're trying to cover a twelve-frame hive.

Or if you go out to a bee yard and you discover you brought those twelve-frame supers and all the hives in the yard are ten-frames. And when it comes to storing all this odd-sized equipment, you'll find yourself in more need or more room.

But back to my ideas on fixing and repair. In the course of my operation, I have a shed where I have a spare corner for my "to be fixed pile." These are the old outer covers where the wood is rotting beneath the tin cover, the old bottom boards I'm converting to screen bottom boards, the old brood boxes that are rotting on the bottom that need to be cut down to a medium size super, and an assortment of boxes that need repainting.

Fortunately, my storage shed is large enough to accommodate all of my equipment, plus those things I normally keep in storage in the course of the year. I usually do not have enough time during the honey season to work on this equipment so it tends to pile up until I have a rainy day or until I get all the honey harvested. Then I sort through the pile and take home certain items to fix and repair.

In order to make my time more efficient, I'll take home all the brood boxes that need to be cut down. In another trip, I'll take all the supers that need to be painted or the frames that need new foundation. Efficiency is the name of the game as you expand your numbers. These items come home to the garage.

I like to have a pile to fix on rainy days or nights, or when I can carve a few spare minutes from my busy schedule. You'd be surprised how spending just thirty minutes at night right after dinner or just before everyone else in the house wakes up in the morning will make a huge difference when you do this for four or five days. When it comes to repair, make every spare moment count. Even if you just spend fifteen minutes wiring three frames, every little bit of action adds up.

Don't waste valuable daylight that is better spent in the bee yard. I sometimes bring home things to fix and they end up in a pile in my garage. There are times

I think I'm going to have time, but something else pops up and I have to deal with it. Then I have to try and work around the mess to get other things done. That's when the cars have to be parked outside and my wife begins to wonder if this hobby of mine hasn't gone too far.

One of my disadvantages is that my storage shed is an open-front cattle feeding shed. It is on my "home" bee yard about two miles from my actual residence. It has no electricity or running water, unless you count the creek behind the shed. While it has plenty of room, I am handicapped to work only in the daylight.

My garage, on the other hand, has the handicap of also housing two automobiles as well as all my wood-working equipment. During certain times of the year when I'm building and repairing, our two cars have to sit outside. This tests my wife's patience, as I may have mentioned earlier.

One of my other beekeeping buddies has a simple tin shed, about twelve feet by eight feet. He bought and erected this tin shed next to his garage to dedicate it for bee equipment only (which then also keeps his garage from getting cluttered). It houses all his extra bee equipment plus his "fix-it" pile. His needs are fewer, so on a nice sunny afternoon, he brings out his table saw from the garage, plugs in a long extension cord, and does all his repair and maintenance on a couple of saw horses in the driveway.

You don't need anything fancy or elaborate. What you need is space and time. You'll need space to store the extra equipment and seasonal items, and have sufficient space to stack up a "fix-it" pile, plus a place to actually do the fixing. Or you could simply fix it on the spot.

I like to "triage" my equipment into 1) those items that I can continue to use even though they need paint/repair, 2) those items that need simple repair, and 3) those items that need major construction skills and replacement parts. But I always have to wrestle with the competition between taking the time to fix something against the money it takes to buy it new.

Recently, as highlighted in one of the national bee magazines, there is a trend to move away from repairing old equipment to buying new. It is thought that your time is more valuable than the cost of new equipment.

Some authors speculate that you'll waste more time fixing an old rotten brood box than if you simply filled out a check and sent off for a new brood box. It is the belief that time is money, and even if you were only paid minimum wage, the paid work you'd have to give up fixing the item is worth more than the cost of that same new equipment.

Economists call this opportunity costs. It is the theory that suggests life is a trade-off of working for money and buying something new, or spending that same time repairing something, which means not working and not getting paid but you don't have to spend the money.

Look at it this way: I can work for $8 an hour. A brood box costs $10 to buy new. The two hours of time I spend fixing an old brood box costs me $16 of lost wages. Or I could work those same two hours, gain $16 in wages and spend $10 on the new brood box. In this case, it is cheaper to work and buy new, then to not work and lose $16 of wages and spend that same time repairing the old brood box to save $10.

But if I can fix ten brood boxes in one hour, those brood boxes only cost me 80 cents ($8 / 10 boxes). Opportunity costs work both ways.

The opportunity cost of working and gaining $16 cash is greater rather than saving the $10 by fixing and repairing that same brood box in those two hours. Then you also have the length that these old, used items will remain is service, which logically, is shorter than the reasonable service of a new item. The newly purchased brood box has a longer life than the repaired brood box. And this idea also has to balance how long it takes to fix things.

As another example, suppose I could fix four brood boxes in an hour, as opposed to throwing them away and buying four new brood boxes. If I were to take an hour of my day and fix four brood boxes, it would be like saving $40, and if I worked my conventional job at $8 an hour, I only have $8 to show for it. I would have to work five hours at my regular job in order to afford the money to buy those four brood boxes.

Though the national trend seems to favor buying new rather than fixing the old, it is my preference to fix the old. It's cheaper, and my time is not always "on the clock" at $8 per hour. I can easily trade those hours I waste watching television for the time I need to spend in the garage fixing old equipment. And if I can shoe-horn fifteen minutes of fix-it time each morning for two weeks, I gain a lot of time I normally do not have.

Fixing and repairing has been my mentality as I've acquired a lot of used bee equipment, some of which was simply given to me, some of which was in pretty sad shape. We seem to live in a "disposable society" in which it is better to buy new than fix what's broken. We seem to have more money to buy new than time to fix what's old.

If this is the way you feel, then go ahead and spend the money and buy new. My theory is this: I have times in which I'm not paid to be working. I have times in which I'm not working. So I can watch television and fill my brain with junk and those programs that pass for "reality" shows, or I can fix up a brood box. For me, to fix the brood box and saving the $10 that it would take to buy a new one is like having someone paying me $10 to fix it. In the end, my time doesn't really cost me anything, whereas buying a new brood box is money right out of my checking account.

Further, spending a rainy afternoon in the garage fixing up old bee equipment is very relaxing. It is my therapy. It reduces my stress levels. And thankfully, I have the skills and the tools to fix, build and repair my own equipment. This whole chapter becomes moot if you have no place to work, no tools (even those you could borrow), and no wood-working skills. Then repairing is somewhat out of the question. When my kids went through "shop" classes in high school (they now call them "Industrial Arts"), I tried to convince them how fun it would be to help me fix up the boxes.

Somewhere, I failed the "dad class" as they never showed any interest, even if I offered them money.

Interestingly, most of my beekeeping acquaintances are also good carpenters and wood workers, at least good enough to build a square box and adjust the depth of the blade on a table saw. But this was not always so with me.

My advice to beginning beekeepers is to start out and buy new equipment. Buy a couple of extra boxes, then copy the measurements, and copy them EXACTLY. If you don't, other boxes won't fit.

As you work with your purchased equipment, you'll be able to use these items as a pattern. Read the old beekeeping books. A lot of them will have sections on the right dimensions for the ten-frame, Langstroth conventional hive. And, if for some reason you want to design your own hive and make your own equipment, you'll have the freedom to keep everything interchangeable. There are some things that already work, and they've worked for hundreds of years. But do not be afraid to experiment as you gain experience.

There have been many years in which I was making my own equipment out of scrap pallets I salvaged out of dumpsters. Agricultural implement dealers always have piles of pallets and shipping crates sitting around. I also haunt the alley of a restaurant supply house for the best lumber that is simply thrown away. I used a regular circular saw until Santa Claus brought me a relatively cheap table saw from Lowes Home Improvement Center (cost around $125).

With this new Christmas gift, my results suddenly showed marked improvement (like straight edges and square corners), though I'm still a long way from perfect. The good news is the bees don't really care (better than a hollow tree!). I am able to make simple cuts and rabbetted corners as opposed to the fancy "dove-tail" or "finger joints" on the commercial boxes.

While I spend a lot of time on developing and expanding my beekeeping enterprise, my time is more available than the cash it takes to buy the equipment. I know those of you who are always pressed for time may find it easier to simply open a shipping box from the supply house and hammer the pieces together. Each of our situations vary.

Along the lines of fixing and repairs come your choice of paint colors. Nearly every convention says beehives MUST be white.

Not in my bee yard.

I travel down to Lowes, Sears, Wal-Mart, even the Salvation Army (which picks up donations of old paint from a local builder of motels and apartments). All of these stores, and any store that mixes paint, has some of the mistinted paint returned. I do not understand this mentality of taking back paint just because the customer didn't like the color, but the stores take back these several cans every season. Top-quality paint that offers a 25-year guarantee along with a $30 per gallon price tag will sell for $2 to $5 a gallon.

The only stipulation is you cannot be picky about the color. So I protect my hives with some of the loveliest colors. And the farmers who have my hives on their farms don't seem to care either. However, a lot of people will take issue and spend the extra money and buy white paint. If you want, paint your hives any color you desire. But I HIGHLY recommend you paint your hives. As I run across old, weathered used equipment, the first thing I do is give them a coat of paint. Old wood usually takes two coats, but in the long run, painting is the best choice to preserve your equipment.

And further, if you find paint in the mistint bin, buy it. These home improvement stores don't always have it in stock, and because it is exterior paint, it tends to have a seasonal availability. You only find it in the warmer months.

And again, you're going to need a place to paint that is protected from the elements, warm and ventilated.

When it comes to frames, I'm at a loss. If you buy used frames, or if one should break, I think your best bet is to toss it away and replace it with a new one. Cut out the wax comb and melt it down, but for my money, fixing frames, especially if they have broken "ears" or those stubs on the ends, it takes more time to fix those, and they'll always be weak on the other side. I agonize over tossing used frames in my kindling box, but with the stress that most extractors exert on the frame, it is less frustrating to simply buy new frames rather than repair them.

If you have a wax foundation "blow out" in your extractor, go ahead and cut it all out and replace the foundation. But if the wood frame is old or weakened from wax moths, then it might be best to pitch it and replace it with a new frame.

I've spoken in another section of "harvesting" old pallets from dumpsters and salvaging the wood to make your own hives. Home improvement stores seem to have the biggest selection of old pallets, however, farm implement dealers seem to have the best grade of pine lumber (easiest to work with).

Also in my area are several manufacturers of pallets, and a couple of manufacturers that have to make their own custom-sized pallets. They simply toss TONS of 2x4 stubs, 1x8 boards less than 24" long, and a host of other wood in the dumpster. A lot of local good old boys like to salvage this wood for their wood-burning stoves. It makes great kindling, even though most of it is pine. I like it as it makes the right wood (at the right price) for making my own bee equipment.

As you move upward, time and money will always be in competition. Whether you choose to save money and fix up the old equipment or spend the money because you don't have the time is a decision you'll be making every day. Fixing and repairing is also a function of a place to do it, but also dependent upon your skills and tools. As we'll take a look in the finance section, start-up costs for beekeeping are high. It's my preference to repair old rather than buy new. It's a decision you'll have to contemplate as you expand.

Beekeeping With Twenty-five Hives

Chapter 6

Finances and Financial Consideration

When moving up to twenty-five hives, how will you finance this move? In other sections of this manuscript, you will hear me preach a method of growing and building. To me, this means growing intentionally and building somewhat gradually. I highly discourage anyone to simply go out and buy the bees and equipment to set up twenty-five hives. You'll be more successful if you can be patient, to build up your numbers as you grow.

But this will require patience, and in the rush to get rich overnight (I think I mentioned this earlier) your patience will be tested. By growing, especially as you learn to make your own equipment, you'll have a better handle on things rather than jumping into beekeeping too fast. But your level of expansion will vary on many different variables and some beekeepers are more adept at scaling the learning curve quite fast.

Working the numbers

To outfit a hive from scratch, buying new equipment at retail catalog prices, you can expect to spend $250 for each, fully-outfitted hive. Shipping will be a big expense as this equipment is heavy. There are commercial grade and budget grades of woodware with different pricing structures. I've always gone the cheaper route when buying and bought the woodware with small knots and blemishes.

Bees, if buying a package, will run around $60 to $75, depending on the strain, race and supplier, and of course, shipping on top of the package (unless you pick them up) is also expensive. If you can, plan on driving to pick up your package bees instead of having them endure the stresses of the postal system. Or work through your bee club and have someone pick up a large order of packages to save the shipping costs and the stress levels.

Nucs, usually four or five frames of bees, brood and a laying queen, cost from $100 to $135, sometimes up to $150.

And of course, if you buy in bulk with a bee club, you can save substantially, particularly on shipping which is cheaper per pound on the larger order. If your order is big enough, you move from normal package shipping to truck freight. The volume of your order will also determine prices as buying in a quantity of ten is always cheaper than one, and if you can afford one-hundred of something, it's cheaper than ten.

One of the bee clubs I worked with bought a large case of Apistan strips. The cost for each strip, when bought by the case, was $1.45 each. Small orders, like for one box of ten for these same strips, brought the price for each strip to around $2.50 after shipping. So the bee club bought a case and sold each strip for $2.00 to their members. You could buy as many or as few as you needed. And for some of the smaller beekeepers who only had two hives, they had no need for a box of ten. It was a good deal for each beekeeper who used

Apistan and the club made a little profit on it as well. Your buying power increases when the quantities rise.

I also found it somewhat interesting, that in the face of mites becoming resistant to the chemical miticides like Apistan, that this respective bee club was still passing out these strips. Albeit, Apistan is an easy way to go, I prefer a different approach. And the good news is beekeepers with differing opinions can coexist.

I have a lot of potential beekeepers and beginners come to me and ask me about getting into the business of keeping a few bees. I quote them the figures above and their eyes widen. It costs money to keep bees, at least the greatest expense will be up front for the first year when you're getting started. And, of course, it's not likely you'll have much of a honey harvest that first year, if any. So the first year you have lots of money going out and practically nothing coming in.

However, as you keep your bees alive and keep them from swarming, the cost is evened out over several years.

I always keep a few catalogs on hand to show these potential beekeepers what it takes to get into beekeeping. It amazes me how people think, since bees are perfectly content living in a hollow tree without any human intervention, that beekeeping ought to be a relatively cheap hobby. Most beekeeping supply catalogs show a blow up picture of a bee hive and all of its components. Every year I draw out a pricing plan to show people who think they want to keep bees what it costs to get started. Starting to keep bees can be expensive. Expanding your current operation can also be expensive.

Mindset of an investor

Think of the expense of getting started or expanding to twenty-five hives as more of an investment rather than as a cost. Yes, you will have to pay for equipment, especially if you buy new at retail catalog prices. And yes, this equipment is not cheap, especially when you tack on the shipping charges.

But what if you looked at this expense as an investment? An investment is money you put down expecting a return in the future. Some investments don't pay off until you sell them. When you buy land, or an antique car, you do not realize any tangible return until you sell the item.

Other investments, like a stock that returns annual dividends, provides a stream of income (perhaps a trickle) for as long as you own it, and may also show some appreciation in price when you sell it.

I think of a bee hive as an income-producing asset or a dividend-paying stock. It starts out as an expense. Let's use the upper figures and say this hive is going to cost me around $325 to get established (equipment and a package of bees), and let's say the first year and every year after that it is going to cost me around $25 to maintain this hive (feed and medication).

So the first year I spend $350 per hive and have nothing to show for it except a canceled check in my check registry. If you get honey your first year, especially if you buy package bees, consider yourself exceptionally lucky. I usually counsel potential beekeepers and rookies that their first year is just to get started.

Like my first start, however, they're already looking around for plastic buckets to store the bountiful flow of honey that's coming in. So the first year, consider the fact that the hive will not produce anything and you'll have no money coming back at you. You might, but I wouldn't want you to count on it.

But the next year, after I invest some time and energy, this hive produces around 30 pounds of honey which I sell for a conservative average price of $2 per pound. Quantities vary, and your unit price on larger quantities of honey will be lower. Small squeeze bears sell for a higher unit price than a quart, and a twelve-ounce squeeze bear will return honey at $4 per pound.

Let's use the average price around $2 per pound just to be ultra-conservative. And 30 pounds of honey is very much on the conservative side as well. But for a beginner, this should be a nice harvest of honey. If you do the math, 30 pounds at $2 per pound nets you $60 per hive. That's not too bad when compared to what you could get at the bank for that same $350 per hive with a CD.

Imagine, for just a minute if you could harvest 60 pounds of honey (not that unusual) and sell squeeze bears to net $4 a pound. Now were talking a return of $240 per hive.

Now before you rush out and buy the equipment for twenty-five hives, consider what happens if all your bees die during the winter. You need to spend another $75 for bees plus the $25 annual expense of maintaining the hive. To re-establish a colony increases the likelihood of harvesting honey, but don't bank on it. If you did, then your $100 additional investment will only bring back $60. You lose money on that hive that year.

Bear in mind, my examples are purely speculative. Reaching 60 pounds of harvestable honey is not difficult, but it depends on weather and available forage.

Now if you only had two hives, then buying two new packages to replace your bees will only set you back around $150 on the upper end of the price range. If you had twenty hives, multiply that figure by ten and you'll need to spend $1500 to get back in business. With twenty-five hives, your mistakes are magnified. This is why you will hear me preach over and over, keep your bees alive (which may require winter feeding) and prevent them from swarming so you have a honey crop to harvest.

For this reason, I keep several hives and maintain a rolling average. Some of my hives will produce over 100 pounds of honey, but they sit next to two hives that won't do diddly-squat. And the next year, I can order new queens and requeen these two under-producing hives. Or I can raise my own queens. More hives means more options.

And further, any good economist would tell you that one needs to look to alternative vehicles for a return on investment. For this reason, consider the money you'll spend on beekeeping equipment, factor in a reasonable return for the honey you intend to harvest and sell, then weigh these figures against something else, even if you left the money in the bank.

This was our dilemma when I was studying agricultural economics in college. At that time, interest rates were obscenely high. It was not uncommon to have to borrow money at 18% interest. Land values for farm ground were holding their own value, but the profit margins on crop and livestock enterprises, over and above expenses, were simply non-existent. It just didn't pay to buy a piece of ground with borrowed money, and if you had the land, it was better (from an economic standpoint) to sell the land and put the money in the bank.

Of course, money in the bank isn't near as much fun!

When we compared two scenarios in my college classes, the decision was easy. One scenario was to borrow the money, buy land, and farm it. The other scenario was to leave the money in the bank and allow it to draw interest. The decision was a no-brainer. It just didn't pay to farm back in those days. It hardly pays to farm today.

So in the light of this glaring reality, the professor asked, "At these kinds of rates, and with these kinds of returns, why would anyone farm?"

There was silence for about a two-seconds, then one student spoke up, "Because I want to." The class erupted in applause and laughter. We all wanted to farm. Farming was a way of life. It was our heritage. It made no economic sense, which was part of the problem why no one could get financing to start farming. There was just no money in it.

The professor, after he regained control of the class, then prompted the young man to explain how he would make farming pay if it made no economic sense. His reply was to depend on off-farm income (translation: a job in town) to fund his living expenses and give his banker some reasonable means of repayment.

It made sense to us. And depending upon off-farm income, usually from their spouse, was how a majority of farmers were able to stay on the farm.

I'll bet once you get the catalogs out and look at the costs, even when viewed as an investment, you may have some reservations. If you don't have the reservations, your spouse likely will object to the money it takes to get started! It would be more sound, financially speaking, to leave the money in the bank. Or, take up some less risky venture like stamp collecting. But most beekeepers I know, even those with two hives, state very plainly: "I don't keep bees to become rich. I keep bees because I want to."

This "want to" attitude is what I call the **hunger factor**. And even if you don't really market your honey to maximize your financial return, even if most of that honey is given away as Christmas presents or simply shared with your neighbors as a generous response on your part, you just want to keep bees because you enjoy it. You just want to do and even though it cost you money in long run, you just want to do it.

Beekeeping is very therapeutic for me. If I had to pay for a psychiatrist to treat me for workaholism or burn-out, it would cost me more than I spend on keeping bees. And it would not be nearly so fun! And if I didn't keep bees, what would I do with my recreational time? It takes more money to play golf or go trapshooting. I know some guys who buy motorcycles and travel all over the country. They say right up front it costs a lot of money. But they do it because they want to do it.

Honeybees and their equipment will cost money. But think about this expense as an investment that will bring in a future dividend. That dividend may be a psychological well-being which cannot be defined by money. This kind of thought helps make that expense a little more palatable.

Equipment

As you build and grow, you're going to need more equipment. Is it worth it to build it yourself? Is it better to buy new? What about buying used equipment that may need repair? A lot of this was covered in the previous chapter, but let's review some things here.

I find this issue has two sides. First, are you comfortable making your own equipment? Can you cannibalize an older box to fix another box of a different depth? If so, and if you have the woodworking tools, then the answer is yes. If not, or if you do not already have the tools, then I would discourage making your own equipment. It will be more frustrating trying to learn how than actually doing so. I should know. I'm a self-taught carpenter...and many times it shows. And I don't think I would necessarily go out and buy the equipment unless you had a longer vision for its purpose in your life.

Second, presuming you are comfortable making your own equipment, are you going to buy the wood to make the boxes, tops and bottoms? If you have to buy the wood, especially at a retail home-improvement store, then you'll find the cost of the wood it takes to build these boxes is about the same cost as buying the boxes themselves from the catalog, which are already cut out and ready for assembly.

But if you want to make your own equipment, I suggest you order a set of brood boxes and medium supers to get their **exact** dimensions. This will help clarify any confusion about their size and how they go together. Then go down and price lumber from Lowe's or Home Depot. Find out how much each box will cost. Then compare to the catalog prices of the woodware that is already cut out and ready for assembly.

What I've found is the price of the wood from Lowes is about the same as the pre-cut catalog pieces, believe it or not. However, I have a huge complaint with the home improvement stores and the so-called "quality" of lumber they bring in and sell to the general public. It's often warped and I have to pick the pile to find something straight. Outside of the quality, the catalog wood comes already cut and ready for assembly. What you could pay yourself for your labor sawing and assembling the boxes is about the same as the price of the shipping. It is, as my mother's common statement suggests, "half a dozen of one, six of the other."

And don't think you have to match those fancy "finger" or "dovetail" cuts like the catalog pieces. There are a host of different end cuts and joints. My preference is a rabbetted cut, but if I'm in a hurry, I'll use butt joints. And with a normal table saw, these cuts are very easy. But if you try and match the cuts from the catalog, it might be more difficult.

Much of my equipment is built from scrap lumber. I built it myself and it shows. I'm not the worlds' best carpenter. But the price of the lumber was right (free) and the bees seem to be no respecter of carpenters.

I've also bought my share of used equipment, a lot of which needed repair. Some of which only needed a new coat of paint. And some of it was only fit for the fireplace.

If there was a down-side to making your own boxes out of store-bought wood, it would be the fact that none of the standard boxes can be made from standard cuts of lumber without some degree of waste. Standardized lumber needs to be trimmed. Scrap lumber is free, but still needs to be trimmed, but those trimmings don't cost me anything when I toss them in the kindling box.

Bees

I've devoted a couple of later chapters to getting started in bees or expanding your hives. Basically, most beekeepers like to buy packages of bees. I don't. I think packages are heavily stressed and the bees are reluctant to accept the queen. After all, they just met on this wonderful "blind date" and the bees are expected to accept her once they find their new home in your apiary. Sometimes it doesn't work.

Most often, bees are bought, which only adds to the financial commitment you are willing to make. Bees also die. When colony dies, you can always sell the boxes and frames and maybe recover a portion of your money. But dead bees are worthless. You can refer to more of my opinions in my later chapter on your options in acquiring bees.

If there was an aspect that gives me the most stress, it would be paying money for bees. And if they die, or if they show up in your mailbox dead from the shipping stress, then you have to buy more bees. Be sure and get your packages of shipped bees insured, if your shipper insures bees. Regulations change every year and the post office is becoming more and more reluctant to ship live bees.

But the downside to replacing dead bees, even those packages that are insured, is that it might be too late in the season to find a supplier who still has bees in stock. I much prefer making my own splits and raising my own queens. More on this later.

Borrow or Spend?

Somewhere down this line of expanding to twenty-five hives of bees, you will have to come up with some money. I tried to make my expansion as cheap as possible. I used scrap wood from pallets thrown in the dumpster. I caught swarms. I raise my own queens. I spend an inordinate amount of time fixing used equipment that I buy from retiring beekeepers. Sometimes people give me old, worn out equipment. Some of this equipment is so old that it takes three supers cannibalized for parts to have enough good pieces to make one good super. Everything I do today focuses on spending as little cash as possible.

This frugal mindset comes from my Depression-era parents who instilled the philosophy of "fix, repair, make do or go without." I'm cheap. And in my early days, I didn't have a lot of money, anyway. And in the early days, I had more time than I do now.

Today, fortunately, I have more money plus I have a stream of money coming in from honey sales. I am moving from fixing old equipment to buying new, in part because time is short and the larger the volume of equipment requires more time. But if the opportunity presents itself, I like used equipment. I need the therapy in the garage.

But there are obviously some people who have quite a bit of money, judging by the cost of the items in the beekeeping catalogs. It appears a lot of people have the money to buy new equipment. And if you do not have the time to repair old equipment, or if you lack basic woodworking skills, or if you don't have the tools, then you will more than likely buy new equipment. And that's okay.

So how do you pay for this new equipment? Most beekeepers just spend the money they have in their checking accounts from their "real" job. But to expand another ten hives, averaging around $350 per hive is $3,500. I don't live in the world where most people have an unencumbered $3,500 to invest in new bee equipment. Maybe you do.

So do you borrow the money? Do you use your credit card? Do you get a weekend job to find the extra money outside your family budget? And if you borrow the money, do you have a way to pay it back if the bees don't work out, or at least, do you have some means of paying it back the first year until your honey sells? These are all good questions to ask.

Taxes and Accounting:

If you make money at beekeeping, even a dollar, you are required to report your earnings to the Internal Revenue Service. You can also use your expenses to offset your reportable income from your "real" job. This means you need some manner of keeping records.

To make my life easier, I use a computer to keep track of my finances. There are sixty million computer programs on finances and accounting from which to choose. I like the most popular accounting package called "Quicken." Then I have one back account I use solely to keep track of my income/deposits and my expenses for my beekeeping.

I am not a tax accountant so what I'm about to say is not to be taken as an authoritative interpretation of the most recent tax code. By the time you read this, the tax code will change. It changes every year. Do you need an accountant? Probably not. The tax code is not that difficult, and there are a lot of good books on business accounting to guide you through the process. But you will need to keep financial records as the law requires.

For income tax purposes, I like to use a Schedule C for businesses. If you think of your bees as part of your farm, then Schedule F is for you. Should you incorporate? Do you file for a LLC? Now you need an accountant to consult with you. How you go about recording expenses, depreciation, etc. is a matter of choice, but once you start keeping records one way, you pretty much have to continue in that manner. I try and keep my expenses and income as simple as possible and a computer program really helps.

Insurance:

I want to close this chapter on finances and financial considerations with a paragraph or two dealing with insurance. Do you need it? It depends.

My initial thought was that I didn't need insurance. I had my bees stuck out in the woods, away from people, away from livestock where no one would get hurt. Then I read a story about how some vandals broke into a vacant house with the intent of robbery and one of them fell down a set of steps and got hurt. Can you believe they turned around and sued the family that owned the vacant house? Can you believe a lawyer actually took their case? Can you believe they won their case?

We live in one screwed up world.

My initial thoughts were that I didn't need insurance. In the early days, when beekeeping was just a hobby and my hives were on my own property, I asked my home-owners insurance agent if I was covered for liability. He said I was. That was good enough for me. And I had liability insurance anyway if the neighbors slipped on my snowy sidewalk or tripped over a garden hose.

But when I began to *sell* my honey, my hobby became a commercial enterprise and my home-owners insurance would not cover my liability.

Then as I expanded to other locations, even those out in the woods, I checked with my insurance agent again. Nope. I'm not covered. And while my hives were located away from people, I had land owners who would follow me out to the hives. Invariably, they would get stung. That was the last time they followed me out. But one of the land owners likes to mow the fence row where the bees are located. I gave him a veil to wear.

And what do you do when someone just gets curious? I had a phone call from a fellow who got stung. He was not an invited guest to my property, but he stopped by my house to buy a jar of honey off my honey stand. He saw the bees up by the fence line. He feels compelled to go up and check out the bees. Without any protection or a smoker, he lifts the lid to the bee hive. And BAM! He gets stung. He was fine, but he called to tell me I ought to put up a warning sign that there were bees in those hives.

Well, yeah. As the comedian on the television says, "You can't fix stupid."

So I start mulling insurance. What if someone gets stung and has a bad reaction? What about their medical costs? What if they die?

And also about this time I approached the local health food store to carry my honey. The proprietor asked if I had insurance. I asked, "What for?"

He said, "In case someone gets sick and wants to sue me."

I said, "Sue you? Over honey? Honey doesn't spoil. It won't go bad. There's no way to get sick. Why would, how could, anyone sue you?"

And he said, "In this world today, people can and will sue you for anything and everything, and often over nothing. There is no lawyer around that won't take a case if he or she smells money. If I get sued, I'm going to come looking for you. And if you don't have insurance, then I can't reasonably protect myself in case someone sues me. They always go for the deep pockets."

We both rolled our eyes at the preposterous nature of today's litigious society. So I told him I understood his point. He was not being unreasonable. I started looking for insurance.

My first stop was my home-owners insurance agent. He said, "Don't tell me you are selling honey from your house. I don't want to know anything about it. If someone gets stung, you are not covered. You have moved from the hobby to a commercial enterprise. I sell home-owners insurance. You need to find business insurance."

So I started looking. I had heard on the Internet that Farm Bureau sold insurance to beekeepers, but my local representative didn't know anything about it, and he claimed he has no way of knowing where to look for it. I can't say I blame him. Bees make a lot of people nervous.

One of the national beekeeping groups had a connection to an insurance company willing to write insurance for beekeepers, but you had to become a member of that group. So I joined, paid my dues, then promptly wrote the insurance company. They sent me some information, then never responded to any other inquiry from me. Perhaps I was too small. Small policies cost the company a lot of time and paperwork.

So I dropped my membership to that national beekeeping group. The only real attractive reason to join was for the insurance.

Then my home-owners insurance agent called. He had, unbeknownst to me, made about two dozen phone calls before he found a commercial agent willing to talk to me. I thanked my home-owners agent profusely. While he could not carry the insurance himself, he was willing to find me the help I need. It's for reasons like this that I like local insurance agents.

It took a few meetings for the commercial agent to understand beekeeping, beekeepers, and what I wanted. The only thing I wanted was a premises and product insurance policy. I did not want flood, tornado or terrorism coverage.

So this agent went to work for me. After about two months, he finally found an underwriter who was willing to talk to me. They were very specific. I had to map out where my hives were located. I had to make maps to their locations. I had to include range and township numbers from the county plat book (check out the reference section of your local library).

My initial cost was $450 which was the minimum premium they charged. Then to renew the policy cost me $50 for the year.

Insurance is hard to find. We don't fit the normal expectations of coverage, and the minute you say, "Bees," the red flags go flying. The idea of getting stung brings childhood horror stories to our remembrance, and ironically, everyone is now "allergic" to bee stings. Which to most people, I find, means that if they have a painful red spot that swells up a little bit, they classify themselves as "allergic." And the horror stories of the Africanized bees does not help us one bit.

Then you read of migratory beekeepers who tip a semi-trailer truck over on the interstate highways. Bees are flying all over the place and they're mad and upset. Fire and rescue personnel are called in. Then those rubber-necked idiots who have nothing better to do than to come to find out what the problem is, get too close and one of them gets stung.

What a mess. No wonder no one wants to insure beekeepers. But they still want the pollination and everybody loves honey.

Is insurance a consideration? In this world, I think so. It is a necessary protection because the world is full of crazy and greedy people.

A while ago, someone tried to put a human finger in a bowl of chili at a fast food restaurant. They never ate the finger, but they tried to sue the national franchise for some perceived damages. It's people like this that make me want to be insured.

And I continue to ponder: where did they get that finger?

And at the risk of sounding like a hypochondriac, or a paranoid, doom and gloom naysayer, it comes back to that magical phrase, "What if?" What if someone got hurt? What if someone got stung? What are our reasonable responsibilities, and in this world today, it seems we are responsible for the stupidity of others. Why I even have to pay part of my auto insurance premium to cover the uninsured motorist who might run into me.

Go figure.

Bees in the wild live free and cost nothing, but they often have no harvest to share. Domestically managed bees cost money to set up and maintain. But they have a great harvest with which we can make money.

There will be some financial considerations to keeping bees. The best thing to do is keep good records. Know your costs. You'll find that the first year's harvest will probably be some of the best tasting, $60-a-pound honey you've ever tasted.

Beekeeping With Twenty-five Hives

Chapter Seven:

Record Keeping

There was a time when I could walk with you down a line of my five bee hives and I could tell you where the colony originated (whether from a package, swarm, etc.), how old the queen was, what color I marked her, what kind of disposition the colony displayed, how productive the colony was last year, and what I planned to do with them this year.

Then as my beekeeping operation expanded and my numbers increased, I moved hives to new locations.

I would refer to their names such as "old swarm from school" and "former hive from the Talley yard." Then as life became more complicated, I couldn't remember which one was which and they all began to look the same, but they didn't all produce the same.

In order to maximize my production, I needed to know what each of my hives needed to make the most of their resources. Some hives had new queens, some hives needed new foundation, some hives had some old drone comb that needed replacing.

And invariably, someone would stop me in the store and say, "How's that swarm you rescued from my rose bush?" I'd have to stop and think which hive body that swarm went to, which yard I placed it in, which location within that yard I set it at, if I requeened it or allowed it to keep the swarm queen, and other such issues.

So in an attempt to be as honest as I could realistically be, I'd say, "They're doing just fine." (People ask me these questions as if the swarm on their rose bush was a unique event in the history of my beekeeping hobby).

But then I would wonder to myself how were they doing? When did I hive that swarm? Was it ready for a super? Was the queen doing any good? Should I give them a little syrup to help them draw out the foundation?

In reality, I had no recollection, even for those hives I just saw that morning. So what could I do to help keep my mind straight on which hives were which, or what needed to be done to which hives? Which hives had an old queen? Which ones needed an additional brood box? Which one did I cut swarm cells out of, and what date did I do that, and when should I go back to make sure they're not making another batch of swarm cells?

It was out of this need that I decided to start keeping records on my hives. Now if you want to really analytical, you can keep track of anything you choose. I wanted to keep track of certain records to keep my hives productive.

There are probably ten million things to keep track of, and I sought to keep track of the things that mattered most to me. I was interested in the origin of the hive, the age of the queen and a relative account of what was done to the hive, when it was done, what the hive then needed or what needed to be done to the hive, and when it needed to be done.

Then, I could sit home and review these records in the evening and decide what needed to be done the next day. This record keeping helped keep me stay organized and made the most efficient use of my time. When you make the most efficient use of your time you are able to keep more bees and make more honey.

There are a host of other things I could keep track of. I could weigh every super as it came off the hive, then make sure all those frames went back in that same super to figure out how much honey came off that particular hive. But this record is not that important to me. I can tell by the queen's productivity if that colony is going to produce a nice crop of honey. I do mark my queens and I like screen bottom boards (SBB) so I make a note of the colony has either of these. If I bought a special queen from a special breeder or noted queen producer, I want that information recorded. If there is a particularly productive, gentle queen I'll make a note of that and plan on using her to raise some queens off of her. If I have a defensive hive, I'll make a note to requeen it ASAP.

But for the most part, my records are a glorified to-do list. I like to keep simple records. Good records keep me from forgetting to do certain things that need to be done. Good records prevent procrastination because you are always reminded of what needs to be done.

If nothing else, my records keep track of what I did so I can plan what needs to be done next. Some hives need special treatment, or an extra super, or a new queen. Some hives have rejected my plastic, one-piece frame and foundation and work best with wax foundation. Some hives are tremendous comb builders. Some hives work better for comb honey production, and some are excessive propolizers (which really does not work if you're producing comb honey). Some hives swarm on me so I need to know they have a new queen that may or may not work out so I need to go back and check the laying ability of that new queen. And I need to make a note to be sure and mark her and with what color I used to mark her. I will also note for next year what I failed to do that caused the swarm.

My idea of keeping hive records is relatively simple. I start out by giving every hive a number. I once tried to keep the numbers in each bee yard consecutive so I could go down the line of hives with 1, then 2, then 3, etc. And then I would move a hive to a new yard and my system would be messed up and my old number 5 in the previous yard would become my new number 1 in the new yard, but I would always know it as "old number 5." This didn't work out so well because I'd then put a new hive in number five's old place. I tried to keep consecutive numbers in each respective bee yard.

Now to keep the numbers straight with the hive, at least in the early years, this wasn't hard because hive number 1 always started on the far left part of the apiary. But as I moved hives to new locations, this was not always so.

So to keep a little better order, I drove a stake along side each hive stand, a simple 1x2" pine board about 18" long. You can buy these pre-cut stakes at any lumber yard or home improvement store. On the stake, I wrote the number of the hive with a felt-tip, "magic" marker.

In a quasi-anal retentive fashion, I still tried to keep my hives in numerical order within that yard. So my first hive I visited was number one, followed by number two, etc., and on down the line. This way I could keep track of which hives were visited, and which hives needed attention on my next visit. To help my increasing mental load, I carried a spiral notebook with me and I numbered the pages for each hive I had.

But then a hive would abscond, swarm, die out, or something else, so I'd have a hole to fill in the numbering system, and a page in the spiral notebook was now out of order when I put a swarm in that location. Then I would move a hive from one yard to another yard and I would have to give it a new number, yet I still wanted to remember where it came from (such as "Old #5 from Talley's Yard").

I was getting way too particular about this numbering system. And if I had to tear a sheet out of my spiral notebook, or if a particular hive was problematic and required a second page, my notebook needed an extra page in the back. And I also found I was not disciplined enough to look over my notes until I got out to the bee yard. Then I remembered I was to bring three brood frames. Oh well, I said, next time.

As I moved up to twelve hives, expanding toward thirty, I would take a notebook for each yard and draw a map on the first page of all the hives, giving each hive a number along with a numbered stake. Each notebook page that followed was then numbered accordingly and after visiting each hive, I jotted down notes on how the hive was doing, with special designation of what needed to be done next on that respective page.

On these pages, at the top, along with the hive number, I noted the queen's race and if she was marked or not. I also made the notation if this hive was started by a split, package, nuc or swarm, and if purchased, where the package or nuc came from. I was under the impression that certain package producers had better bees than others, and in some years, they do. Unfortunately, I discovered a great inconsistency between queen producers.

As I moved up to several yards in remote sections, I carried a different notebook for each respective route, and within the notebook a page for each hive. It helped me keep track of what needed to be done when, and what was done.

This system worked fairly well, as long as I didn't move hives from yard to yard. One notebook, one yard, and keep the hives consistent. But as hives died off or swarmed or whatever, my spiral notebook would fall out of order. It was also prone to getting spotted with honey and propolis.

And my stakes were fading, some were rotting off, and much to my consternation, I would trip over one of them occasionally, usually when I was trying to balance myself with a heavy super in my hands.

At one point, some of the old-timers introduced me to the "brick" system. This system of keeping records uses a brick on the top of the hive to describe how the hive was doing. Setting the brick on the front of the outer cover means one thing, setting it in the middle means another thing. Setting the brick on edge means another thing.

This seemed fine with ten hives, but with more hives, and more situations trying to be described with a brick, it was simply too confusing. Then I would forget to put the brick back in place to keep my records straight. Sometimes the brick sat on the outer cover and it wasn't used to designate anything. Some good that did me!

I remember all too well the advice given to me by an older man who was wrestling with the normal aging process and his forgetfulness. He carried a small notebook and simply said as he jotted himself a few notes: "If it doesn't get written down, it doesn't happen." That was the extent of his record keeping and it worked for him.

Some beekeepers simply write on the hive body itself with a pencil as to what's going on. I guess this would work if the weather doesn't erase it. Some beekeepers keep a note card stored between the inner cover and the outer cover. When they open a hive, the card is retrieved and reviewed, then the appropriate action is taken and the results recorded. Then the card is placed back between the inner cover and the outer cover when the hive is reassembled. I guess this would work if it wasn't too windy when you lifted the outer cover.

While these systems work for some beekeepers, I don't like them because they don't prepare me for what I need to bring with me before I arrive at that bee yard. Some of my outwards are quite some distance away and it's more trouble to go back and retrieve some forgotten item than it is to try and remember it for the next time. Everyone needs a system that works for them, and what works for me may not work for you, and vice versa.

My encouragement in this chapter is to consider some kind of record keeping, if not for yourself, then for the bees, but in the end, you'll find it helps you and the bees. And you only have to keep track of what matters to you. I guess, as I go back to my original question as to your purpose of keeping bees, if you were keeping bees for fun and you don't care how much (if any) honey you harvest, then record keeping is something you probably don't even worry about.

I keep bees and I want to maximize my efforts and make the most efficient use of my time (as opposed to those who complain they don't have enough time). As my trial and error evolved, here is the system I now have in place.

Every hive keeps at least one brood box on it. So I made a brood box to go with my screen bottom board that will stay with that colony. I used a permanent "magic" felt-tip marker to write a number on the brood box. I started out with consecutive numbers, but the number corresponds to a page in a loose leaf notebook rather than a spiral notebook, and each number corresponds to a particular hive irrespective of it's location in a respective bee yard.

Step one is to give every hive a number. I gave up trying to keep consecutive numbers in each bee yard. Each hive gets a number no matter where it is. When a colony dies out or absconds, the hive body is either refilled with a swarm or it goes back in my shed until I make a split.

What you use to make this number is irrelevant. I thought about stickers (like they sell at the hardware store for mailboxes). I thought about buying consecutively number ear tags for cattle and attach them with a drywall screw. To keep my costs low, I simply hand-wrote a large number on the bottom brood box with a broad-tipped, permanent marker, beginning with the number 1 and moving up the system as I added a new hive to my apiary.

I started out writing numbers in my first yard consecutively, then moving on to my next yard in continuation. But as I added hives from splits and swarms, I simply gave them the next number in the over all sequence.

If the first step is to give every hive a number, the second step is to create a loose-leaf notebook or a three-ring binder with each page given a respective number corresponding to each hive. It doesn't matter which yard the hive sits in, each hive has a number and a corresponding page in my loose-leaf notebook.

I call this loose-leaf notebook my *"log book."* It doesn't matter which bee yard has which hive, or which hive has which number. The pages in the loose-leaf notebook go in order so the notes on that particular hive is easy to find. When you make a note for a hive, you need a place to make those notations. Each hive has a corresponding page in my loose-leaf log book. And because it's a loose-leaf notebook, I can add pages, take out old pages on hives that die out, add a second page on really productive hives or those hives that require a lot of notations. If I pull a hive body from the shed and make a split, I can start that colony off with a fresh page.

But as I took this loose-leaf notebook with me on my visits to the bee yards, it was getting sticky with honey and propolis. I also found myself scribbling abbreviations and other such gibberish that didn't make sense. I was usually in too much of a hurry to remember what I meant the next time I reviewed my notes.

So I went to the office supply store and picked up a spiral notebook that I take out the bee yards. I call this notebook my **"field notebook"** and it the notebook that I take with me. In the field notebook I make my notations for each hive I visit. I make the notes without concern for having one page for each hive. Some pages have similar notes for three hives. I just make notes in a continual fashion. Some hives take quite a few notes and other hives simply are given a "looking good" comment.

For each hive I visit, I make notes in the field notebook on how the hive is doing and what else needs to be done. This field notebook will become sticky with propolis and honey. I make rather unintentionally obscene abbreviations that only make sense to me. And I don't worry about this. These notes are just for this day. I make sure and note what needs to be done next for each respective hive on my next visit.

When I get home, I take out my loose-leaf log book (which now stays at home) and transfer the notes I made in my field notebook to the corresponding page in my loose leaf log book. Each hive has one page in the log book and each page is numbered to correspond to the number of the hive.

I date my entry in my log book and transfer the notes from my field notebook. This gives me a good idea on the progress each colony is making. Then I tear out those sticky pages from the field notebook and throw them away. Their job is done. The information that is important to me is written in my log book.

I go through my entire log book (at least once a week) and review all my hives. I'll take my field notebook, and on a clean sheet, I start making notes on what needs to be done next, in which yard, and to which hives. On this page, I start making a "to-do" list for that coming week. I jot down notes on which bee yard I want to visit next, or what bee yard needs the most immediate attention, what hives I need to visit, what equipment I'll need to do what needs to be done. Then I look at my calendar to find a block of time that I need to visit the bee yard in the coming week.

On that day that I've blocked out time, I already know what I want to do. Hopefully, even before I load up the car with what I need, I've organized a pile of supers, excluders, etc., the night before so I don't waste valuable daylight searching for the things I need.

I got this idea from a time-management idea called the $25,000 idea. The legend behind this story originates from an industrial plant back in the early part of the last century. The executive offered his employees an incentive to make the plant more efficient. He said he would reward the employee with a cash gift of 10% of the savings that came with their new idea.

One day an employee came to the executive and said, "Here's an idea to make you more efficient, and to make all of our departments run more efficiently." The executive was all ears.

The employee continued, "Every manager with some level of responsibility needs to sit down at the end of the day and think about what needs to be done the next day. To keep from being overwhelmed and distracted, the manager needs to limit his list to six things. No more than six things are allowed, and those six things need to be numbered in order of importance." The executive nodded his head to affirm he was following the employee's advice.

"Then," the employee continued, "at the start of the next day, the list is picked up and the manager starts his day with item number one. Only when that item is finished is he to go on to number two. As the day goes on, he might not get to all of this items on his list. So at the end of the day, he starts a new list with six things to do for the next day. He takes the things that did not get done this day and he puts them at the top of his list for the next day. And only six things can be listed."

The legend suggests that the company saved over $250,000, and hence, this time-management method became the $25,000 idea based on the 10% incentive given to the employee.

Now I don't know if the legend is true, but this idea has saved me a lot of time and energy. As I peruse my loose-leaf log book, certain items and tasks comes to my attention. At least once a week, preferably on a

Sunday night, I'll sit down and look over all the notations I've made on my hives so I know what needs to be done in the coming week.

So on any given night, I will sit down with my loose-leaf log book and make plans to visit a certain bee yard the next day. On a fresh sheet in my field notebook, I jot down what yard I want to visit, which hives need to be seen, what tasks need to be done to these respective hives, and what tools I need to accomplish my tasks. I take into account how much time I have and what needs to be done with the most importance. Then I usually go out to the garage and assemble the tools and supplies I need (that I have on hand) and I make a list in my field notebook what needs to be picked up at the storage shed.

With this system, I don't have to visit every hive in every yard. I don't have to open a good hive that doesn't need anything. I only address the hives that need something.

Your record keeping system does not need to be elaborate or fancy. If you can keep twenty-five hives straight in your head, or if you only have one yard and know what you want to do to all the hives at the same time, then you may not need to keep records.

And then, you may not want to keep records. My purpose in keeping records is to give my hives the best possible opportunities to make the most honey, which in turn, makes me the most money.

The purpose of my record-keeping system is also to make the most efficient use of my time. Additionally, my records help me...

--to prepare my visits to one of several out yards,

--to know what needs to be done so I don't waste time wondering where to start (especially helpful when I can only work a portion of the hives in any particular bee yard),

--to insure I bring with me the tools and equipment I need to get the job done, and

--to make sure I make a note of what needs to be done on my next visit or which yard needs that next visit.

My objective of keeping records is mostly to know what I need, when I need it, and what was done to make my trips to remote bee yards more efficient and effective. Many times I have gone out to a bee yard only to find I failed to bring with me what I needed that day. This means another trip back to my central storage shed and wasted time.

The location of your bee yards will impact what you need to bring with you, and may cancel your plans that afternoon if there is something you forgot. I can recall too many trips to certain bee yards, only to find I left my smoker in the garage when I needed to make room in my van when I hauled some pallets to another bee yard. When I went out the next day, I presumed the smoker was still in my van.

The location of this particular yard was too far away to warrant a trip back home and back out to the bee yard. There was just not enough time to make all these trips. Plus it would be a waste of gas. That's why keeping records is as important to the location as the location itself. A long list is better than a short memory.

As certain needs evolved that were required irrespective of which bee yard I visited, I began to set up remote storage areas. One bee yard had no special place to store anything, so like that beekeeper in Iowa, I set up a bottom board, stacked several extra supers and queen excluders and topped it with an outer cover.

Then next to it sits an empty hive body on a hive stand. Inside the hive I set an extra smoker, smoker fuel, an extra hive tool, and matches in a sealed canning jar. I've done this at a couple of remote yards. Basically I have a small shed with the essentials. If the mood strikes me during the day or if I find myself with a moment of spare time and I want to make the trip out to this remote bee yard and tend to my hives, I have the equipment out there. I know some beekeepers who keep an extra hive tool under the outer cover of a few hives just in case they lose their hive tool in the grass.

Whatever you choose to do, you'll want to make sure you have the right tools when you need them.

Along with the need to bring what the bees need is the need to keep records. I carry my field notebook in the van with me at all times. I also try and keep my smoker, wood chips, veil and hive tool box with me in the van at all times as well (and it drives my family crazy to wrestle around all this stuff). But sometimes these items get removed for family responsibilities.

With good record keeping, you'll always know what you have out in the yard, what your needs are, and what you may have on hand. By making notations with each visit, you'll know what to bring with you on the next visit. You can also keep track of which hives need an extra super, which ones look like they need to be requeened or split.

When I only had five hives, I could tell you, off the top of my head, what hives were doing well and which one was doing poorly. I could tell which queen was in which hive and when she was introduced when I requeened the colony. But I didn't have intentions of staying at five colonies. And my mind is growing older and more, uh, oh yeah, forgetful. Some days I can't hardly remember to put my shoes on when I leave the house! Then I ponder why my feet are so cold.

My objective of keeping records is mostly to know what I need, when I need it, and what was done to make my trips to remote bee yards more efficient and effective. There are no special criteria to which records you keep as long as you stay abreast of what each colony needs, and you record somewhere (even mentally) what need to be done.

As you climb and expand to twenty-five hives, efficiency will be a challenge. More hives take more time. You have to become more efficient. Good records will help you to become more efficient.

Beekeeping With Twenty-Five Hives

Chapter Eight:

Location, Location, Location

Where does one put twenty-five hives? Perhaps the better question is how many hives can one area support?

The answer is simple: "it depends."

The number of hives any one area can support depends on many things. Obviously, the plant sources and vegetation will make a huge difference. I would think varied plants species, blooming at different times of the season would be ideal. Cultivated ground sown to hundreds of acres of single crops would present a bigger challenge, especially if the crop (such as corn) is not a major nectar producer. Even if it is a good honey crop, single varieties of crops produce small windows of nectar, then they quit and produce the seeds/vegetables. A varied crop location is best.

Placing hives in suburban areas where much of the ground is covered by asphalt and cultivated areas mown regularly to prevent blooming would not benefit the bees. Not that grass yields any nectar, but those of us with clover in our yards keep it mowed too regularly to benefit the bees. And yet suburban areas often have sufficient trees that balance the asphalt and concrete. Suburban areas can and will produce a honey crop.

And then, on top of plant species, what are the other inherent dangers that make a location restrictive? I think of chemical sprays and pesticides. Keeping bees around golf courses or commercial orchards has certain limitations. Large bodies of water such as lakes do not contribute to the honey production, and yet they do provide some water for the bees' needs. I have some hives near the interstate highway. The long, seldom mowed, ditch banks provide wonderful plants and shrubs for nectar.

However, it does make me wonder: Do bees fly low enough to get hit by all the passing cars?

So if you had the ideal ground, a mix of cultivated row crops, woods, hay and pasture, fence rows and ditch banks, gardens and lawn, how many hives would it support? How many hives can you have before the bees start competing with one another for the nectar sources?

I don't think this question has a real answer, but at twenty-five hives, you are probably safe from saturating the area with the maximum limit of foraging bees. I have a couple of yards with fifteen hives. My main yard, which I also use as a holding yard to establish swarms, has between thirty and forty hives.

And yet the established hives in these yards still produce an ample amount of honey. These areas are also quite rural, pastoral and covered with a wide variety of land use (some crops, some woods, some pasture, some government set-aside ground, some ditch bank along the highway).

I don't know what the maximum number of hives this ground will support. But sooner or later, as I continue to add hives, I will reach a saturation point. I have no idea what this number might be, but I'm relatively confident that having twenty-five hives in one location will not reach that point. This should not be a burning question in your mind. Conceivably, you could keep all twenty-five hives in one location, even expanding to fifty hives without detriment. But it depends on the crops and the variety of plants in the area.

However, in order to spread out my hives to insure they have plenty of plants to forage, I generally shoot for a minimum of eight hives to a maximum of twenty hives per location. But having multiple locations also means I have to travel between the yards. I probably would do better having all my hives in one location. Despite the time involved in traveling between yards, I am more comfortable spreading my hives out.

Here are my criteria for placing hives.

Plant species

Obviously, you want to place hives where lots of flowers bloom. Preferably, I like a wide spectrum of plant species, blooming all through out the season. My ideal would be lots of nectar-producing plants as some plants produce more nectar per plant, or more nectar per acre than other plants.

But this is not always so. Some of my locations are great fields of soybeans. This means my early production of honey is rather limited until the soybeans bloom. I have a couple of areas where the soil is light and sandy. Here in southeast Missouri, it means July and August will likely produce no nectar. Everything dries up.

Some of my locations are close to the interstate highways, some locations are close to the woods. For the diversity, for spreading out the time that certain plants bloom in certain areas, I like to have my hives in different areas, knowing that each area will have a respective time to produce nectar.

As bees will fly several miles to find nectar, I cannot fully control all the plants in their respective flying zone. But by having bees in different areas, I feel I spread out my risk of drought or plant species, as well as varying the soil type.

As you consider locations, think first about the plants that will be in bloom. Look for a diversity of blooms as well as plenty of ground planted to nectar-producing plants. Stay away from places like golf courses, land fills, industrial sites or certain crops that require pesticides (orchards, etc.).

My time

If I only had twenty-five hives, I would probably do well to put all of them in one yard. Then, when the bees needed to be worked, I could make one trip and do what needs to be done.

As I have around one hundred and fifty "production" hives (at the time of this publication, not counting nucs and queen mating yards), I have spread out my hives to a dozen different areas of the county. All of my hives are within seven to ten miles of my home, with the exception of two locations which are eighteen miles away.

However, these two locations are within three miles of each other which makes the commute tolerable. On a sunny afternoon, it's no big deal to get in the car and drive to any of my locations, tend my bees, finish up and get back to the office or my home before dinner. Most days, this is how I spend my lunch hour. I can get to, get in, get out of a bee yard in about an hour.

During the busy seasons, I try and visit several yards in an afternoon to do all that needs to be done. I broke my locations into "zones" or routes. My routes look like a five-leaf clover with my home in the middle where the leaves adjoin the stem. On a given day, I will drive out and cover all the hives in that "leaf." Then the next day, I'll cover another "leaf." And a lot of this is dependent on my work schedule, family obligations and of course, the weather.

As I consider future locations, I want to make sure they fit in my routes, or I may have to make a new route. I want to consider the time it takes to travel to the bee yard so I'm not eager to place my hives too far away. Additionally, most of my customers continue to hammer me with questions about how local is local honey? I market honey from the location, and each location produces a different tasting honey. The honey varieties are kept separate, which makes for more work, but it really makes the honey sell quite well.

Secondarily, if I have hives in a remote area, I want enough hives in that area to justify my travel time. For this reason, it is my preference to place eight hives as a minimum in any one area. Yes, there are exceptions. In one location I have six hives, but a mile down the highway, I placed two hives in the garden of a good friend. She wanted two hives to pollinate her flower beds, even though she does no seed production. She just likes the idea of having bees in her garden. However, she lives next to a dairy farm with hundreds of acres of alfalfa. Unfortunately, the alfalfa never really gets blooming before its cut down for hay. Still, these two hives do produce a nice crop of honey.

If these two hives were way out by themselves, it wouldn't be worth my time to drive to the location to tend to just two hives. But I've bunched them up with some others and put them on a route to make the best use of my trips. And yes, to a certain extent, those two hives are like a favor to a friend.

As you find places and locations for your hives, take into consideration the time it takes to get to them, and make sure you have enough hives to justify the travel time and gasoline.

Access

Most of my hives are located on farms. I like to keep my hives away from the residence, away from livestock, and far enough away that the family and their children do not feel threatened.

This usually means my hives are placed somewhere on the back fence line. This means I need to drive past the house (and let them know I'm going back into the field). This means I need to open some gates and make sure those gates get closed. The roads going back into the fields are not paved and subject to muddy conditions if we've had a recent rain. Even a four-wheel drive vehicle has trouble so I often have to wait until things sufficiently dry up.

Then when I'm done, I come back, making sure I close all the gates, then I drop by the house to let them know I'm done, and that I've made sure the gates are closed. I always share my appreciation, but stopping by the house usually means time invested in "landlord relations." Sometimes the landlord likes to follow me out and see the bees. This is fine with me, but often the conversation is lengthy and takes precious time away from the bees. I consider these tail gate conversations, "social rent." It's just part of keeping bees on someone else's farm.

Along the lines of access, and some of the hardships of getting to remote locations, is the threat of vandalism. Thankfully, I've never had a problem with vandals. Some of my hives sit quite close to the highway. Some of my hives are visible from country roads, easily accessible to me, but also to vandals. I want hives that I can get to, but I don't relish the idea of making my hives too accessible for vandals. This is a trade-off you'll have to deal with. And thus far, I've been very lucky, blessed, and fortunate not to have problems with vandals. Access works both ways.

If you keep bees anywhere on your own property, you must always keep in mind the neighbors and how close your bees are to the property lines.

Obliging generous people

I've been blessed in that people have approached me to put bees on their property. I have not had to beg or persuade farmers for locations for setting up a bee yard. The farmers have come to me as they like the idea of keeping a few hives on their farm. They believe the bees pollinate the crops and the farmers benefit in that way. As I've stated above, I like to put eight hives as a minimum, but this is not always the case.

When someone approaches me to put hives on their property, they generally have no further interest in pollinating the family apple tree, the large garden, or just the general feeling of "good will" that comes from having bees on the property. There are some old-timers that feel it is a sign of prosperity to have bees on their farm.

I've tried to oblige people, especially because they are so generous. It's hard to look a gift-horse in the mouth! I will try and shoot for eight hives, as I mentioned earlier. If I can work them into my route, if I can have good access with protection from vandals, I will try and put hives on their property. Then I may work up to twenty hives for the efficiency of time.

Neighbors

I keep some of my bees next to my house, right up next to the property line. A chain-link fence separates the property. This is no big deal as my sub-division has no codes, covenants or restrictions preventing me from keeping bees, plus my neighbor used to keep bees as a kid. And I only keep five hives in this location.

Neighbors can be a problem, or more correctly, their fears can be your problem. Their fears do not even need to be legitimate or rational to cause you problems.

If you can, shield your hives with a privacy fence so at least they are out of sight. Tell neighbors you have bees. Educate your neighbors, share some honey, know the rules and regulations, especially if you live in the city limits. The best rule of thumb, if you live in close quarters to your neighbors, is to be a good neighbor. Sometimes your bees will be up visiting the neighbor's dog bowl or swimming pool. Provide water to your own bees if you have to, but always, always, always be a good neighbor. Remember you are also an unintentional bee ambassador.

I heard one funny story where the neighbors didn't like the idea that the beekeeper was keeping bees on his property. The yards were spacious in this subdivision, but still, his bees kept visiting the neighbors for water. More of a concern, they were drowning in the neighbors swimming pool.

Finally the neighbor had enough. He called the beekeeper over and showed him the pool filter filled with dead bees. The neighbor demanded the beekeeper keep his bees out of the pool. The beekeeper said, "Well, let me see those bees."

As the irritated neighbor handed over the pool filter, the beekeeper reached into the pool filter and brought out a bunch of dead bees. He rolled them around in the palm of his hand with his index finger.

He pursed his lips, shook his head slowly, then said, "No, I'm sorry. I can tell by the markings on these bees that they're not mine. They must have come from somewhere else."

The neighbor was dumbstruck. The beekeeper brushed off the dead bees into the grass, shrugged his shoulders, and said, "Sorry, they're not mine. I can't help you."

That was the end of that conversation and the beekeeper never heard another word.

Disquieting fears of the unknown

I had one location where I started out with four hives. We had no written agreement, but the husband felt it would be fine for me to set up more hives later in the season. Little by little, as swarms were caught and hived, I increased the number to ten.

Well the husband thought this was fine. The wife thought otherwise. Ten hives seemed like too many. She could not, or would not, put a finger on why she didn't like ten hives. They were over the hill and out of sight, away from the residence. But she didn't like the idea of having so many hives. "What if they swarm?" she would ask.

I tried to educate her on swarming, trying to assure her that the bees would not necessarily head straight for the house. I tried to tell her swarming is a reproductive action, not a defensive or an aggressive "attack" action. But it was no use. She was nearly hysterical.

I cut back my hive numbers to four to keep the peace. It was a great location with a wonderful variety of plants and a running stream nearby, but without good landlord relations or people that understand the benefits of having bees around, you'll be running into problems.

Whenever you place hives, someone will get nervous. They don't know what they're nervous about, but they just don't want to get too close to the bees. When I work my bees, I seldom wear a veil. I use ample smoke, work slowly and gently, and I work my hives on calm, sunny days, provided my schedule coincides with sunny days. Some days are overcast and you just have to go out and work them and you know they'll be hostile.

Sometimes the best relationship with a landlord is to let them watch you work the bees. When you get a chance, show them the queen. Show them the brood. Let them poke their finger in some fresh honey and let them lick it off.

Good neighbor relations take work to dispel the rumors and the fear-mongering. I can't count the number of times I've moved hives onto a new location or added onto an existing location without someone asking, "Those aren't them African bees, are they?"

I calmly reply that they are not. Then we take some time to educate in a very patient manner.

Water

Bees need water, and if a water source is close, so much the better. If a water source is not close, then you'll have bees visiting bird baths, pet water dishes, swimming pools, etc. Depending upon the location and the neighbors, this may be a problem.

I've had a few locations without good water sources. I have not had any problems, or maybe the bees found a source of water I didn't know about. You can fix this problem by using an entrance feeder filled with water. It won't cause any robbing problems and you will supply the water they need right close to the hive. You can even set this entrance feeder on top of the hive and allow the bees access to it as they wish.

Storage

Whenever I head out on one of my routes, I have to remember that I need to bring everything that I may need. For this reason, I want to reiterate the need for good records. I need to bring sufficient supers, feeders, top and bottoms, queen excluders, etc. This means my van is my traveling storage shed. I also need to know how many of each thing I need, so I frequently bring extra things along just to make sure.

This also becomes a good reason to make all your equipment the same size, or at least keep your supers mediums or shallows, but not necessarily both. Or commit one yard to the shallows and one yard to mediums. And for heaven's sake, do not do as I did one time: I was pulling frames of honey from medium supers, and inadvertently replaced a few of the medium frames with shallow frames. The bees filled in that little strip on the bottom of the shallow frame with burr comb, and when the boxes were later separated, the brace and burr comb, now filled with honey, broke and made quite a mess.

If you have remote yards, you'll probably benefit from one main storage area or a central storage point. But as you travel and commute between yards, you'll recognize the need to keep yards standardized with respect to the supers and frames, and you'll also learn to bring along what the bees need.

Along these lines, you will need a location for storage. I carry with me at all times my smoker, smoker fuel, veil and gloves, and a working tool box with hive tools, queen marking paint, twine, duct tape, etc. And there are times these items get removed from my van, especially if my wife needs the van for a project with the kids.

But I need a place to store all the supers and bottoms and queen excluders. Fortunately, one of my locations, an old cattle farm, has an old, three-sided shed. It makes excellent storage. I also use my garage and workshop to fix and repair, but I need the shed for my storage. And you would be surprised how much space it takes to store all this equipment.

The ideal storage space has a concrete floor so you can use a cart or dolly to move stacks of supers.

Additionally, it helps to be mouse-proof, and obviously, it needs a good roof to keep out the rain. It needs to be accessible at all times when you need bee equipment so some of these rental lots where you have a garage-sized space that you rent by the month may not work.

Thankfully, my storage facility is centrally located. It is like the stem of this five-leaf clover. I can conveniently stop by the shed, pick up what I think I'll need, then proceed out to the bee yard and do my work.

If you can keep all twenty-five hives in one location, you probably will be better off. If your storage facility is also at this location, you will never be without the tools you need. But if you desire, and if the opportunity presents itself, you will find yourself with multiple locations.

If you want to see how it goes, thinking perhaps of moving up to fifty hives, find another location. Be mindful of zoning laws and city ordinances. But find a new location and set a couple of hives there. See how it goes to make visits to this new remote location. See how it goes to bring all the things you need.

Then as you grow more comfortable with this prospect, you can either add some more hives or find another location to start another set of hives. Over time, add hives if you can legitimately warrant the travel time.

But if you start small, you won't be overwhelmed. And think about keeping that honey separate. You can make a different label and market it under a different name for each different location. Make sure you educate your customers as to the source or location as if the honey was something special, because it is!

In the real estate trade there is a saying, that the three things you need to be successful in real estate is location, location, location.

I think the same applies with honeybees. A good location can make the world of difference in your success.

Beekeeping With Twenty-five Hives

Chapter Nine:

Nucs, Packages, Swarms and Splits

Where do you get the bees you need for twenty-five hives? The good news is you have several options.

So you've made up your mind you're ready to move up and increase your colonies to twenty-five hives. Presuming you've worked out the financial aspects of acquiring the woodware, boxes and frames, and you've found a suitable location, where are you going to get your bees?

I find most beekeepers, when they want to expand their operations, look first to buying packages.

Packages are shipped, usually with two, three or four pounds of bees and a caged queen. Installing the packages is easy. Packages are great ways to introduce beginners to beekeeping. But let's not get the cart in front of the horse.

One of the big keys to getting bees settled, even before you find them or buy them, is to have all your equipment ready, assembled, painted (and dried), and preferably in place on the hive stands wherever you are going to have them established. It's hard to move bees once you get them in the hives (though the professionals and the commercial guys do it all the time).

I do not favor moving bees from crop to crop unless you invest in a trailer and have the bee hives mounted on the trailer. But this is already too far for you to worry about--you don't even have your bees yet!

There are four basic ways to acquire bees. The irony is that the easiest ways to acquire bees is the most difficult way to succeed. Well, maybe not the most difficult to succeed but it is the method that will make success hardest to come by. And likewise, the hardest way to acquire bees is the easiest way to succeed, but it does require some special skills that you may not necessarily have at this point, but it doesn't rule you out.

The easiest way to get bees is to buy a package. The second easiest way is to trap or capture a swarm of bees. The second hardest way is to find another beekeeper and see if you can buy a "nuc." The hardest way being making a split from your own hives.

Either one of these four ways will work. Some ways are harder. Some ways require better luck. Some ways are cheaper, even free, and then some methods will cost a bundle (and every year the price goes up). All of them will test your patience and none of them will guarantee your beekeeping success.

Packages:

Most beginning beekeepers order a package through the mail. It is the easiest way to get bees, though it takes some planning ahead of time to insure you get your bees reserved and a delivery date confirmed. If you want to expand with packages, my strong advice is to order early. Your order is taken in the order it is received, and within reason, most package producers will try and accommodate your order.

Any time I've ordered packages, I've tried to schedule delivery around the first part of April. Invariably, cool weather in the south prevents young queens from mating, or there is some other delay.

One year I ordered packages from a southern beekeeper. The beekeeper was bringing his hives back from California. The bees were pollinating fruit trees and this beekeeper thought they would be strong, populous hives encouraged by the influx of nectar and pollen. He imagined them full of young bees and brood, ready to shake into a box.

However, the fruit trees were treated with a fungicide. The fungicide did not kill or harm the adult workers bees as they foraged the flowers. But as the foragers brought back the contaminated pollen, the larvae all died. This beekeeper opened his hives to find nothing but adult worker bees.

There was no sign of any larvae. If he shook his bees into packages, he would decimate his colonies and have no bees for the rest of the summer. So he called me and told me I'd have to wait at least three weeks until the queen could lay some eggs and some young bees emerged.

I told him I fully understood and those are some of the risks you take in ordering packages.

If you look in any number of bee magazines or catalogs, there are lots of Southern beekeepers who offer packages of bees for sale early in the springtime. Some will offer two-, three- and four-pound packages with a mated queen of your choice.

Some will offer shipping and some will demand you to come to their warehouse and pick up the bees. Most northern supply houses order a truckload of packages and when they come in, you need to show up and pick up your packages. Some will offer volume discounts.

One of my complaints about packages is the price for the shipping. Packages are heavy. At the current prices, your first package will cost around $60 to $75, plus $20 to $30 for shipping through the mail. But if you order two packages, or even three or four packages, the supplier will nail lathing strips to the packages to make them one shipping unit. On four packages, even with the increased weight, your shipping charges will be $40 for all four packages. And as I checked around, four packages are the most they can bundle together with lathing strips. Basically, the more packages you can order, the per-package-cost goes down.

To avoid this high cost of shipping, I also would encourage you to drive, if possible, and pick up your packages to reduce the amount of stress put upon your bees. Fortunately for me, I've always had good luck with our local post office. I've gone down the week before my expected delivery to tell them the packages are coming and to call me first thing when they arrive. I don't want the bees trucked around the county in a drafty delivery truck. I don't want them sitting by the side of the road next to my mailbox.

Packages of bees are nothing more than a new queen bee (in her own cage), and a couple of pounds of bees literally shaken from the frames of an established hive. The bees get to meet their new queen as they are shaken from their home hive, kind of like a blind date. When you release the bees into your hive, they'll need some additional time to get acquainted with this new queen. There are plenty of books that will teach you how to install a package of bees and how to effectively introduce a queen bee.

The beekeeper who sells packages shakes frames of bees into a wire screen cage with a can of sugar syrup for food. He inserts a caged queen and takes them to the post office and sends them through the mail to you. All you have to do is send a check to the beekeeper ahead of time and your local post office delivers them. Nothing could be easier, except succeeding, that is.

What makes packages so difficult, especially if this is your first year with these bees and you have nothing to offer them but foundation, is that your bees, stressed through the mail, have to draw out the comb from the foundation before the queen can start laying eggs. Then they have to get the queen out her cage by eating the candy plug (this allows her "scent" to become familiar), then get her to lay her eggs.

Your queen can't come right out of her cage because she's basically still a stranger to these shaken bees. The bees have been plucked from their nice home and shoved into cramped quarters. They've been on a marvelous tour of the country side, from sorting stations to warehouses to your residence. You receive them, take them out to your bee yard and release them by turning the package upside down. You expect them to go to work, but often the early spring weather doesn't give the bees good weather to fly in.

Package bees require feeding. I tell beginning beekeepers to have all their material assembled and painted, set up on the hive stand, ready to receive the package and have syrup mixed up and cooled down ready to feed to the bees immediately after installation. Do not place your hope on enough leftover syrup from the package.

Now it takes a little while before the queen can lay her eggs because she won't lay eggs until the bees can gather the nectar and pollen to support the new family (queens are really responsible in this way!).

This usually means the bees begin to lose confidence in their queen, this queen they just met and hardly know. Sometimes the bees will "abscond" the next day and simply leave your hive because they haven't bonded with the new queen. If this happens, they're gone and you're out the bees.

Sometimes the bees will let the queen out of her mailing cage and allow her to lay an egg (one!) which they designate as a "supersedure" cell, the process in which they will begin to replace her by feeding this egg royal jelly. As soon as the egg hatches into a larva, they may kill the old queen or they may drive her from the hive.

I've opened a hive about four days after the package was installed to insure the queen was released, then I came back about two weeks later to find no queen, no eggs, just a (one!) nice plump queen cell waiting to emerge.

If the bees initiate the supersedure and try and replace that strange queen sent along in the package, the new egg needs sixteen days to hatch and grow into a queen. She needs about seven days to mature, four more days to mate before she starts laying eggs.

If this happens (and it's happened to me), your new queen will not begin laying eggs for the first month. The new eggs that she lays need three weeks to hatch into workers, who in turn need three weeks to mature before they take flight as foragers to replace the aging bees that came in your package.

To me, buying packages is a lot like taking your family and putting them in the back of a pick-up truck. Without warning, you suddenly have four or five neighborhood families join them, all crammed into the back as well. You are riding in this pick-up truck for three days with a cooler of sandwiches and bottled water to drink, which may or may not last the journey.

When you finally reach your destination, you are released, along with these neighbors, to a house site that has a brick foundation, and a pile of two-by-four studs and four-by-eight plywood sheets. There's a box of food and stove, but you still have to build the house, hook up the electricity, and all this time begin to wonder when you're going to eat your first meal. Life might get kind of cranky.

But through it all, you might get the house up and covered. It may take a little while to get the stove hooked up after that, but soon you can cook meals. And sooner or later, you will have the household organized with people getting jobs and bringing in an income to finish the house and buy fresh groceries.

That's what it's like buying package bees. Yes, you can make it, but the risks are so great and the odds are against you. I've ordered packages in which the queen was not mated, didn't lay eggs, and the poor workers couldn't even get an egg with which to begin the process of supersedure.

There is nothing I can do, except hurry up and buy a new queen (through the mail, which takes some time, on top of the time I wasted waiting to see if this existing queen will lay her eggs). The best thing to do is to kill her and combine the workers bees with another hive. Every day you wait means a few more of those adult worker bees die off.

Still, some packages come out rather well and even produce honey that first year. Every package I've started with, however, on average, simply drew out the comb on the foundation and established themselves that first year and prepared for the next year. Packages are the easiest to buy and set up, but success is often elusive and your delayed gratification works against your enthusiasm and perseverance.

I'm not a big fan of package bees, even though this is how many beginner beekeepers get their start. It's how many beekeepers fill their winter dead-outs. It is the easiest way to expand. But I think the financial costs as well as the opportunity costs are just too high.

One tip I would pass along, if you going to go this route of buying packages. If you can bring in a frame or two of drawn comb from an established hive, especially if it has some honey and pollen stored in it, and put it in the hive just before you shake the package into the hive. This will really help the package bees get a jump start.

Further, if you have a frame of **_SEALED_** brood to "borrow" from a strong hive, this will bring on a generation of young bees very quickly. I would warn against bringing in a frame that contained eggs and young larvae. Because the queen has not been released from her cage, there is too great a temptation for the bees to start making queen cells thinking the queen in the cage is no good.

Swarms:

The second easiest way to start with your bees is only modestly successful, and that's to try and catch a swarm of bees. I've been fortunate enough to get my name established with the local police department and with local exterminators. I put my name in with the Department of Conservation and with the Extension service. I offer, for free, to come and pick up a swarm of bees that is hanging on a tree or mailbox.

For whatever reason people may have, they feel the need to call the police when they encounter a swarm of bees. So the police call me and I go out and attempt to rescue the bees and start a new hive.

Catching swarms is tricky because you have to get right out there or they may fly away. As the swarm hangs on a bush or branch, scouts bees are vigorously scouring the countryside looking for a new home. The trick is to shake them from the branch into a hive body of your choosing, making their choice for them.

The swarms I've caught often happen in early May (just before the first smaller blossoming of local flowers, called the "early (or minor) honey flow"). The second swarm season happens in mid to late June which follows the main blooming of flowers in my area, or the "main honey flow."

(In reality, honey doesn't "flow." It's an expression to reflect the flowers that bloom and provide the nectar that will be converted into honey.)

I've also been honing my skills using a pheromone-baited swarm "trap." It's a box that holds about five or six frames. It looks a lot like a nuc box. It smells and looks and feels like the perfect place for a swarm to set up residence. The design was perfected by entomologists working to trap Africanized honeybees and prevent them from migrating into the United States. It also works really good for catching our local, "European" honey bees.

I highly recommend hanging a few swarm traps around your bee hives to catch the swarms that come

[306]

from your hives. However, it is my hope to monitor the hives to keep them from swarming in the first place.

Catching swarms, whether by a frantic call from the police or by using a trap, is fun and the bees are "free" for the cost of the trap (reusable) and your time (non-refundable, especially if the swarm takes off before you get there). Swarms are primed to take over a new residence and they set up their new residence with seriousness unrivaled by package bees.

Catching swarms is like getting a package of bees for free. A swarm is usually twice the size of a package of bees and will do better. They already know their queen and they are ready to go to work.

In fact, they seem to have a frantic urgency to get to work where a package of bees seems to be disoriented and unfocused. If given the choice, I'll take a swarm over a package any day. There are, however, serious questions as to the age and productive life of the queen bee.

Catching swarms, however, does not often coincide with your plans or your schedule. You cannot schedule an appointment for a swarm to come to your empty hive. The age of the queen is questionable, though early "prime" swarms are almost always headed by older queens. Later swarms are "after" swarms and are invariably headed by unmated, untested virgins.

But despite her age, I often find some late swarms (swarms that usually issue after the honey flow begins to subside) do not have what it takes to build a big enough family to keep the hive warm enough to survive the coming winter. Swarms may, if caught early enough, produce a workforce to bring in a super of honey, but then they seem to fade out as the summer nectar dwindles. In retrospect, I like swarms but I will plan on either using a swarm queen to raise new queens or I'll simply plan on replacing her.

Further, honeybees in the wild are decreasing due to mite infestation. Swarms are not as available as they used to be, so catching a swarm is not as dependable as it once was just twenty years ago. You just cannot depend on the swarms, nor can you schedule a swarm to come to your attention early enough to make enough harvestable honey. But since the price is right, I never pass the chance to at least hive a swarm, and if I don't plan on leaving it to its own merits, I can always combine it with another colony to strengthen it.

The old time beekeepers used to say that a swarm caught in May is worth a load of hay; a swarm caught in

June is worth a silver spoon; but a swarm caught in July isn't worth a fly! Catching a swarm is tricky, and harder than buying a package of bees. But if you can catch one, at the right time of year (which is not nearly as dependable as the delivery of a package), you have a greater chance to expand your hives.

I've had better success with swarms than I have with packages, but the ones that have been successful are the early spring swarms, which are not always plentiful nor dependable. You also have to be in a place where someone will call you to tell you to come get the swarm. People need to know you want to retrieve a swarm and they need to know how to get a hold of you. In this day of cell phones, the latter should not be a problem.

In my early days, I would come home around dinner time, find a message on my home answering machine from the police about a swarm that was at someone's home around one o'clock that afternoon. So giving my wife an apology about missing dinner, I'd hop in my van and trundle on over to the swarm location.

Guess what? It had already left. I'd return home to a late dinner and a fussy spouse. Today I give my cell phone number to those who need to call me. I pack a hive body in my van at all times during the swarm season. In my storage shed I have several hive bodies with secure bottoms and ten frames of comb/foundation ready for a moment's notice.

Nothing is as painful as having to rush home, find a hive body, attach a bottom board, locate ten frames, etc., and rush on over to the swarm location. I have learned that if I want to collect and retrieve swarms, I have got to be ready. I also have to have my equipment ready.

Additionally, swarms are nothing more than free packages. Most of my swarms are much larger than the packages I pay for, but they are still a bundle of homeless bees that need to establish comb from scratch, get the queen laying eggs, get a new generation ready to take over, etc., etc.

You can give the swarm a jump start the same way you handle packages. A frame of drawn comb, even sealed brood would be helpful. Swarms initially benefit from feeding supplemental syrup. But because they have a higher population of bees, and their queen is accepted and ready to lay eggs, they always seem to do better than a package.

And they are free.

However, as you make plans to expand, you don't have to limit yourself to just one means of starting new hives or expanding the number of your colonies. If you wanted to add eight hives, you could order four packages to be delivered on a specified date, then hope to capture four more swarms to fill out the eight hives you need to expand.

What I have done, when I've chosen to expand my bees with a purchase of a package, is to set up the package in early April. My delivery date is confirmed with the producer of the package bees. When they come in, I set up the package like most of the books on beginning beekeeping suggest. Then I diligently monitor the bees and feed them sugar syrup to get them going.

Then in May or June, or even July, when I capture a swarm, I set up the swarm in a separate hive body on top of the package hive. I use a solid divider board to keep the two colonies separate. It has a shim around the edge with a notch for an entrance. I give the swarm two or three weeks to get established and allow the old swarm queen to lay eggs. This time frame usually means I'll have brood ready to emerge.

Then, after these two or three weeks, I'll see which colony has the better queen. Usually the swarm queen will be showing me better egg laying ability, but then she has the advantage of being related to all those worker bees in the swarm. She may also be a newly hatched virgin swarm queen and not have had sufficient time to lay eggs. Unless my package queen is an absolute failure, I'll go through the swarm hive and find the queen and kill her (squeeze her quickly and humanely—if that's what you want to call it). I'll take out the solid divider board and replace it with a sheet of newspaper. On top of this newspaper, I'll set the swarm hive and put on the hive top.

It will take a day or two, but the two hive communities will eat through the newspaper and meet. By this time, they have "adapted" to one another and absorbed each other's "scent." Since the swarm hive has no queen, they'll assimilate into the package hive and begin to work for the package queen. The result of combining the two colonies will result in a synergistic boost that will almost insure your success, even to provide extra honey your first year.

However, these manipulations may be more than you're willing to attempt your first year of expanding. These kinds of manipulations are referred to as "bottlenecks." There are some days when I get two or three swarm calls, and I go after them. There is something irresistible about "free" bees. And as I chase these swarms all over the county, I create a bottleneck of things I need to be doing back in my bee yards.

When I hive a swarm, I usually kill the swarm queen off sometime after the honey flow, and if I don't already combine the swarm with a package, I'll want to requeen the hive with a queen of known age. I don't know how old that swarm queen was, and invariably, if she was real productive this year, she seems to play out and next year she isn't worth a hoot. I've been caught with high hopes. This year I'll have a productive queen and my hopes allow her to live until next year. But sadly, she is often done. I've learned to use those queens to raise other queens.

My package queen is supposed to be a relatively young queen, and time and time again, you'll hear how beekeepers requeen their hives with new, young queens. Queens are really only good for two years, seldom three years, though there are exceptions. I strive to raise my own queens and put new queens in my hives every fall. More on this in the next chapter.

But let me also add the necessity of marking your queens. Marked queens are always easier to find, and using a color scheme, you can always tell how old they are. Sometimes the bees will supersede the old queen and you don't even know it. This is a good thing and the bees have blessed you by requeening the hive with a new, young queen. But if you don't mark your queens, you'll never know how old she is, and you won't know which queens have been replaced for you, free of charge.

Lately, I've been raising a few extra queens to sell to other beekeepers. Raising your own queens is not something you should worry about your first couple of years, but it's something that adds a remarkable dimension to keeping honeybees. Again, you don't want to create too many bottlenecks in your first year of expansion.

So buying a package of bees is easy, but your success is risky. Catching a swarm is tricky, but your odds seem to increase if you can catch a swarm early in the season. I feel the best way for you to expand, if you insist on purchasing a package, is to also buy a swarm trap in the hopes of catching swarms. Also, put your name in with the local police telling them you'll come and get a swarm if they should get a call from a nervous homeowner. This way you can combine the early swarm into the package and you'll coast into the summer with a strong hive.

Nucs:

There is, however, a third manner in which you can acquire bees that dramatically increases your success, but acquiring these bees is more difficult. This method is called buying a "nuc."

A nuc is short for "nucleus." A nucleus is nothing more than a smaller version of the bigger hive. It has several frames of drawn comb, sealed brood, larvae in different stages, and a mated laying queen.

Several beekeepers produce nucs by buying young, mated queens from Southern queen breeders. The beekeepers take this queen and make a new nuc, by taking four or five frames of bees from an established hive and introducing the new queen.

They introduce the queen in the queen cage, but the frames of bees already have the comb drawn out and should have sealed brood on them. In a couple of days, the queen comes out and begins to lay eggs. When you buy a nuc, it is like buying a package of bees established on a set of frames. The queen is out and you won't have any problems getting her accepted. All you have to do is transfer those frames of bees and brood from the nuc box to your hive body.

Buying packages is easy. Just make a phone call in the late winter and send the southern beekeeper a check. No questions asked. Buying a nuc means you need to stand in the presence of an experienced beekeeping who may size you up and wonder if you have what it takes to take care of honeybees. He'll probably want to give you some free advice. (And my advice is to take it, even if you disagree.) He'll want you to succeed, but he may insult you by telling you exactly how you need to proceed (which will likely be **his** way).

Nevertheless, accept his advice with the grains of salt I offered earlier. Pay the beekeeper for his nuc and be on your way. You'll have more to learn than he can tell you on the morning you drive out to his beekeeping property.

I like nucs. Nucs take off like a rocket. They get to their productive destination ten times faster than package bees. Package bees are like going to the barn, chasing the horses into the stall and getting them harnessed to the wagon. Then you take that wagon to town and it's going to take you a decent amount of time.

With packages, you eventually get to town, but by the time you get the horses harnessed and leave the farm, the nuc is like an automobile and is already at the big city doing business. The nuc may even have time to get back to the farm before the package even has the horses harnessed to the wagon.

With packages you miss out on a great deal of development, but packages are easy to acquire and establish, provided you have patience and good luck. You can get a package with a phone call and a check or credit card.

Nucs, however, are seldom available through the mail. You have to know a beekeeper and drive to their place and pick up your nuc. You may have to provide your own hive body, top and bottom, and six frames. Some beekeepers who produce nucs give you a price for four frames "placed in your equipment." This means you drive to the beekeeper's place.

You take out your hive body (with a screen over the front opening and six frames on the inside). The beekeeper will open his nuc, show you the queen so you know for certain you have her, then he'll place that frame and three others in your hive body. I don't care for this arrangement as you miss a lot of the foraging field bees.

The hive body is now heavy, a little hard to manage, but you have a growing population of bees with a laying queen ready to start filling out the rest of your hive body with new bees. The four frames of bees will quickly expand to the other six, and before long, you'll be adding a second hive body.

Some nuc producers have you drive out to their farm, drop off and leave your equipment for a week, then ask you to drive back and pick up the established colony. It's a little more difficult as it takes two trips. And you may have to feed nucs to keep them going while the weather is still cool.

One trick with nucs once you get them home is to weave the outside frames into the middle of the established frames to stimulate the queen to lay more eggs. The queen, in most cases, lays eggs in the middle frames. Each week, I take one of the outside frames, then slide four or five frames from the middle over to the side, creating a vacant slot in the middle of the hive body. The outside frame goes in this slot.

One week I take the outside frame from the left side of the hive body; the next week I take the outside frame from the right side of the hive body. This method works wonders, and will likely work also for packages, but you can only do it every two weeks since your work force is limited with packages.

Nucs are the most successful way to start with bees, but finding someone close to you who will set one up for you is trickier. Nucs take time to establish, and the beekeeper needs to arrange for new queens to be shipped. Sometimes you'll have to make a deposit or pay in advance.

Nucs cannot be mailed or shipped so you have to arrange for delivery or pick them up yourself. You can also expect to pay a little more for a nuc than a package, but this cost seldom includes your time to go get them. At the time of this manuscript, nucs are selling for $70 to $110, but compared to packages, the extra cost will be returned your first year.

If there is any drawback to buying nucs, it would be the delay the nuc producer experiences because the queen producers in the south were delayed because of bad weather. You can get nucs early in southeast Missouri, around the middle of April to the first part of May, but the time table really depends upon the availability of queens and the weather. April in southeast Missouri is famous for cold, drizzly days accompanied by gusty winds.

If I had my choice in my expansion plans between packages, swarms and nucs, I would always, always,

always take nucs. They cost more, but they will respond better the first year and will likely produce a super of honey without too much problem. In a nutshell, they pay for themselves that first year. And you can schedule them fairly close to an early season's date.

However, I am cheap. And I like hiving the free bees I get when I answer a swarm call.

<u>Splits</u>:

There is a fourth way which is hardest of the four methods, but this is my real means of expanding my number of hives. The process is not really that hard, but it does create another bottleneck in the expansion process.

Basically, I am going to make my nucs. I am going to order queens from a southern queen producer. When the queens arrive, I'll go through my hives and pull out three or four frames of bees and brood. I'll either set them aside in their own nuc box, or I may top the old hive with a solid divider board, and start the nuc on top of this divider board (captures some of the heat from the bottom hive).

The trick, of course, is to order your queens with enough notice so they arrive on the date of your choosing. April 1st is a really good date to receive queens in southeast Missouri. By the time the queens get acclimated, introduced and accepted, the nuc is ready in the matter of three weeks to set by itself and to take over as an established hives.

Further, when you make a split, you give the old hive more room and reduce the chance of it swarming. You inadvertently checkerboard the bottom hive to make your split in the top of the hive with the new queen.

For me, as I expand or add to my numbers, I have a real hard time arguing against a split. Queens are very expensive. The rumors floating around the country suggest queen prices are going to take a major jump this next spring, and of course, spring is when EVERYBODY wants queens and weather delays can make them even more difficult to purchase. Rumors of $25 to $45 per queen are surfacing.

I really like to make my own nucs. I highly recommend nucs for your initial expansion, but finding a beekeeper who will make them up for you is the hard part. You may not have a local beekeeper who is comfortable with ordering queens and making splits to sell as nucs. Why not you? While I'm not advocating you to make additional nucs to sell at this point in your expansion (though you could) there's no reason why you couldn't order the queens and make your own splits.

All you need to do is open the old hive, find the queen and confine her so she stays in the bottom of the hive. Split the hive with a divider board and introduce the new queen to the top half of the hive. It's really that simple, but to the inexperienced beekeeper, it may seem a bit overwhelming as you are also likely trying to assemble the bottom boards, hives, etc., that you'll need for these new splits.

Before you do or try this method, read extensively about requeening. One bit of advice I leave with you is when you introduce a new queen in a queen mailing cage, be sure and take out the attendants that come with her. If you can take out all the bees that come with the queen, the new hive will accept the queen with greater success.

With all this said, the next chapter deals with requeening. The conventional wisdom says to make splits in the spring with mail order queens. Yes, this will work. But I have a method I prefer of raising your own queens in the summer, and having that nuc ready by winter so you don't have to order any queens, you don't have any requeening problems, you have no weather delays. I think I have the best kept secret to my success in expanding the number of my hives without incurring the cost of an arm and a leg.

Concluding Thoughts:

I have one last piece of advice when it comes to queens, nucs or packages: order early. Today is not early enough. By January, most commercial beekeepers and queen producers have most of their orders booked and reserved for delivery later that spring. If you're going to order queens and packages, do so today.

Most producers operate on a first-come, first-served basis. Weather is tricky and often results in delays and the cancellation of late orders. Put your order in early, and request delivery for a week before you really want it. If the queen producer or package beekeeper is delayed by weather or has to cancel due to winter deaths, please be understanding as these factors are out of his or her control and a normal occurrence in business. If the weather turns sour, the queen slows down and fewer bees can be shaken. It's life, and every beekeeper has to accept this reality.

Also, by ordering early, you avoid the likelihood that the package producer will be sold out. There are many would-be and wanna-be beekeepers that think they can simply order a package in May when the weather settles. By this time, it's really too late, though not impossible.

One late March I had some dead outs. I wasn't ready to trap that many swarms so I checked around to find a package producer who would sell me a package of bees. The earliest shipping date was the middle of May. By this time our main honey flow would be coming on, and my package would not have a work force built up to take advantage of it.

In addition to ordering early so you can receive your order early, you also put yourself in a position to order replacement packages or queens if something fails (like getting a package with a dead queen because the other bees have killed this strange queen in her shipping cage). Almost every package or nuc producer insures their shipments and will replace or fix your problem. But if you don't order early, then you'll really be late getting established hives up and running.

One last option to get more bees for your expansion plans is to simply buy a functioning, established hive from another beekeeper. Because they weigh so much, this is likely a single brood box with a top and a bottom, with the front entrance screened off. You can expect to pay more for an established hive than for a nuc because you have the equipment cost in the established hive.

However, this method is almost a guarantee of success as everything is up and running. However, moving an active beehive is something only a professional should do. Plus, they can weigh a ton if filled with good honey stores.

And one last word about which kind of bee to order. There are several kinds of honey bees. Each variety or strain of bee is different with different strengths and weaknesses. Some bee breeds build great comb, other varieties survive the winter better than other varieties. Some of the varieties are showing a resistance toward the parasitic mites. Some bees are gentle, and bees of that very same variety are mean as hornets.

I've found beekeepers are like dog owners. Each dog owner has a certain preference, each breed of dog has strengths and weaknesses, yet depending who you talk to, their breed preference is the best.

As you start to expand, you may want to order a couple of different breeds of bees to see which one you like. Some bees bring in lots of honey, but they're a bit ornery. Some breeds are gentle, but they don't aggressively seek the nectar.

The bottom line is this: at this juncture, until you learn more about bees and which one you prefer, just order the bees that you can afford or whatever bees your local beekeeper likes to use. Later on, you can begin to select which breeds you prefer, then you can tell everyone who asks you that your breed is the best!

Beekeeping with Twenty-five Hives

Chapter Ten:

Requeening, and Raising Your Own Replacement Queens

During my early expansion phase, I used mostly packages to increase my numbers. But this method of creating more hives was quickly supplanted by trapping feral swarms. In addition to offering to retrieve swarms from nervous homeowners, I put my name on the list at the police department, etc. to solicit these calls.

Why did I choose swarms? Mostly because they were free, and by all appearances, they seemed healthy and ready to get down to work right away with the intent of producing multiple supers of honey for me.

This raises a question: When you start expanding and begin to "get serious" about your production schedule and your honey marketing, what race of bee is the best? If you talk to any one of the hundreds of commercial beekeepers, even the larger sideliner beekeepers, there is a strong preference for Italians. They are gentle and productive, though susceptible to diseases and mites.

Turn to the pages of the bee magazines and you'll find hundreds and hundreds of ads for a variety of races, hybrids, crossbreeds, and inbreds with a host of characteristics like hygienic behavior, mite suppression, disease resistance (and the list goes on and on).

What race should you choose? I don't think it really matters. My suggestion is to choose a line of bees, or experiment with several, or just pick one. I don't think it really matters in the short run. But when you find a line of bees that fits your personality (most of us like gentle bees) and your goals (most of us want a ton of honey from each hive), then go with that race of honeybee.

What I have found for my operation is to expand with feral swarms from the surrounding area in southeast Missouri. Some people don't like swarms as a method of increase. They think they carry diseases, which I've NOT found to be true. I find they carry a certain level of resistance to mites that fits my management practices, and they are free.

But the downside was always poor quality queens, largely because they were older. Obviously, if a colony is strong enough to swarm, then they must have had some level of population, and in my mind, good health. My guess is that I'm getting an older queen that comes with the prime swarm. She's pretty much worn out and played out, and my experience with her has been short-lived.

However, even with the packages from reputable queen breeders and package producers, queens that came with packages always seemed to start slowly (even with drawn comb from a winter dead-out), and by the next year, they were doing poorly and I wanted to replace those queens.

The swarm queens were always a wild-card, and the late swarms, though I hoped they'd get down to business and raise me a couple of supers of honey (yeah, right) they practically laid down and coasted right into a mid-summer doldrums. These late swarms were likely "after" swarms headed by virgins that needed to be mated, and as they swarmed into the summer when nectar and pollen slowed down to a dribble, the queens would not lay very many eggs.

As a result, these late swarms that I hived never seemed to do any good. Though swarms always gave me a big dose of hope, for the most part, queens were always a disappointment. In many cases, these late swarms never produced anything and usually got robbed out during the nectar dearth, then absconded.

With swarms headed by older queens, and late swarms headed by queens that seemed to slow way down during the summer, I wanted to inject some new blood into my gene pool.

The idea of requeening came to my attention, and initially, I tried to go the conventional route of ordering queens in the spring and killing off the old queen 24-hours before introducing the new queen. I wish I had better success with this method, but I never did.

Queen quality was poor, and it seemed I never ordered my queens early enough to get them when I wanted them (like around April 1st). Further, spring weather in Southeast Missouri is really fickle. We'll have three days of 70 degrees followed by a week of 30 degree weather. There were times the queens came in but the weather did not warrant opening the hives. Then those queens camped out in my basement, a cool and dark place, until the weather settled. Then when I put them in my hives, I lost about a week waiting for the queen to emerge and start laying eggs.

Some beekeepers feel buying mail-order queens is a waste of time and money. If you can get the queens introduced and accepted early enough to produce an aggressive work force, then the cost of the queen can easily be worth it. If you harvest two additional quarts of honey, that new queen can pay for herself.

But you have to get that queen early enough, and unfortunately, every large beekeeper in the country is looking for those same early queens. Larger commercial beekeepers have established relationships with commercial queen breeders. You need to order early as you can as you are in direct competition with big orders, and if you wait until the last minute (like early March) most queen producers are sold out. If you're thinking about ordering some queens when you need them (like mid-April or May) you will find you cannot get them.

However, if you find yourself in a bind and need a queen, start making some calls. Someone will have a queen for you somewhere, but only ordering one queen will cost an arm and a leg. The postage alone will just about kill you.

As I expanded with swarms, I felt the need to requeen. I went the conventional route of ordering spring queens and requeening from conventional, commercially raise queen producers. It was very expensive, and as I've noted, queen quality was somewhat random and unpredictable. I felt there had to be a better way, but at the time, I was following the methods that everyone said you were supposed to do, that is, ordering queens and requeening in the spring.

Then something happened that changed my whole perspective. At the time of this incident, I was experimenting with screened inner covers. I made an inner cover with a 1" outer rim made of wood, the same size as the normal hive. I covered it with 8-mesh screen (8 squares to the inch) and secured it with staples. I covered the top of the hive with this screened inner cover.

Then, when I put on the outer cover, I would prop open the outer cover with a small stick between the inner and outer covers to provide better ventilation. The screen prevented robbing and bees escaping out the top. I'm not sure all of this was really necessary, but it was an experiment to see if better ventilation helped ripen the honey faster.

One time I accidentally trapped a queen on the top of a screened inner cover. As I remember, it was still early May, and as I took apart the hive to inspect the bees. As it would happen, the queen was on the underside of the screened inner cover.

But I didn't see her, and as I put the hive together, she had moved to the upper side along with a few bees. She got trapped between the screen inner cover and the outer cover. And as I was likely either in a hurry or nervous, I didn't pay her any attention. Because she could still make contact with the bees below her through the screen, she made no effort to try and escape at the place where I propped the outer cover open with a stick.

I came back a few weeks later and opened the hive. Much to my surprise, I immediately found this marked queen under the outer cover, crawling around on the screened inner cover. I caught her in a queen catcher and began to tear apart the hive. This was not an overly populous hive, and it wasn't long before I found an unmarked queen in the hive below, which I presumed to be a new queen.

Not sure what to do, I moved the old marked queen to a nuc box with a frame of bees. From there, nothing happened and I can't remember that nuc doing anything at all. It probably just whittled down to nothing and the bees absconded or it got robbed out. However, what I do remember is the hive with the new queen seemed to explode with bees and produced a nice super of honey. All this, despite having to raise a queen all on its own.

From this rather accidental queen rearing and /or requeening incident, I came to trust the bees to raise their own queens. (This is something the experts will strongly advise against doing). But this was back in the days when mail order queens cost $8 plus $5 for shipping. If you ordered ten queens, they still cost around $6 each, but the shipping was now around $12 for the order. Ten queens was a very large order for me at that time. The idea that the bees could, and would, raise their own queen was very intriguing. Of course, they've been doing this for centuries long before humans figured out how to manipulate them to raise queens for us.

And as I grew, the price of queens kept going up. When the price of queens hit $13, I started looking into queen rearing. I bought one of those graft-less, queen rearing kits, but it took me about five years to perfect my method. At twenty-five hives, I would encourage you to buy one of these kits. They cost around $100 with the necessary supplies. But you only have to produce a few queens to make them to pay for themselves. However, they are tricky. If you want to raise your own queens (which I **HIGHLY** recommend) there is a simpler way and you don't need one of those kits.

In the meantime, as I continued to fuss and fume with the trickiness of the queen rearing unit, I experimented with the method of allowing the bees to raise their own queens. I had in mind pulling out three frames of brood and bees and setting them in a nuc box, then moving the nuc to a new yard. In those days I only had three bee yards so it wasn't that easy.

But I made some very nice, three-frame nuc boxes out of used plywood. I pulled out three frames from the original hive making sure at least one frame was full of eggs. And at least one frame needed to have pollen and honey. And my preference for the third frame was to have a good amount of sealed brood and attached bees. In the absence of their old queen, the bees will take young larvae and make a queen for themselves. Three weeks later, I had a nice, new queen in that nuc box that was mated and beginning to lay eggs.

And here's a tip: you have to move the nucs at least two miles from their original location. If you don't, you can bet most of the bees will return to the original hive and ignore the larvae and eggs you brought to the nuc.

Much to my surprise, and to the chagrined surprise of my beekeeping buddies, the queens these nucs produced were very productive. I gather my success was related to the fact that I raised queens when nectar and pollen was abundant. This meant my bees were well fed, and as you read in the beekeeping books on queen rearing, good nutrition is the key to raising good queens. As my queens were raised in a nuc box, they were never confined to a queen cage in a "queen bank."

A queen bank is a queenless colony in which forty or fifty queens are isolated from each other in queen cages. The queenless colony feeds those forty or fifty queens, and as they are kept separate in a protective cage, they don't kill each other. But they don't get to lay any eggs and I believe the confinement is detrimental. That is my opinion and others will argue against that opinion.

After my queens started laying in their three-frame nucs, I went back to my slow producing hives and late swarms and killed off the old queen. Then, after waiting twenty-four hours, I covered that hive with newspaper, set a new hive body on top of it and set in it the three frames from the nucs along with some other frames to make a total of ten.

When you requeen a colony after twenty-four hours of queenlessness, and when you introduce a mated, laying queen with brood present, your acceptance is practically fool-proof. And you never lose a single beat waiting for a queen to come out of her cage. There is no gap in the production of the brood.

This new hive (old hive combined with the nuc and the new queen) is allowed to continue through the rest of the summer, fed for the fall and then carried through the winter. Then in the following spring, this one-year old queen is laying, ready to go. She is not subjected to the stress of a queen cage nor is she shipped all over the country moving from air-conditioned warehouses to hot trucks in the delivery process. And as the weather turns nasty, she is snug as a bug in a rug inside that hive. She doesn't have to vacation in my cool, dark basement waiting for the weather to turn nice or my schedule to free up.

Now, before I proceed, let me warn you. There are other beekeepers who hold other opinions. There is a belief that you need freshly mated queens shipped up from the South and they can't be more than two months old. In the opinion of other beekeepers, my queens that were raised in the summer of the previous year, raised in a nuc and transferred to a hive in anticipation of this coming year, are too old.

I disagree.

The benefits that I gain from a queen already accepted and laying, not to mention she has been protected from shipping abuses and confinement to a queen cage, far out weigh the fact that she is perhaps nine months older than her mail-order counter part. I've raised my own queens from this method, and compared to the queens I've bought through the mail, mine are superior.

I have quit buying queens and raise all of my queens, plus offer a few to sell to my buddies. Technically, I let the bees raise their own queens. If it is done during a time when nectar and pollen are abundant, you will raise some really good queens.

As you work your way up to twenty-five hives, you should consider some kind of requeening schedule, even the possibility of raising your own, locally adapted queens. I requeen now on an annual basis. Some beekeepers still adhere to the every-other-year requeening schedule. You can still buy your queens through the mail and try and requeen in the spring, but this plan is very labor intensive and comes at a critical time which may result in a bottleneck.

When working your way up to twenty-five hives, your labor, time and energy will be your biggest bottlenecks. I also find spring is way too busy for me to be trying to introduce mail-order queens and the weather is always something with which I am forced to contend.

Here's how I've taken to raising my own queens.

I start with the idea that a worker bee egg takes three weeks to hatch, then that newly emerged bee spends three weeks as a house (nurse) bee. She then moves up to the ranks of a forager (field bee) for the remaining three weeks of their lives. As our nectar flow is pretty much finished by the 4th of July, an egg laid in the third or fourth week of May hatches in mid June (three weeks later).

After spending three weeks as a house bee, from mid-June until the first week in July, she is ready for field duty around the 4th of July. But by this date, the nectar flow is dwindling, and she is not going to be much help contributing her efforts to the honey harvest. She's ready to go to work but there is just no nectar to gather.

With this schedule in mind, any egg laid after the third or fourth week in May will pretty much be a non-productive bee, that is, as it pertains to the honey I want to harvest. So I usually peg my queen rearing schedule to the last week in May, but this date is not firm and depends upon my schedule. Nectar and pollen are plentiful so the larvae are getting a good nutrition. I have most of my supers on the hives and I've got my hives settled to fill up the supers.

So around the third or fourth week in May, I pick a hive that is doing well, speculating, to a certain point, that a healthy productive hive will also produce queens that carry on that same tradition. This is not always true, but it has worked for me.

I pick a hive and set the supers off to the side in one pile. Then I begin to work through the brood boxes and find the old queen. As I will preach to you over and over, a marked queen is easiest to find. Spend the money to buy marked queens or better yet, learn how to mark your queens. It's not that hard.

After I find the queen and hold her in a queen catcher or a glass jar of some sort, move the brood boxes to another pile. Do this during the middle of a calm, sunny day when the foragers are out and it will go fairly smooth.

I set a new brood box on the hive stand. I pull out two or three frames from the original brood boxes, and I'm looking for older comb that is filled with nectar and honey. To these existing frames I add the compliment of new frames to fill out the hive body. At this point, these new frames can be foundation or drawn comb, it really doesn't matter. I like to intersperse the new frames between the old frames which helps the bees to work them faster. This is especially true with new foundation.

On top of this new hive body, I set a queen excluder, then release the queen under the excluder. Here she will continue to lay eggs and keep the colony going. She is the glue that keeps everything together. On top of the queen excluder I set the honey supers, then on top of the honey supers I set the brood boxes (usually two of them). I add the compliment of frames that were removed and placed in the new hive body on the bottom. If four frames were removed, I'll add four frames to the top brood boxes.

If you read any of the literature, especially from years ago, this process is called, "Demaree." It is named for a specific swarm prevention method which removes brood and larvae from the presence of the queen, basically giving the queen more room to lay fresh eggs. As she has more room, the hive is less congested and they are less likely to swarm.

The drawback to the Demaree method of swarm prevention is that the bees in the upper brood boxes, in the perceived absence of a queen, will want to make queen cells. In the conventional Demaree method, it is recommended that these queen cells be cut out.

But guess what? We don't mind if they make queen cells, in fact, we want them to make new queen cells. That is the whole purpose of moving the queen down below and moving the brood up above.

In the course of the next twenty-four hours, the bees will sort themselves out. The foragers that were in the brood boxes will work themselves down to the bottom brood box and honey supers and any house/nurse bees will work themselves back up to care for the brood. Let the hive sit for twenty-four hours. Get your nuc boxes ready.

The next day I come back and start making up my nucs. It's very easy and quick as the old queen is in the bottom brood box, contained by the queen excluder. I usually figure each brood box will make up around three, maybe four nucs. I prefer six-frame nuc boxes. As I will be pulling only a couple of frames of brood and eggs from the original hive, I will need more empty frames to compliment the six-frame nuc box. It really doesn't matter how large your nuc box is, just fill it out with enough frames to take up any extra space.

Whether these frames are drawn comb or foundation isn't that important, at least at this point. The bees you put in the nuc box will focus on raising a new queen, not filling drawn comb with eggs or nectar.

After I fill the nuc box with a couple of frames of brood and at least one frame per nuc box with eggs, add the additional empty frames. Then I duct-tape the opening to the nuc box to close it off, and I run duct-tape around the top of the nuc-box cover. My covers to my nuc boxes have a three-inch opening in the lid (cut with a "hole saw") which I cover with 8-mesh wire screen. This will provide the nuc box with ventilation.

I make up all my nuc boxes and load them in my van. Then I move them to a bee yard at least two miles away. I keep the duct-tape on the nuc box for an additional twenty-four hours to confine the bees which gives them the opportunity to acclimate themselves to their new home. It's a good idea to set the nuc boxes in the shade, and if you are short on shade, store them in a cool shed for these twenty-four hours. Since you are not going to release the bees for these twenty-four hours, you can really store them anywhere you want. Just keep them cool.

Then the next day, I'm back to release the duct-tape on the opening, and I give each nuc a quart jar of syrup. I like to feed an inverted jar with very small nail holes punched in the lid. A regular canning jar fits nicely on top of the 8-mesh opening in the nuc box lid. Though the bees have ample stores on the frames in the nuc box, I like to keep feed on them until the new queen comes out and starts laying eggs.

You won't see much activity as you observe these nuc boxes. All of your field bees are still at the old hive. By waiting twenty-four hours after you moved the old brood boxes above the supers, you allowed the hive to sort the nurse bees from the field bees.

There has been some news recently about creating special yards of hives that are used to produce drones. These mating yards have hives with queens that will produce the drones you want to mate with the virgin queens from your nucs. I think it's a good idea, but you may not want to, or need to, be so selective in your pedigrees. I like to move my nucs to a new yard as it keeps the bees from flying back to the old hive, and it also introduces the newly emerged virgin queens to a host of unrelated drones.

I can leave these nuc boxes in place for the next three or four weeks without much concern. Once a week or so I'll replace the syrup jars. The bees will take a worker bee larvae and convert it into a queen by feeding it royal jelly. They may actually raise several queen cells, but the first one to emerge will sting her awaiting competition. Only one queen will rule the nuc box.

In the course of the first three weeks, not too much will happen. The queen will emerge and all the remaining brood will have hatched out. Some of the older bees will convert to field bees and begin bringing in nectar. Under normal circumstances, you will probably have enough open cell space give the queen an opportunity to lay eggs. As you've been feeding the bees syrup (I prefer 1:1 syrup), they will have drawn out some of the frames if you added the compliment of foundation to the nuc box when it was made up.

Here in Southeast Missouri, I begin my honey harvest around or right after the 4th of July. We experience quite a dearth of nectar until early September so there is not too much happening in the hives. I will remove and harvest my honey and take the supers from the hives. What I have left after the honey harvest is hives with brood boxes and old queens, and nucs with new queens. At this point, I have two options.

My first option is to go into the established colonies and kill off the old queen, then cover the hive with newspaper and add the nuc to that established colony. The new queen will be accepted with incredible ease. The colony will coast for the summer, then pick up some fall nectar (not really worth harvesting around here). I'll winterize them, and by the spring, I'll have a strong colony ready to go with a new, young queen.

My second option is to transfer the nuc boxes to a ten-frame single, then rob some extra frames from the older, established hives to balance everything out. This process will convert the nuc boxes to an expanded, ten-frame single brood box, and will also reduce the older hives to a single brood box as well because you borrowed frames from them to make up the expanded nuc box colony. My ideal is to equalize the colonies. This will reduce robbing. If you have bees of Italian pedigree, they will be very inclined to rob their neighbor.

Since I also harvest my honey aggressively, I will have some brood-sized frames of honey to harvest. These drawn frames can also be added to the expanded nuc boxes after I extract the honey.

After everything is equalized, I will feed my colonies. I harvest my honey aggressively, then replace it with syrup. Other beekeepers have different opinions about this process. I look at the price of syrup (50 cents a pound for the sugar) and the price of honey ($2.50 to $3.00 a pound) and the decision to harvest aggressively and replace the harvested honey with sugar is pretty easy.

The bees also sense the incoming syrup and the queens will continue to lay eggs when they normally shut down during the nectar dearth. As the queen continues to lay eggs (and Italians queens are real good producers even during a nectar dearth) the colony will be producing a continual stream of young bees. Younger bees survive the winters better.

In my region of Southeast Missouri, our honey flow is over by the 4th of July. The fall nectar flow is minimal and I prefer to leave this honey for their winter stores. Your region may vary, but for the most part, there is no real action in the bee hives from July until the following spring. It often amazes people how compressed the honey season is, when in fact, the rest of us are enjoying a hot, humid summer.

This second option is the best for expansion. By the following spring, you'll have some hives headed up by two-year old queens, and then a bunch of new queens that were raised in your nucs. While these queens are really one-year old queens, they are only about nine months older than the queens you can buy through the mail.

However, they are acclimated and you don't need to battle the weather getting them introduced and accepted. Best of all, you raised them from you own stock and they were free. And because you pull the brood frames from the hive at the peak of the honey flow, you really do not infringe on the colony's ability to produce several supers of honey.

Then this next year, you can repeat the process with raising another batch of your own queens in the nucs, and requeen the colonies headed up with the two-year old queens. Each year will you will have a portion of your colonies headed up by established two-year old queens and a portion headed up by one-year old queens.

And again, mark your queens. If you have a colony that supersedes your old queens you don't have to worry about requeening that colony. But if you don't mark your queens you have absolutely no idea how old she is. You may inadvertently kill off a new young queen that never got the chance to show you how productive she could be.

As you move up to twenty-five colonies, I feel it is important to keep young, vigorous queens in your colonies. Not only are they more prolific egg layers, but young queens also reduce the swarming impulse. And as obsessive as I am about marking queens, I am ballistic when it comes to allowing your colony to swarm. Never, never, never allow your colonies to swarm. When your bees swarm you have just kissed your honey crop good-bye.

But it also gets back to your purpose in keeping bees. If you want to put in the minimal amount of labor and get whatever you can, then your bees will swarm and you'll maybe get some honey. If this is your level of expectation, then I think you'll do just fine.

But as I've told many wannabe beekeepers, my bees work for me. I put in my time and energy. I expect a honey crop in return. The person who can afford to allow their bees to swarm has more wealth than me. Never let your bees swarm, unless of course, you're just keeping them for fun.

I am likewise a big stickler for keeping young, marked queens. The young queens you just raised in your nuc boxes will be anxious to lay eggs, especially if induced with syrup during the mid-summer months. These queens will bring a colony filled with young bees into the winter, and this colony will stand an excellent chance of surviving the winter.

As you move up to twenty-five hives, and even further, you will begin to learn a lot. The more you learn, the easier it will be to keep bees, the more joy you will experience, and the more money you will make.

There a several different ways to raise bees. Sometimes you will find yourself buying packages and other times you will want to raise your own queens. I like this method of "emergency" queen cells. When done during the peak of the nectar flow, you will produce some healthy productive queens.

And that $100 queen rearing kit? Yeah, there's a learning curve to it. I'm still learning. It will allow me to raise a lot of queens, but in the end, I still need to borrow frames of brood and make up nuc boxes. It really is easier to let the bees do the work for me.

Beekeeping With Twenty-five Hives

Chapter Eleven:

Harvesting and Marketing

Harvesting and Storing Your Crop, and a little on

Marketing Your Product for the Greatest Return

I wrote earlier about marketing, really about having the end in mind, namely, where is all this honey going to go? Let's spend some time looking at how you're going to get all this honey off the hive and into storage. As a smaller beekeeper, this was probably something you took care of on a Saturday afternoon, and by that evening, you even had the place all cleaned up and your crop secure. With a weariness, it felt good to have all this work behind you. Prepare yourself for this same feeling, only ten different days of it.

Increasing the size of your apiary to twenty-five hives requires an attitude of "getting serious." You have to remind yourself of your purpose and why you want to be this size. While that sounds a little austere if not downright ascetic, let me assure you that it doesn't mean you won't have fun. Seriousness is more about a "devoted intention" rather than a lack of enjoyment.

When it comes to harvesting your honey, there is plenty of room to have fun, to make the process enjoyable, but like so many aspects of twenty-five hives, there's a lot more work to be done and the real secret to operating twenty-five hives is to gain efficiencies. Someone once compared the hobby beekeeper as woodworker who does his work with a hammer, a hand saw, and a piece of sand paper taped to a block of wood.

The sideliner beekeeper is like the woodworker who uses a nail gun, a circular power saw, and an electric sander. Both do the same kind of work, and produce the same kind of results. One just does it faster and with greater efficiency. The more hives you have, the more efficient you must become.

This chapter is about harvesting your crop of honey and marketing your product, and the need to be efficient. But more importantly, as there are a hundred different ways to harvest and market your honey, this chapter is to give you an idea of what it entails to move from a hand saw to a circular power saw, from the hammer to the nail gun, what you must do to gain efficiencies in order to handle twenty-five hives.

Let's start with pulling the supers. In my earlier days, I used to go out to the apiary and select the hive from which I was going to rob the honey. I had with me an empty super and a wheel barrow.

After smoking the entrance and top liberally, I would take the top off the hive and set it on the ground. Then I would pull out a frame from the top super, inspect it to make sure it had no brood or open nectar cells. If it fit my criteria, I would violently shake the frame in front of the hive entrance. Most of the bees would fall off, some would circle madly, but they soon started to funnel back into the hive.

I would place the frame in the super on the wheel barrow and repeated the process for the next frame.

When all ten (or sometimes nine) frames were removed to the super on the wheel barrow, I would remove the empty super from the hive and place it on top of the full super on the wheel barrow and repeat the process for the next set of frames.

I would imagine I removed 90% of the bees, but after two supers, I was getting into the frames in my supers that had brood in them. I was also finding unripened frames of open nectar. Since I basically allowed my queen full reign of the hive, figuring the bees would store honey in the top and the queen, if she laid any eggs in the top supers, she would eventually work her way down by harvest time. Still, I had to watch each super for brood.

If there was a downside to this method of pulling supers it would be the time involved. This is a time-consuming process. Adding more hives meant I had to increase efficiencies. So I moved up to a bee escape board. Since I already had the inner covers with that nifty little oval hole in the middle, all I had to do was order the plastic bee escapes to fit into the holes.

Bee escapes work, but they usually take at least one day. If you can retrofit one of these "Porter" bee escape boards with an 8-mesh screen so the bees in the super can see the bees below them, these escape boards work much better. These bee escape boards have been improved by the use of small wire cones, and another model uses triangled shims. Check out any bee supply catalog for their full description.

The idea behind these bee escapes is very simple. Go out on one day and slide the bee escape under the super. Come back the next day and simply pull the super off. For the most part, you don't even need to fire up your smoker on the second day. But if there is any brood in the super, bees are **VERY** reluctant to leave.

And while it requires a second trip to the bee yard, the time you spend actually removing the supers from the hive is quite improved. One downside I found with shaking the bees from the frames is that such action seems to literally inspire the bees to start robbing from the open supers.

As a beekeeper with twenty-five hives, using one of those "bee-blowers" doesn't really seem practical or economical. I've tried cordless leaf blowers but it didn't seem to have enough blowing power to work effectively.

As I increased to the one-hundred hive level, and as I didn't have enough bee escape boards to cover all the hives I wanted to rob in one day, I began to look into those smelly fumigants that chase the bees from the super. You take an outer cover and glue a piece of old carpet to the inside. Spray or pour a small amount of fumigant on the carpet, then place this "fume board" over the hive. It works real well. After five minutes, the bees leave and move down into the hive.

There are two commercially manufactured products on the market and both work very well. One really stinks and the other has a nice smell that reminds me of almonds. I tried to use four of these fume boards when I go into a bee yard. I pour a little bit of fumigant on all four boards and place the four boards on hives. I give them about five minutes to work.

As I pull off the first fume board, I take it off the first hive and walk it over to my fifth hive. Then I take the super off the first hive and load it into the van. Then I move to the second hive and remove the fume board. I go down to hive number six and put that fume board on that hive. Then I remove the supers from hive number two. I rotate the boards to the next available hive, and the time it takes me to remove the previous supers is sufficient time for the fumes to do their trick.

If there was any drawback to these fumigants, it would be their lingering odor. My van will stink, even with the pleasant smell of almonds, for a week after I'm done hauling supers. My extraction room where the supers sit awaiting extraction also smells of that lingering odor. I'm not a big fan of this odor.

But Holy Cow, Batman! These fumigants really move the bees out of the hive. No matter which method you choose, there is always an upside and a downside, both advantages and disadvantages. You have to weigh both and choose which method works best for you. Personally, I like the bee escape method, but there are days in which I just don't have that kind of time.

In my schedule, I like to put in an early day at work, then leave the office around 3:00 in the afternoon. I go out to the bee yards and pull enough supers to fill the van, then I head for home. After dinner, I start uncapping and extracting. I uncap twenty frames, let the cappings fall into a lovely stainless steel tray from a deep fat fryer, then let the frames drip over a catch pan. The catch pan holds twenty frames. Then I move these twenty frames to my twenty-frame extractor, and while it spins, start in on the next twenty frames.

Often the question comes up about uncapping knives. I have never used a heated knife on my honey. When I watched other beekeepers uncap their honey, they take this heated uncapping knife, thermostatically controlled, and slice off the cappings. The first "bite" into the honey comb releases a small, but violent wisp of smoke from the scalded wax and honey. The air is suddenly filled with an odor of scorched honey. Then about three-quarters of the way down, the knife cools and bogs down in the honey because the knife is not very sharp, and it has cooled. It relies on heat to cut through the cappings.

Then the beekeeper will wrestle and plow, wiggle and saw that cooling knife through the last quarter of the frame as the knife struggles to reheat, then as they set it down, the knife heats up again (the thermostat was finally triggered) and the residue of wax and honey on the knife blade are reduced to another wisp of smoke.

If you want to use a heated knife, go to the extra trouble and buy a steam knife. They look just like the other uncapping knives except they have a place for two small hoses. You hook one hose up to a pressure cooker to generate the heat, and the other hose goes down to the floor to allow the condensing moisture to escape.

The heat is even and constant, and it doesn't violently heat up and scorch the honey. Of course, you need a hot plate with the hose attached to the pressure cooker filled with water, but these knives work like a dream.

I prefer, and I always have preferred, to use cold knives. If you go to any fancy culinary/cookware store at the outlet malls, you can shop for bread knives. The best cold knife to use on honeycomb is a bread knife with a scalloped blade. A serrated blade will tear too much of the comb, but a scalloped blade cuts like the honey comb was butter.

There are also a couple of brands, one is called "Cutco" which sells serrated knives with "D" shaped scallops. These knives are the best, but they cost $50 to $60 a piece. They are sold on the Internet, but aspiring college students trying to raise money for college will also try selling them door to door. We have a couple of these knives, but my wife won't let me use them on the honey comb.

So I'm waiting for the neighborhood kid to get ready for college. Then I'll have my own knife. My wife can keep her Cutco knives and I'll keep mine reserved for the uncapping tub. Yeah, they cost more, but I'm also helping send the neighbor kid to college.

I still have the original, two-frame tangential extractor I used in the very beginning of my beekeeping career. Later, I acquired a four-frame tangential extractor in a deal with a bunch of used equipment from a deceased beekeeper's estate. Both of these tangential extractors are the kind where you have to stop the basket after a few spins, reverse the frames, then continue spinning to release the honey from the opposite side. Both were hand-crank models. And with a bit of minor modification in the size of the drain, I would spin frames in one machine until the honey backed up in the bottom, then I'd spin frames in the other machine while the first one drained. Both extractors drained into five-gallon buckets.

I did just fine with these two extractors, alternating back and forth as I could extract and spin the frames faster than the honey could drain out. I poured these 5-gallon buckets into another bucket with a nylon panty hose over the top. And when I tell people all I do to my honey is strain it through nylon panty hose, I get the smirking jokes if the panty hose was new or did I use my wife's old ones?

Yeah, right. REAL funny.

I store all my honey in 5-gallon buckets. When I want to pour honey into some bottles or jars, I have a 5-gallon bucket with a honey gate on the bottom. After filling this latter bucket, I allow the honey a few hours to let the bubbles rise to the surface. The honey is poured into jars and squeeze bottles. The honey gates allow that 5-gallon bucket to become my bottling tank.

This system works for me. As I expanded, I found a twenty-frame extractor with a motor. The price was right so I purchased it. But in the long run, you do not have to have a warehouse full of stainless steel commercial equipment to extract honey.

I really like to bring home a van load of honey, then extract that load that evening after dinner. It's not uncommon for me to extract and strain honey all the way up to midnight. I mostly work alone, and the work is fairly tedious for most people. I find it enjoyable, even therapeutic.

Then the next day, weather permitting, I'm out pulling more supers and extracting that night. If your weekends are free, maybe you want to pull supers during the weekdays and extract all day Saturday. Or if you're a weekend beekeeper, maybe you want to pull supers on Saturday and extract on Sunday.

I find you can extract a ton of honey with a simple, two-frame extractor. It may take a little longer, but it is really about as efficient as the big extractors. The downside is you have to hand crank these models.

I had opportunity to watch a large, commercial beekeeper extract his supers in a sixty-frame extractor. The extractor spins about twenty minutes to cycle through the removal of the honey. He uncapped more frames during this time. Then he unloads all the old, empty frames and loads all the new frames full of honey. The time he takes to unload and load is his bottleneck.

This is where I think I can keep pace with his sixty-frame extractor because most of the time is really spent loading and unloading frames. It's just that my cycles are shorter and quicker. But the cranking is what wears me out. My twenty-frame extractor is motorized.

Though it may seem you spend more time extracting with a smaller extractor, I believe you can keep pace with the big boys. You just don't need the big and fancy equipment as you move up to twenty-five hives.

But to have the room to extract in is another story. I have the luxury of an extra room on my house where I can set up my extractor, straining pails, capping buckets, and stacks of supers awaiting extracting. Seasonally, I take over this room.

I've known smaller beekeepers who extract in their mechanical shops, their garages, their kitchens (mostly when their wives are out of town for the weekend), even their basements, but this is assisted by a walk-out entrance. I don't have a walk-out basement, so I once tried carrying supers up and down the basement stairs. Never again.

I've toured some of the big operations. Most of the larger sideliners and smaller commercial guys have dedicated buildings to assemble their equipment, extract honey and store supers. If I had the money and the available land, it's what I would do. But my resources are somewhat limited.

At twenty-five hives, you don't have to have all the dedicated buildings and large-scale commercial equipment. But you do need to recognize the larger you get, the more this hobby is going to encroach on the rest of your life. It is far better to have spousal cooperation than to try and fight these battles.

A fallout from my initial extraction endeavors was those little clusters of bees that insisted on hanging around the supers. Between the van and my extraction room, they mysteriously multiplied, so when I was done extracting, there was a small bunch of bees circling the lights, hitting the windows, and generally causing no small stir in my family. They came as uninvited guests and wouldn't take the hint to leave!

As I mentioned earlier, I store and pour my honey from five-gallon buckets fitted with a honey gate. I can move these around faster than I can a large drum. I also keep my honey segregated from different areas because the honey tastes different based on the different crops in each respective areas.

I've seen some sideliners who pour, and continually pour, their five-gallon buckets into a larger, stainless-steel, 300-pound (capacity) bottling tank. They always keep enough honey in the tank to allow the air bubbles to rise to the surface.

While this works great for them, I am less inclined to homogenize my honey. As I have different locations, the honey is different. In marketing my honey, I will make a big deal about location, location, location. I offer taste tests and comparisons. While it takes more energy and more time to selective segregate your honey, I think it pays quite well to keep it all separate.

And sooner or later, you will have a bucket granulate. Now what? Well, again, the bucket is easier to re-liquefy than a drum. I built a small box out of scrap lumber, a box large enough and tall enough to hold two, five-gallon buckets, side by side. I wired the box for two light bulb sockets, and placed 100-watt light bulbs in the sockets.

Along with the wire, I bought an adjustable thermostat that fit an electric hot water heater (available at most hardware and farm supply stores). I can put two buckets in this box, plug in the lights, and the heat-sensitive thermostat will cut the electricity off at slightly more than 100 degrees. Then as it cools down, it clicks back on at 86 degrees.

I also bought a digital, minimum/maximum thermometer to keep track of the heat. I don't want it too hot. Others have used an old refrigerator with a single light bulb. They monitor the temperature manually and the refrigerator acts as a great insulated box. Unless you can sell all your honey at the harvest, it will likely granulate. You need to have a means of warming it up.

Which brings us to the marketing aspect of twenty-five hives. When you get this much honey, you need to have a means of selling the honey. As a smaller beekeeper, you have great flexibility. Really small hobby-beekeepers don't have the volume to really market their honey for a good price.

Large commercial beekeepers typically have so much work, and such a volume of honey, they cannot devote the energy to marketing their crop other than to sell it by the drum for a low price. They sell to 'packers' who spend their energy marketing the honey rather than producing it.

As a twenty-five hive beekeeper, your volume is just on the edge of some serious, personalized marketing. Instead of settling for wholesale, you have the option of working the retail prices. You can sell direct at farmer's markets, flea markets, gas stations, barber shops, or whatever.

My wife always carries a box full of squeeze bottles because wherever she goes, people know I keep bees and have the best honey in the county. But that's a reputation that needs to be built, and it takes time. People can always buy honey, but you're selling yourself.

I suggest you gather up a bunch of bee supply catalogs and purchase a selection of squeeze bottles, bears, queenline jars, etc. It's hard to tell what customers want, and to a certain extent, the wide spectrum of different sizes can be dizzying. But I would suggest you have at least six different sizes to offer your customers. Price your honey according to the ounce, then factor in the price of the bottle. You'd be surprised what portion of the total cost is taken up by the container.

Even if you have no artistic bones in your body, you can still design a label. I suggest you go to your local office supply store and shop for "Avery" brand labels. They come in a hundred different sizes. Find a label that fits your container. I use a program called "Microsoft Publisher," but I gather any desk top publishing program will have a pre-formatted label making application.

And if you truly do not have an artistic bone in your body, you can always enlist the services of a commercial printer. In doing so, your options will be limited. In general, a one-color label will cost around $30 for 1000 labels. There might be a set-up fee of $30. Then for each color you want, add in another $30.

And this is for one design and one size. With my own computer, I can make several designs and only print one label, or one sheet of labels, up to as many as I want until I have to replace the ink cartridge. Or as one of my beekeeping buddies does, he has me make up his labels! Since I have the computer and the blank labels, and since he has few computer skills and not enough product to warrant buying a whole pack of labels, he just has me do it.

Most labels require you to have the product name (honey), the net weight (in pounds and ounces), and some means of getting a hold of the producer (that would be you). Even the beekeeping supply houses have a stock design that they can imprint your information on for a small fee. Consult any of the several catalogs to see what is available.

When you start thinking about twenty-five hives, keep in mind that everything will be bigger and take longer. You need to take a more serious note, a more dedicated interest and a greater commitment toward disposing of your honey. It gets back to my original point of defining your purpose.

If you don't care how much, or how little, money you make keeping bees, then the harvest and marketing will not really be much of an issue for you. But if you want to make this hobby grow and make some kind of a financial return, then you need to increase and elevate your seriousness.

One last thought: when to harvest your honey. I like to harvest my honey right after the 4th of July. The nectar flow is practically over, and I like to harvest my honey aggressively then feed sugar syrup to the bees to replace the honey I've robbed from them. Some of the local beekeepers like to wait until Labor Day and spend all weekend extracting. But I find if I wait, the bees will begin to consume some of their handiwork. I want that handiwork in glass jars for me to market.

The real advantage to harvesting a little early, aside from getting the honey crop off before the bees eat it, is that you are now free to treat your bees for mites and disease. Although harvesting honey in the heat and humidity of July is not pleasant, I now have all of August and September to make splits, equalize hives, treat for disease, analyze and observe mite counts, treat for mites.

The downside is if I harvest too aggressively, then I will need to feed. But here in southeast Missouri, with our summers hot and dry and devoid of nectar-bearing flowers, I usually want to feed anyway.

If I wait until later on to harvest my honey, then I'm bumping up against colder weather. Menthol only works at warmer temperatures on those pesky tracheal mites. I like to fog FGMO (or in reality, canola oil infused with therapeutic essential oils), I will also give my hives a couple of doses of powdered sugar (it takes several) to knock the mites off, plus a few puffs of smoke from burning sumac seed heads in my smoker.

In other words, harvesting early gives me more flexibility, and I'm not sold on the conventional chemical approaches to treating my hives. Further, the mite population really picks up in August and September. If I don't harvest until Labor Day, then I've pretty much allowed the mites population to grow unchecked.

But your season may vary and your goals and purpose may be different. I know a lot of beekeepers who love keeping bees, but they hate the harvesting work, they detest the influx of all that honey, and they are not too keen on selling it. But they like keeping the bees. I like the money the bees bring in when I sell the honey.

When you build your apiaries up to twenty-five hives, harvesting will be the hardest work you've ever done. It is manual labor and requires a strong back. You may have to hire some young high school boys to assist you with the heavy lifting. The days are hot and the nights extracting the honey are long.

But in the end, the rewards are very sweet.

Beekeeping With Twenty-five Hives

Chapter Twelve:

Bottlenecks and Trouble Shooting

Well, if you've gotten this far in this manuscript, you're doing well. Beekeeping is serious business and there is a lot to consider. We've covered a lot of ground and there is still a lot more that I can think about, but some things you just have to learn as you go. And there are some things you just cannot anticipate. And there are some things you just have to find out for yourself. And as your situation is going to be different from mine, then there are some things I just cannot tell you how to do.

In this chapter, I want to challenge you to "get serious" about keeping bees. No doubt, as you've picked up this book to see what it takes to grow your operation and expand to twenty-five hives, you already are thinking about getting serious. Now is the time to **GET** serious, not just **THINK** about it.

Most of keeping bees is, as my father used to say, a "continual continuation." Which simply means you keep going, and going, and going until you reach your destination. And often that destination is nothing more than the next step to the next thing. Then you develop a new game plan for the next level of a continual continuation. Success is really a moving target.

And so it is keeping bees. You keep going, and going, and going. At some point you reach a level which you previously thought would define yourself as a beekeeper. But that place is but a stepping stone to your next thing. In all things we find success when we work at a continual continuation.

But plowing along joyfully in your continual continuation is not easy. It takes perseverance and patience. Interestingly enough, the word, "patience," is not in the King James translation of the Bible. The word the KJV uses in place of "patience" is "long suffering."

And I think any success in beekeeping (or anything that takes work) is a result of long suffering, but more than the idea of "suffering," is the ideal that you will keep going no matter how tough it gets. Suffering is related to enduring. And what do they say?

When the going gets tough, the tough get going, and the rest of us find something easier to do.

But if you want to be a successful beekeeper and master the twenty-five hive level of production, it will take endurance, patience, and yes, maybe even some suffering. My father-in-law's advice to me on my wedding day was,

"Nothing important merely happens."

Without a doubt, there are great rewards to those who can work through the tough times, and in beekeeping, there are plenty of seasonally tough times, times in which you will have a million things to do and hardly a minute to do them in. Not only will you have a million things to do, but most of them really need to be done **NOW**. Beekeeping is not for procrastinators.

You may feel overwhelmed, especially if you have made a substantial leap in the number of hives you're keeping. There will be times you wonder why you got into this mess. And over the long haul, there will be times when you feel all alone and nowhere to turn.

These are what I call "bottlenecks." Bottlenecks are usually seasonal crunches when there is a lot to do and very little time to do them. These are the times when several things need to be done TODAY, or you have to be in two places at the same time. These are the days I wish I could clone myself!

One way to prevent bottlenecks is to always be prepared. If you keep good records, or at least keep a notebook on what tasks need to be done, when you're going to do those tasks and what tools and resources you need to accomplish each task, you will do well. Anticipating the needs of the bees is highly important. Most beekeepers fool around, fiddle and diddle, squander their sunny days and all of a sudden they see a swarm fly out of their hives. They kick themselves and say, "I was going to put those supers on last week, or was it the week before that?"

Then these same beekeepers are scrambling around, grumbling and complaining about how they don't have any supers on hand or how they had to hurry up and assemble a bunch of frames only to find out they didn't have enough foundation. Then they're asking me if I have any spare foundation, or glue, or nails to fit their brad nailer. And naturally, by this time, most of my extra resources are already on the hive. By the time they order new foundation, their bees have swarmed again or the flow is about over.

When another person calls with a great urgency due to their procrastination (and beekeepers do not have a monopoly on procrastination), I am reminded of an old saying:

**Procrastination on your part
does not constitute a crisis on my part**

What this means is that if you procrastinate or fool around and don't get things done on time, don't come to me and expect me to drop everything I'm doing to try and mend your mistakes. I'll help, and I'm glad to help, but I will always put things in their proper perspective. The bottom line is you shouldn't be having these problems if you took care of business four weeks ago.

Bottlenecks happen even with the best laid plans, and I have my share as does everyone, but you need to stay on top of things to minimize the effects of these stressful times.

But if you keep good records, if you plan ahead and prepare for what you think you need to do at the right time, you will avoid a host of problems, namely that horrible feeling of "heading around with your chicken cut off" (which is worse than running around like a chicken with your head cut off).

When I said in an earlier chapter that beekeeping is not for procrastinators, I meant it. Even if you don't fool around and procrastinate, there are times when there are a TON of things that have to get done. Bottlenecks happen. We all get busy. Procrastination only makes them worse, but sometimes these seasonal tasks sneak up on you. There was not always an intentional avoidance of what needed to be done at these times. Things happen or even our best intentions fall short.

And there are those times when you think that box of leftover foundation is plenty for the frames you want to put together, or that box of shallow frames turns out to really be a box of medium frames. Time gets away too easily and the next thing you know

EVERYTHING is chomping on the bit. We've all been there.

And it's not the keeping of the bees that is difficult. It's the bottlenecks and the times you just can't keep ahead of the game that will cause the greatest frustration. Sometimes these bottlenecks are caused by the weather. Other times your "real" job or family obligations will curtail your beekeeping activities. And there are times great personal issues will come to bear and become a mental or an emotional distraction.

But no matter what is on your agenda, there will be times when you just don't have enough time. It's just physically impossible to get everything done. And if you don't give the bees the attention they warrant, there will be consequences. These are what I call bottlenecks. Here's a small smattering of bottlenecks you may encounter when you expand up to twenty-five hives.

Swarm Prevention:

As I moved up to twenty-five hives, swarm control was my biggest, and most critical, bottleneck. And there is a difference between swarm control and swarm prevention. When you start finding swarm cells, you need to shift into swarm control. It's too late for swarm prevention. But hopefully you can take care of the prevention before you need to instigate control.

Swarm prevention starts way back in late winter when the queen is laying and spring is still a distant hope. Nectar and pollen from the early tree bloom is starting to fill empty honeycomb. The queen is beginning to lay more eggs every day. The brood will tie up that cell for twenty-one days. In the course of those three weeks, more nectar enters the hive. The queen increases her egg production as the weather warms and more nectar and pollen are coming in. Somewhere there is a point at which the competition for cell space will prompt the bees to say, "Hey! It's getting congested in here. Let's start making plans to split and we'll send our old faithful mother and half of our siblings out into this wonderful world to find a new place to live."

What is going on is that something has to alleviate the congestion. If the bees could remove the excess honey to make room for more eggs, they would. If they could shorten the brood cycle to create more vacancies, they would. If they could somehow put an "addition" on the hive, they would. But they can't do any of these things. So they start making plans to raise a new queen. They start talking about swarming.

And the beekeeper has no clue what is happening. At this point, you may inspect your hives and be quite pleased with the brood production. You have no clue what's going on, until the swarm cells are found. Now it's time to start panicking.

Swarm prevention is a bottleneck because you can't see the congested cells. You can't see the frustrated queen searching for empty cells to lay an egg. You can't read the minds of the workers who start preparing swarm cells because that dilute nectar is taking up a lot of space. And for the most part, the weather is still a little too cold to get out and open the hive on most days. And what makes this a bottleneck is that all of your hives need more room. You need to cross that fine line that defines winter and spring, then get more brood space on all your hives ASAP.

The answer to swarm prevention is to add more space, namely drawn comb. But don't confuse **congestion** (the competition between eggs and nectar for available cell space) and **crowding**. Crowding is just a high density of bees for the given space. Crowding is good in the early spring as it generates lots of heat to keep the brood warm. Crowding doesn't cause swarming. Congestion causes swarming. Congestion happens when foragers want cells to place incoming nectar, and the queen wants more cells to lay eggs.

And simply giving your colony a fresh box of brand new foundation won't immediately help. The bees are looking for cell space. It may take a few days to draw out enough comb to put nectar in. I've seen packages start drawing out the comb on foundation and the queen was willing to lay eggs in half-drawn comb.

Adding a box of foundation will alleviate crowding, but crowding is not your problem. Congestion is the culprit and it will take a few days for the bees to draw out enough of the new foundation such that it can be utilized by the bees for nectar or the queen for eggs.

Also this time of year, lots of beekeepers are likely to feed their bees a light 1:1 syrup to stimulate a nectar flow, and to hopefully, stimulate the queen to lay eggs. There are those beekeepers who will argue against feeding syrup in the spring because it will cause the bees to swarm.

This is partially correct. The rapid influx of syrup acts like a major nectar flow. The bees take the syrup and start storing it in cells. The queen comes along and says, "Hey! I was going to lay eggs in those cells!"

Now you have congestion, the competition between nectar and eggs for a limited amount of drawn comb.

The rest of the worker bees notice what's happening and the plans for swarm preparation are made. One thing I always try to tell beginning beekeepers, and even a few of the older beekeepers, is that swarm preparation happens long before you see the swarm cells. Swarming doesn't just happen. It takes time for the colony to make the appropriate provisions to set the stage to swarm.

If you don't feed 1:1 syrup, a week of warm temperatures in the spring will also flood the hive with nectar. One day you look and there's plenty of room, the cluster is small and the weather is still pretty cool. Then by the weekend, the warm temperatures all week give the bees the opportunity to fly and forage and the nectar flows freely. The next thing you know, the combs are filled with that dilute nectar. Beekeepers forget how dilute nectar is and how much cell space it takes.

The best way to alleviate congestion is to bring in frames of open drawn comb. You need more available cell space. If you bring in frames of bare foundation, you do not increase the available cell space until the bees can draw out the foundation.

I prefer to intersperse the new frames of drawn comb between the existing frames of brood. It doesn't always work to simply add a brood box of drawn comb above the brood nest. The bees don't always move up, and they won't if you have a rim of honey, a honey "ceiling" along the tops of the frames of brood in the existing brood box.

By interspersing empty frames of drawn comb, you break the ceiling and provide a stairway for the queen to move up. In most hives that go into the winter, there is a dome of honey that will keep the bees in that brood box. Merely adding a new box or even reversing brood boxes will not necessarily get the bees to move up.

My plan for swarm prevention is to come to a hive with an additional brood box with ten (or nine, if you prefer) empty frames of drawn comb. You can make this work with foundation, but drawn comb is better. After I take off the outer cover and set it upside down in the grass next to the hive, I set this new brood box on top of the outer cover. Then I pull out four or five frames from this new box and set them aside in the grass. With those remaining frames in this new brood box, I'll space them apart so I can slide a frame of brood from the old brood box between them.

From the existing brood box I'll pull out four or five frames of brood and place them in the new brood box, interspersed between the empty frames of drawn comb. Then I'll take those four or five empty frames that are sitting in the grass, and place them in the existing brood box, interspersing them between frames of brood.

Obviously, this works extremely well when you over-winter your bees in single brood boxes, even double brood boxes. This method then expands your single brood box to a double, or your double to a triple. If you over-winter your hives in a double, then this will add a third box. Or as an alternate plan, since the bees will be mostly in that upper box, pull the two brood boxes apart and intersperse frames of brood with empty frames of drawn comb (which will be mostly in the bottom box).

If you find large amounts of honey, pull these out of the hive and replace these frames with empty drawn comb, or if you don't have comb, foundation. The bees will not need much stored honey at this point in the life of the hive. Leave the two outer frames with honey, but every other frame in the hive needs to be open drawn comb, ready for the queen to lay eggs in, and ready to give the hive a buffer for the incoming nectar until you get your supers on.

This swarm prevention method makes a lot of beekeepers nervous. They feel breaking up the cluster will chill the developing brood. I have not found this to be true. If you have a strong hive, the bees will cover the brood and leave the empty frames alone on those cool days and cold nights. As the temperatures increase, more eggs will be laid. I think we totally underestimate the bees and their ability to manage their developing brood. But, of course, I'm not talking about doing this procedure until the weather moderates.

Then, as an additional swarm prevention measure, don't be afraid to add supers IN ADVANCE OF THE HONEY FLOW. I mean it. Don't wait for the weather to really warm up before you add your honey supers. When warm weather comes to your region and the nectar starts flooding in the hive, the bees will store it in the brood chamber until you get those supers on.

And if the nectar is placed in the brood chamber and the queen is coming around looking for cells for her eggs and nothing is available, guess what? You have a recipe for swarming. If your bees swarm, you can kiss your honey production good-bye.

A lot of beekeepers are unfamiliar with this method, and they have no clue why it works. Let's walk through this again. I like to pull frames of brood out the existing box, replacing them with empty comb. Then I take the frames I removed from the brood box, put them in a new box and add in more drawn comb.

This process has been called "checker boarding," as your hive will look like a checkerboard when viewed from the front. A real checkerboard has alternating red and black spaces. A checker boarded hive has alternating frames of brood and empty combs. This has been championed by a man names Walter Wright who nick-named this process, "Nectar Management."

There is a web page devoted to all of Walter Wright's articles recently published in the leading bee magazines. You'll have to run an Internet search as many of these pages are posted to web sites, but web sites come and go about as fast as expired cheese in the deli case.

Some people still believe the best way to alleviate congestion is to alternate, or reverse, their brood boxes. This helps, but if you read Walter Wright's material, and if your top box is full of winter stores of honey, reversing doesn't alleviate the swarm impulse. And if you have a really strong hive, a colony that has both brood boxes full of bees, then a third brood box is a necessity.

To alleviate swarming, you need empty comb to give the queen room to lay eggs. And if your hives are still full of last year's honey, and you don't have any frames of drawn comb, you may have to have an early spring extraction party. You may have to fire up the old extractor and start uncapping frames. Then you'll have empty drawn comb to give back to the bees to fill up with eggs.

And at this point in the beekeeping season, extracting honey only creates another bottleneck. And if you feed sugar syrup like I do, there is a good chance this extracted "honey" is a blend of sugar syrup and should be fed back to the bees, ideally, after you take off your honey supers.

As much as I preach the gospel of Walter Wright's theories on cell space and honey ceilings, I cannot seem to get it through the heads of 99% of the beekeepers that they need to get that excess honey out of the hive. The bees don't need it. Every frame full of honey is a frame the bees cannot use to store nectar or the queen to lay eggs in. The bees' greatest need is open cell space on frames of drawn comb. Your greatest need as the beekeeper is to prevent the circumstances that lead to swarming.

Swarm prevention is a bottleneck because you have to get out and give your hives new frames of drawn comb. Obviously, this means you need to have drawn comb in your winter storage shed, protected from mice and moths. I hope you haven't created an additional bottleneck by failing to store your equipment in an orderly fashion. The thing to remember is that many of our bottlenecks are self-made!

Don't create the swarm prevention bottleneck by procrastinating. There is a fine line between the cold of winter and the rush of spring. Check your storage shed to make sure you have the frames of drawn comb. One day it will seem there is snow on the ground and the bees are all clustered up tight as can be. You'll sit around thinking you still have plenty of time before you have to work your bees and get them tuned up for spring. The next day the trees and blooming and the pollen and nectar are stimulating the queen to start laying eggs.

And this often happens right around Easter, a busy time in the life of the church and most families. You will have to find the time to get out and give your hives some extra space. And to make this time a little harder, the days are still relatively short so you don't have a lot of day light to work your bees, plus the mornings are still cold and the evenings cool down way too fast. It's hard to find time to work your bees.

If you don't have the drawn comb, you could offer sheets of wax foundation and give them some feed. I find in the early spring, the bees will draw out wax foundation quite readily, and much sooner than plastic foundation. But the debate between plastic versus wax foundation is another story. If you offer sheets of wax foundation, be sure and give them a little syrup (emphasis on LITTLE). And I also find the bees will draw out wax foundation faster if a sheet is inserted between two frames of brood.

But do bear in mind that bare foundation, until the bees draw it out, is not the same as drawn comb. It will take at least a week for the bees to draw out that foundation, then it will only take the queen a couple of days to fill it full of eggs. And then remember that those eggs will tie up all that newly drawn foundation for three weeks.

Swarm prevention is something that has to be done. Swarm prevention eliminates future bottlenecks such as swarm control.

Swarm Control:

The best way to alleviate swarming is by prevention. But if you don't practice swarm prevention, you are going to find yourself with a swarm control problem. Swarm control is the bottleneck when you have to go through all your hives and cut out swarm cells. And if you are finding swarm cells in your hives, you have to act right now. If you find swarm cells in one of your hives, chances are real good that more hives have them as well. And if you don't get out and get this done, your colony will swarm.

In no way shape or form do I think swarming is a good idea to allow it to happen in your hives. If anything, swarming only hurts you and it will greatly diminish your honey crop. If you find swarm cells, you're in big trouble. You're behind schedule already and the pressure is on. You have yourself a bottleneck.

I define a swarm cell as those enlarged, peanut-shaped cells typically found along the bottom of the frames. You'll find them in clusters extended about a ¼" below the bottom edge of the frame. The bees make these swarm cells, which are really queen cells, in anticipation of the old queen swarming off with half of the worker population.

If the old queen leaves, the colony needs to have some provision for her replacement, so they make these new queen cells. And technically, they are not swarm cells but "stay behind" queen cells. These cells contain the replacement queen for the old queen that leaves with the swarm.

However, if your colony has made ten, fifteen or twenty swarm cells (which is not uncommon), then the "prime" swarm will leave with the old queen. You will then have subsequent "after" swarms, swarms that leave with one of these newly emerged queens as she departs with half of the remaining population. Then another swarm cell will open and that queen will leave with half of the remaining population.

This will continue with each newly emerged queen and further deplete your workforce. Each new queen will emerge, and after a short while, take her leave along with half of the half of the half of the remaining population of worker bees with her. Then the next queen emerges and depletes the workforce further. Then, somehow one of those newly emerged queens recognizes she is the last to emerge. She'll stay and become the new queen of the colony, or at least, what's left of it.

As this swarming process continues, your workforce of foragers is decimated. Your chances of harvesting any honey later that summer drop to ZERO. This is why I am so adamant about swarm prevention and swarm control. If you can't, won't, or don't manage the swarming issues, you will have no return on all your labor, time and energy.

The best you can do when a colony swarms is get it up and running in preparation for next year. The good news of swarming is that your have a nice, young queen for next year.

Swarm control is a problem bottleneck because the influx of nectar and the warm spring weather have caused massive congestion problems. If you have one hive making swarm cells, chances are real good all your hives are constructing swarm cells. You can start cutting out the swarm cells but you better plan on doing it to all your hives as soon as possible. And because you didn't give them enough room earlier, they still have in their little minds that they need to swarm. Cutting out swarm cells today means you'll have to come back in ten days and cut them out again. This creates another bottleneck. And those bees are stubborn. If the old queen has not left yet, and if you are successful in cutting out all of the swarm cells, you have dodged a major bullet.

But those bees are stubborn. As that old queen is still present and still laying eggs, they will work to construct a whole new set of fifteen or twenty new swarm cells. Thankfully, you have ten days before you have to come back and cut them all out again. And I hope you don't miss one, because if you do, the presence of one missed swarm cell will result in a swarm.

Typically, the presence of a sealed queen cell usually means the old queen has already left, though not always. You're too late with swarm prevention. It may be too late for swarm control. You may have missed the prime swarm.

But you don't want to kill off all the swarm cells or you may kill off all chances of a single queen leading the colony.   If the old queen has left, meaning you cannot find her (a reason for marking your queens) then there will be no queen to lay any fresh eggs.

If the old queen is still there, then cutting out the swarm cells will only cause the workers to make more swarm cells from fresh eggs after the queen lays some more. Once the urge to swarm starts, it's really hard to eliminate it.   So you can either continue to cut out swarm cells or you can create an artificial swarm.

If you can find the old queen, (and I trust you have her marked so you know which one is the old queen), it's best to remove her to a nuc box with a few frames of bees to satisfy the swarming urge.   Once removed, you've taken care of the prime swarm urge with this artificial swarm.

Now you need to cut out all swarm cells but one. And if you should miss one or two swarm cells (they are not always on the bottom of the frame), you'll probably end up with part of your remaining work force swarming. Again, this is why prevention is better than control.

Or, instead of cutting out all but one swarm cell, divide the colony into nucs, and in each nuc place one frame with one swarm cell on it, respectively.   Cut out all but one swarm cell on each frame. Each nuc will raise the queen and you have a nice way to multiply your replacement queens.

What this does is artificially simulate a swarm. You have removed the old queen and left one queen cell in the old hive. Give the original hive about ten days to two weeks to allow the new queen to settle herself, then kill off your old queen that's in the nuc box, then add those frames from the nuc box back to the original hive.

Combining the workers from the nuc box (and on these frames will be fresh eggs and emerging brood from your old queen) will salvage your honey crop. It's hard to imagine that the nuc box and the original hive from which it came would be strong enough to produce a crop of harvestable honey.

However, if the colony starts making swarm cells early and you have a good season, you may end up with honey to harvest. If nothing else, you have a colony with a new queen and a nuc box that will likely need a full-sized single brood box in short order. But the key to this system is to remove the old queen and cut out all but one queen cell.

If you don't cut out the extra swarm cells, the colony will throw several "after" swarms. The colony will send out a portion of the remaining worker bees and the available work force could just dwindle down to nothing.

An ounce of swarm prevention is worth a pound of swarm control. And if you have one colony swarming on you, it's a good chance many more colonies will follow in the coming days. This is a critical bottleneck, for if your colony swarms, it is highly unlikely you have any honey to harvest.

In my beekeeping practices, I seek a zero-tolerance when it comes to swarming. Some beekeepers don't mind the swarming as it gives the colony a chance at raising a new queen. And if these beekeepers can catch the swarm that leaves their hives, then they figure they are starting a new hive. And of course, the original hive won't produce any honey, but the swarm might if it swarms early enough.

These beekeepers who allow their colonies to swarm, or suggest that they don't care if the colony swarms, have to be the richest, most wealthy beekeepers in the country. Obviously they have more money than I do because I cannot afford to have a colony swarm.

When I see one of my colonies swarm, I know the old hive will not produce any harvestable honey. When

I see the swarm fly off into the woods, I see the potential of a full super of harvestable honey leave my bee yard. That swarming procedure will set the original colony back and prevent it from producing at least a super, about thirty pounds, of harvestable honey.

Thirty pounds is about ten quarts of honey. I sell my quarts for $12.00, so I figure that every swarm that leaves my bee yard costs me about $120 in lost revenue.

I can't afford to lose any swarms. But those who say swarming is no big deal must have more money than I do because they can afford to have their bees swarm. It appears they can afford to allow $85 fly off into the woods. I can't.

Honey Harvest:

There is another bottleneck when it comes to harvesting honey. My usual harvest day is to put in a normal work day at the office, then leave the office around three o'clock in the afternoon, earlier if I can get away. I head out to one of my bee yards and pull in the supers. I bring them home to my honey room and set them aside, protected from any robbing bees from nearby hives. After dinner, I start uncapping and extracting. It's not uncommon for me to extract from seven o'clock all the way up to midnight. Though it is a slow process to extract, I find it very therapeutic.

Then the next day I return those supers to the hives and let the bees clean them up before I remove them for storage. I like to harvest my honey on the same day I pull the supers off.

The honey still retains much of the summer heat so it extracts real easy. If I delay, I run into problems with cool honey and the potential for wax moths. And lately, small hive beetles have been known to infiltrate honey rooms of stored supers awaiting extraction.

Further, unless you have a warm honey room, supers of unextracted, capped honey will pick up moisture from the summer humidity. You run the risk of your honey fermenting, but even higher moisture content will cause the honey to granulate faster.

Extracting honey is highly dependent upon the weather. If it's rainy, I can't get out. Further, when it's hot, I'm not always in the mood to drive to the bee yards and pull supers.

But extracting honey just has to get done. In my operation, as soon as the supers are pulled and extracted, then set back to get cleaned up, I put the supers into storage after treating them with a biological preventative spray. Then I start making my splits for my summer hives. In my operation, I hope to start my extracting after the 4th of July and have it wrapped up by the first of August.

But even within my honey harvest are several bottlenecks. My biggest bottleneck is the cappings. I uncap my frames into a wire basket. The basket is made of stainless steel and was once used as a food basket for a deep-fat fryer. It has lots of little holes and it works great.

But this basket is not that big. But no problem, I have three of these baskets.

But three uncapping baskets are not enough for my needed capacity of uncapping, and further, cappings really take a couple of days to drain. And I'm uncomfortable about leaving the capping exposed too long to the hot, humid air of a southeast Missouri summer. So what should I do? Finally, I found a better solution.

I took a regular plastic bucket with the normal 5-gallon capacity. I put one of those plastic honey gates on the bottom. Or if you're not handy doing this, you can buy plastic buckets with these honey gates already installed on them from any beekeeping supply catalog.

Then I went to my local bakery (or visit the deli and/or bakery department of any large, full-service grocery store). They have buckets of varying sizes. I chose the bucket that looks just like that 5-gallon bucket, only it's more squat. It's actually a three and a half-gallon bucket for cake frosting. It is the same size as the 5-gallon bucket, only shorter, so it will fit right down inside and "nest" inside the 5-gallon bucket.

The rim of the frosting bucket is the same as the 5-gallon bucket so they stack beautifully, and because the frosting bucket is shorter, it leaves about a 2 gallon gap underneath it. So I took my power drill and a ¼" drill bit and drilled about twenty holes in the bottom of the frosting bucket.

I pour my cappings into the frosting bucket as it nests in the 5-gallon bucket. Then, when full, I snap on the lid to the frosting bucket. The cappings are protected from absorbing any humidity from the air. I have enough buckets like this where I can set them aside and allow them to drain for days, or at least until I'm caught up on the extraction. And the honey gate on the bottom of the 5-gallon bucket allows for quick and neat removal of the honey.

After the honey is drained from the cappings, I take large trays about 18" by 30" and spread out the cappings. These trays came from an old pizza parlor that was going out of business. I inquired at my favorite pizza place (which is still in business, thanks in large part to my family, I'm sure) and they are willing to sell me any quantity of these trays. The trays are used to allow the lump of pizza dough to rise before they work it into a pizza crust.

I pick a shady spot in the yard (do not drain cappings in direct sun or they will melt and stick to your tray), spread the cappings out on the tray, and allow the bees to glean every last drip and drop of honey.

Then I take a crock pot to melt the cappings into a nice 8" disk that weigh around 2 to 3 pounds. This is a nice marketable size for selling beeswax.

I've seen commercial beekeepers with wax melters and sumps with baffles. I'm not ready to invest in this kind of equipment. I'm still very manual in my operation.

Frame Assembly:

Another bottleneck I have is frame assembly. For most of my hives, I use the standard frames made of wood. The bees really like wax foundation so that means putting in horizontal supports of tinned wire.

Yes, I know you are not supposed to need these horizontal wires when you buy the pre-wired foundation with vertical support wires embedded in the foundation, but I like the added stability of horizontal wires. Wire takes extra time and effort, but when I was young and still a small beekeeper, it was something I liked to do.

But more and more, I am replacing my wax foundation with plastic inserts. As I buy new frames, I've skipped the wax foundation and the wiring and gone to plastic foundation. And when I have a little extra money I am buying the one-piece plastic frames.

But assembling the frames was always a bottleneck, especially in the spring when I realized I needed 250 more frames for 25 supers. To make this assembling easier and quicker, I made a square wooden box that holds ten frames side by side. I manually assemble the frames, then stack them side by side in this square box. The box holds ten frames to make nailing quicker and easier. As I need two hands to drive a nail, this box supported the actual frame so I could nail it.

You can find these framing jigs in any beekeeping supply catalog, or just make one. This isn't rocket science and all you need is a box that is the same size as ten frames. Or if you want to make one for twelve frames, or eight frames, or whatever.

Measure however many frames you want to nail together at one time, then make this box just large enough to slip right next to the frames on all sides. The height of the box should be just below the ends of the top bars so the top bar has room to seat firmly into the groove of the side bar.

I made three boxes that fit the respective heights of brood frames, medium super frames and then shallow frames. If I were to do it all over again, I would get rid of these shallow frames and shallow supers and stick with brood depth and medium depth frames. But I got them, mostly from retiring beekeepers, so I might just as well use them.

In addition to the framing jig, I finally broke down and bought myself a "brad nailer." I always thought this little nail gun was something of a luxury. I've seen roofer use larger nail guns on home construction and I thought that application warranted such a power tool. But nailing frames? Please!

Well, I finally broke down and bought one. They range in price from $45 to $100, and I picked one that would shoot a smaller range of brads (small nails). I didn't need one to shoot anything more than 1-1/4" nails (for the top and bottom bars) and 5/8" nails (for the wedge bar). But be careful. Some brad nailers only handle the 5/8" nails.

I always thought the expense of the nails, which come in these convenient strips--real easy to load into your brad nailer--were too expensive. And another thing that prevented me from really enjoying a brad nailer was the fact that I had several boxes of frame nails.

In one of those "deals" I got from an old man who used to keep bees, I got several boxes of frame nails with a bunch of his old equipment. I felt it was good stewardship to at least use up his nails before I squandered the money to buy a brad nailer.

Well, what I really found was that I was squandering my time nailing all these frames by hand. And when I priced the strips of nails that feed the brad nailer, they were not that expensive. And my goodness!

The time I saved was worth it. There are some things that will save time and some things that save money. Life is a trade-off, and while I'll take the time to fix and repair worn out supers, I am in love with buying new frames.

Hauling and Delivery:

There is another bottleneck that you will never see coming until you start making trips out to your bee yards. Hauling and delivery.

I discovered this with a remote bee yard, one of my far distant yards. I went out to pull supers. Since I'm still working my way into this sideliner aspect of keeping bees, I still use my van to haul bee equipment. I have a 1996 Ford Windstar. The seats pull right out and give me an area about 4' by 8' to carry my supplies. I made a wooden platform out of plywood which helps keep drips off the carpet, and it makes the back end level which stabilizes my load inside the van.

I went out to pull supers, and the thing I really like about my van is that I can close the door to keep pesky robbers out of the honey I intend to take back and extract. The down side is I have a limited space and weight is an issue for my van. This is a passenger vehicle, not a commercial-hauling vehicle.

So at any rate, I drove out to this bee yard and I started pulling supers. Everything was going well, but about halfway through the line of hives, my van was full. I had no choice but to quit, go home and unload. Then make the return trip to take off more supers. After the second load had filled my van, I still had two more hives to pull supers from.

Since I like to keep all the hives in my yards equalized, I debated whether or not to leave the two and come back later on another day, or make a third trip back that same day. Since I like to market my honey by varieties and location, I went home, unloaded the van, came back and finished up just before it got too dark to see. Boy, those bees in the last two hives were hostile toward my honey robbing. Removing supers is so much more enjoyable in the middle of a calm, sunny day. The closer you get to sundown, the more protective they become of their honey!

What I really need is a truck, but that's still not in my budget, at least not just yet. I suppose I could rent one, but that's still pretty pricey and my honey harvest is so much governed by the weather. I could use a trailer, but a lot of my hives are out on gravel roads, and in July, the dust raised on these roads is an environmental hazard.

I would not want the dust blowing through the trailer, anyway. Plus, I would be leaving the supers on the trailer open to inquisitive bees looking to start a robbing frenzy (yep, been there, done that!).

And there was that one time I left the van doors open for that last trip back to get a few things. Well that led to a few more things, and one more thing, then one more last thing.

Next thing I know as I come back to the van is to find a van full of robber bees. The best thing I could do was go home wearing my bee veil. When I got home, I removed the supers from the van and put them in the garage. I instructed the family to stay out of the garage and leave the lights out.

By early evening, most of the bees had vacated the supers and were flying up against the window in the door to the walk-in entrance. I opened the door, let the bees fly out, and hoped they would find a hive in my yard with which to drift over to.

Obviously, they were too far from home to fly back. And then there were several small "knots" of bees hanging around my van. (Those poor lost bees really freak out my children's friends who think honeybees have some kind of aggressive killer instinct.)

I am still working on this hauling and loading. When I am adding supers, I have the same problem. The space in my van limits how much I can haul. When I am feeding supplemental syrup, it's the weight. I can easily fit twenty-five buckets of High Fructose Corn Syrup into my van, but that's 600 pounds in the back end. It really pushes down my shock absorbers. I think my next purchase will be for a covered trailer, but for the limited time I need it, I'm just not sure yet. Hauling and delivery is still a bottle neck.

Mixing Sugar Syrup:

I harvest my honey aggressively, that is to say, I take a lot of honey from my bees, then plan to replace it with supplemental syrup. Syrup is easy to make, especially in large quantities in a large tub.

But it's a bottleneck.

I bought a thirty-two gallon, heavy-duty, plastic trash can. It was a Hefty-brand "Rough Neck" trash can I bought from Lowes Home Improvement store. I drilled a small, 1" hole on the lower side, close to the bottom of the tub. With my plumbing experience, I bought several plastic fixtures to make a drain with a faucet-style ball valve.

It's really simple: I add hot water, pour in the sugar, then use my electric drill with a paint mixer on the end and I mix up my sugar solution to feed the bees.

I take my hot water directly from my water heater in the basement. A five-gallon bucket of hot water weighs forty pounds. If a pint is a "pound the world around," and there are eight pints per gallon, a five gallon bucket of water weighs forty pounds. (8 pints per gallon x 5 gallons = 40 pounds)

I pour the water into the trash can. If I am making 1:1 syrup, I add one fifty-pound bag of sugar. At today's prices, one of these bags costs $33 at Sam's Club. In reality, this ratio is closer to one part water and one-and-a-quarter parts sugar, but since this is not rocket science and I'm not making rocket fuel, it will have to do. In the long run, it's not going to ruin the bees or send them on some kind of sugar high.

(And, by the way, there have been boat-loads of arguments that honey is better for the bees than sucrose syrup, and most of those arguments have been debunked. I see my honey selling for $2.50 to $3.00 a pound (depending upon the size of the container) and sugar sells for 50 cents upwards to 66 cents a pound. Do the math. It pays to harvest aggressively, but you will have more labor replacing that honey.)

Forty pounds of water and a fifty-pound sack of sugar will give me slightly more than four buckets of supplemental feed. I feed my syrup in an inverted 2-gallon bucket I picked up at the bakery department at my local grocery store. They formerly contained cake frosting. They cost 50 cents each.

I drill five or six 1/16" holes in the lid, turn the bucket over the hole on the inner cover, and let the bees feed. And yes, you will need a pretty stout inner cover. I make my inner covers from 3/8" plywood.

The cost of one bucket of syrup for one hive is $6.60, plus my time and labor.

Now sometimes I want the heavier, 2:1 ratio of syrup. So to my 5-gallon bucket of hot water I add 100 pounds of sugar (two 50-pound sacks) and mix with my electric drill. By the way, you can get these monstrous paint mixers at any hardware or home improvement store. They make them to mix up and stir five-gallon buckets of paint. It will take a little longer to mix this syrup up, and yes, it's more like a 1:2.5 ratio, but this isn't rocket fuel. The bees will do just fine, plus, not all of the sugar gets dissolved. This ratio will give me slightly more than 5 buckets of heavy syrup at a cost of around $8.80 per 2-gallon bucket.

Compare this cost against the value of the honey you are removing from the hive! It pays, though it is more laborious, to take the honey, make the money, then buy sugar.

And in my large tub, I can make up two batches of either ratio. But after mixing it up, I find I need to let the syrup cool and settle. If I pour the syrup into my buckets still warm and cloudy, the sugar will settle, crystallize, and plug my feeding holes in the lid of the bucket.

So what I used to do was mix up a double batch of syrup, then let it cool and settle. I would come back the next day and pour my eight or ten buckets of syrup. Then I'd mix up another double batch, then leave it to cool and settle. Then I'd come back the next day and pour those eight or ten buckets, mix up another batch, etc., etc., etc.

And in between some of these batches, I'd have to make that trip to Sam's Club and buy the sugar. And since I wanted to make one trip out to selected bee yards, I have to wait until I had enough syrup made up, then some days the weight of the syrup in my van became the unexpected bottleneck.

Now days, I go with High Fructose Corn Syrup. I have it delivered in 55-gallon drums (they yield 600 pounds of syrup), which I transfer into my 2-gallon buckets. HFCS costs less than sugar, doesn't have to be mixed, and the bees seem to prefer it to sucrose syrup.

But you have to find a place that sells it, then you normally have to drive that distance and pick it up. I found mine through a bakery supply business that makes regular runs through my area. I used to feed my syrup in quart jars when I had up to twelve hives. This was a bottleneck! And now, even with 2-gallon buckets, it's still a bottleneck.

Marketing vs. Producing:

I guess another bottleneck would be the competition between marketing my honey and producing the honey. It's really just your standard bottleneck of not having enough time in the day to do all you want, plus the fact that most of our time is needed during day-light hours.

I market a lot of my honey at the farmer's markets. Right now, we have two farmer's markets in our area. These are your traditional, open-air markets set up on parking lots. The markets are open Wednesday mornings and Thursday afternoons, and both markets are independent, run by different boards and meet in different locations. There is a third option on Saturday mornings at a local diner/coffee house.

All three of these markets are valuable for consumer education, giving away free samples, defeating the notion that "store-brand honey is just as good," and meeting people. I really enjoy the experience. But these markets take time. I sell a lot of honey this way, but I talk to a lot of people. I introduce a lot of people to locally produce honey. I get out what I put in, but they take a lot of time.

Invariably, during the slower times of the markets, my mind drifts to my bee yards, especially the ones I haven't seen for some time. I know I need to get out, check on some new queens, check for super space, maybe even bring in a few supers and remove the honey.

I'm like that pastor who was sitting in his office. In his mind he was thinking, "I've got to get out and visit the shut-ins and the home-bound church members." But when he was at the home of matronly member, who in her hospitality was serving cookies and coffee, his thoughts were, "I've just got to get back to the office and work on that sermon."

We always find a conflict of time. We feel torn to be two places at once. In my youth I drove a delivery truck. Some of my deliveries were 100 miles away. As I watched the rolling countryside out the windshield, all I could think about was an old song by a country-western artist named Eddie Rabbit who sang a song about a truck driver. The chorus of that song went, "I'm driving my life away, looking for a better way, looking for a sunny day."

And that's how I felt. Ironically, as I drove along those rainy highways, the windshield wipers were "slappin' out a tempo, keepin' perfect rhythm with the song on the radio," and I felt I had to keep on a rolling. But my heart was back home with all the work I needed to be doing.

Just as conflicts are inevitable, so will our conflicts with time and schedule, weather and incessant to-do lists. And just when you feel you've caught up with one thing, something else pops up.

That's life.

I think the reason I feel so overwhelmed is because the bees have their own schedule. Their schedule is often in response to the events of their environment and the call of nature's unique and unpredictable rhythms. And when the bees are scheduled to start, or stop doing something, they don't wait for us. They'll start without us.

And when it's time to put on supers or prevent swarming, if we don't get going the bees will move on to the next thing on their agenda. Perhaps our real sense of being overwhelmed originates from the fact that we don't keep bees; they keep us. They keep us busy. They keep us jumping. They keep us guessing what we need to be doing next.

And I know there are some beekeepers who "hire" extra help. Sometimes this extra help is the neighborhood kid who mows grass all summer and is strong enough to huck supers on the back of a pick up truck.

Sometimes this hired help is a couple of retired men, just a couple of good ol' boys from church or the coffee shop with more curiosity than common sense, but they're still an extra set of hands that come in handy.

But finding this help is not always reliable—at least is has not been for me. Much of beekeeping in my life has had to be on my schedule, and on my time. There are days when I need to go out on my lunch hour and other help is just not available. There are those nights in which I extract from dinner time until midnight. Few people are available. My weekends are full when most others are free, and of course, we are always driven by the weather.

There are two quotes to pull this chapter to a close. The first is by Jim Rohn. He said:

"Success is nothing more than a few simple disciplines, practiced every day."

This is what my father suggested about success (in any endeavor) is merely a "continual continuation." Remember the words of the prophet Zechariah (4:10), "Do not despise small beginnings." And remember how Jesus implored his disciples that all they needed was a very small amount of faith, even that which was as small as a mustard seed had the power and the potential to move mountains.(Matthew 17:20).

And mountains are often moved, one shovel full at a time. But if you don't pick up the shovel, it will never be moved.

The second quote comes from Elizabeth T. King who said:

"I find that it is not the circumstances in which we are placed, but the spirit in which we face them, that constitutes our comfort."

No doubt, you will find yourself overwhelmed with the bottlenecks. They are inevitable. But how you handle them will determine your long-term success at beekeeping.

Beekeeping With Twenty-five Hives

Chapter Thirteen:

Looking Before You Leap: Do You Have the
Right Stuff?

Some Philosophical Thoughts Before We Get Too Far

There are three existential places we keep bees.
We keep bees in our heads, our hearts, and our back
pockets. You may be thinking about the back yard as
your place to keep bees, but in an existential sense, we
keep bees in three places: our heads, our hearts and
our back pockets.

When I say we keep bees in our heads, I mean our minds, our intellect. This is where we keep "**knowledge**." This is where education files away all the hundreds of interesting facts about bees. This is where we put all the information about when to super, what needs to be done to prevent swarming. This is where we think about bees when we're driving down the road and we pass by a huge field of uncut hay or a blooming meadow.

When I say we keep bees in our hearts, I mean our insides, our "gut." This is where we keep "**passion**." This is the place where experience fuels desire. I might also call this my "hunger" factor. This is the place that answers the question of why I keep bees. This is the place that people ask, "Just what makes that man tick?"

When I say we keep bees in our back pocket, I mean our wallet. This is our "**bank account**." And this is not always measured in dollars and cents, nor is it quantified in financial terms. This is where we balance the work (debt) against our joy (income). You may keep bees and give away all your honey, but the joy of sharing the fruit of your labor is what finances the time and energy. When beekeeping becomes work, then it may be time to reassess where you want to go with your bees, or perhaps, you need to look at where your bees are taking you!

I have found an odd ignorance with people who want to keep bees. Since bees are found in nature, holed up in some hollow tree, they begin to believe that there are no costs to keeping bees. And I guess if you can cut off that section of the tree, convert it to a level stand, these bees will be free and their housing comes at not cost as well.

But bees cost money when you have to buy the resources to build those boxes. If you aggressively harvest the honey, then you'll need to feed sugar syrup. You'll likely have some losses and need to buy replacement bees (and a package costs around $60 to $75 bucks).

People act surprised when I show them how much it costs to start beekeeping, and then they also wince when I show them how much it costs to maintain them, plus buy the appropriate jars to market the honey, plus the cost of the extractor, etc., etc., etc.

And then first year beekeepers start getting impatient when their package of bees uses a lot of their resources to draw out wax comb. By the time fall rolls around, their honey reserves are so low, they have little chance of surviving the winter. So I tell them they need to buy a bag of sugar and mix it up, two parts sugar to one part really hot water.

That's when they start complaining about how they can't afford to feed their bees. I point out that a twenty-five pound bag of sugar costs $13 at the grocery store. That will probably give the bees enough resources to last through the winter.

My best guess is that a twenty-five pound bag of sugar will mix up around three gallons of syrup. When fed before the weather gets too cold, the bees will take the syrup and store it in the comb. This ought to get the bees through the winter.

Again, the complaint comes from new beekeepers as to how they never knew it cost so much to keep bees. I tell them they can buy the sugar now, or buy replacement bees in the spring time. Let's see, $13 now or $70 later. However, there is no guarantee feeding the bees will get them through the winter if you haven't treated for mites or disease. But $13 is a nice insurance policy on the investment you've made in your bees.

Plus, if the bees die, that opens the door to wax moths. If you get wax moths, you've been reduced back to a first year rookie beekeeper.

Somewhere people are under the delusion that if bees can live free in the wild, then all this honey will be free as well. They have ideals of a 100% profit. There are some funny assumptions out there.

As I climbed the apicultural ladder to twenty-five hives, up to sixty, later to over one-hundred hives, each of these three "places" (my mind, heart and back pocket) were significant. You need all three, and all three need to be in balance. You need the right knowledge (one that always thirsts for more), the right passion (balanced in proportion against your knowledge) and the right bank balance (because you're going to have to pay for some things).

As I write this manuscript, I have assumed, heavily and perhaps incorrectly, that you have a good working knowledge of bees, bee biology, hive activity and the seasonal demands of keeping bees. As you expand, your knowledge will need to increase. One thing is for sure, at twenty-five hives, you will quickly learn all the things you don't know.

Knowledge is the first key to keeping twenty-five hives of bees, and a good beekeeper is always a student, always reading, always asking questions. But knowledge, in and of itself, is not enough. You also need passion.

I have also assumed that there was some driving impetus that is moving you to want to expand to twenty-five hives. There is a reason why you picked up my book. Perhaps you are contemplating the time and energy demands of twenty-five hives.

Maybe it's something you think you'd like to do but you need more information. A quest for more information is not enough. You have to be hungry enough to do something.

There needs to be a balance between knowledge and passion. You need to know how to do something, and you need to be appropriately motivated.

Years ago there was, in our small town, three "service" stations. These were the old fashioned gasoline stations where you pulled up and this guy bolted out from the office and asked you what kind of gas you wanted. They pumped the gas, then took your money. Then they brought you back change. The ideas of paying at the pump with a credit card didn't even exist in our imagination. These guys also changed flat tires, changed your oil, repaired water pumps—in a nutshell, they offered "service."

Well in this small town with three service stations, there were three different opinions as to the service they offered. The first service station was run by a man who had knowledge of cars and engines, but he was lazy and unmotivated.

The second station was run by a man who had very little knowledge, but he was more than willing to give it the old college try, even though he had no moral right to be picking up the tools to attempt to fix your car. The third man, well, he had neither the knowledge nor the motivation, but he was willing to offer gas at a penny per gallon below the other guys.

The first guy had knowledge, but not passion. The second guy had passion, but not knowledge.

It was said of the first man, "He could, if he would, but he won't, so he can't"

It was said of the second man, "He would, if he could, but he can't, so he won't."

And the third guy, it was said that he did it for less and made it up on volume.

There needs to be balance between knowledge and passion. And sadly, over the course of time, all three went out of business, collapsing and surrendering to the self-serve, pay-at-the-pump, "convenience" store. But that's another story.

My point is this: knowledge by itself is not enough. Passion by itself is not enough. You need both, and they need to be balanced. You need to be willing (passion) but also able (knowledge). And many people are able but they are not willing. They have knowledge but they just can't seem to get motivated. And then there are some people who want to keep bees but they just don't have any knowledge or experience.

Most times they don't have the patience and they'll rush into buying some expensive equipment and some packages of bees. The end result is usually disastrous. But for these people, I want to cheer them on. If given the two qualities, knowledge or passion, passion is more important of the two. Passion will bring you into knowledge for your ultimate success, but to start out, passion is wonderful but you'll soon need knowledge as well.

There is an old axiom that reads: **"Only those who truly hunger lose weight."**

Sounds odd, doesn't it? But until someone really and truly hungers to be thin, until they desire weight loss more than anything else, they will forever battle the scales. Hunger is passion.

If you want to be thin, if you want to keep bees, you have to want it, you have to want the goal of twenty-five hives. Passion is the second key. Let's look at the third place we keep bees. It's time to check your bank balance. The third place we keep bees is in our back pocket, our wallet.

My third assumption is that you have the resources to move up to twenty-five hives. These resources need not necessarily be cash, although you will quickly learn that to outfit a hive, if everything is purchased and bought at normal, retail prices, each hive will cost from $200 to $250, and this does not include the bees. Add another $60 to $75 to this figure.

But who said you had to buy everything, or buy everything at once? In an earlier chapter I've explained more of the financial details, but you may need to take a sober look at what it costs to establish a new hive and maintain a seasoned hive before you get in too far. This is especially true if you are borrowing the money to start your bee enterprise. Not only will you need the woodware and the bees, there are medications to buy. There will be times you need to feed sugar syrup, and I'll tell you right now, feeding sugar is laborious, but a twenty-five pound bag of sugar from the grocery store is a heck of a lot cheaper than buying replacement packages the following spring.

I highly recommend subscribing to the two leading magazines, *The American Bee Journal* and *Bee Culture*. But subscriptions cost money. So why not convince your local library to subscribe? Or do as I did. I found a buddy who liked *Bee Culture* and I was already subscribing to *The American Bee Journal*. Every month we traded our magazines after we each had a chance to read them. This way, we each got two magazines for the price of one subscription.

You need knowledge, you need passion and you need resources, but these resources don't always have to be financial, though for the sake of my body analogy, I've referred to the "back pocket" as this place of keeping bees. Remember, you can always barter and trade your time, energy and services to an older man who quit keeping bees several years ago. You can work for a beekeeper and receive the old equipment or nucs as payment for your services. Or you can find an existing beekeeper, work with them and trade your time for more knowledge and experience.

As you move up to twenty-five hives, your emphasis and purpose will change. Mostly, you will be moving from keeping bees for fun to keeping bees for profit. Twenty-five hives will incur more costs, and you'll be looking for more return to cover those costs.

But never lose sight of the fact that keeping bees is fun, and with twenty-five hives, it can still be fun, even more fun than keeping four hives. If it isn't fun anymore, then maybe you need to do something else. How do you keep it fun, especially when twenty-five hives starts to become work?

John D. Rockefeller the III wrote,

"The road to happiness lies in two simple principles: find what it is that interests you and that you can do well, and when you find it, put your whole soul into it -- every bit of energy and ambition and natural ability you have."

What this statement says to me is this: find what you want to do, then put the appropriate amount of energy into it. And what Rockefeller says is appropriate is **"your whole soul."** That's passion!

If you are not willing to invest the sufficient time and energy that it takes to be success, then it will become work, a drag, a constant frustration. If you're not willing to do what needs to be done, when it needs to be done, then maybe you need to do something else. If it's not worth doing well, then it's not worth doing. And I think if you enjoy keeping bees now, then it will be worth doing well as you expand to twenty-five hives.

We all have, in many areas of life, things we love to do and things we despise doing. I have found that if I'm willing to plan and prepare and invest the appropriate amount of energy into a project, it is fun. If I procrastinate and fly by the seat of my pants, then it becomes work and I usually do a poor job. Then I receive the appropriate criticism.

And that's not fun.

And this is true whether I'm preparing a sermon, leading the Boy Scouts, giving a presentation on fund raising, planting my garden, taking my son to a ball game or setting up the concession stand for the local swim team. Procrastination is a recipe for frustration and stress for me.

Anything worth doing is worth doing well. And the better you do it, the better it will get done, and the more you will enjoy doing it. Beekeeping is no different. To make keeping twenty-five hives of bees fun, and to prevent it from become a slave master that lords over you, there are some very simply things to do to keep it an enjoyable, and profitable, enterprise.

Earlier I mentioned the idea of making every day count. Beekeeping is seasonal and when the season arrives, there is a lot of rushing around. There will be bottlenecks. Preparation is the key, and as you'll hear me preach over and over, beekeeping is not for procrastinators. You have to be prepared.

And to paraphrase a favorite piece of the Bible from the third chapter of Ecclesiastes, there is time to super and a time to harvest; there is a time to requeen and a time to watch for swarm cells; there is a time to treat for mites and there is a time to feed to supplement winter stores. There is a time to rest and a time when there will be nothing but work.

There is a time for everything, but above all, make sure you do it! Time waits for no man and the bees don't sit around waiting for procrastinators. Procrastinate and you'll be paying the price.

I found as I kept thirty hives, time and energy were my main concerns. As I became more efficient, time and energy were easily managed so I expanded. Because I increased my efficiencies, I could handle more hives. Now my biggest stumbling block is organization. I've managed my time and energy, but keeping everything straight to do what needs to be done, when it needs to be done is my biggest challenge right now.

That's why I am so adamant about keeping records. And records do not have to be boring and overly detailed. But you have to keep some record of what you've done and what yet needs to be done, plus what you need to accomplish those tasks.

This leads me into an interesting perspective on beekeeping: being reactive versus being proactive. Bees are very reactive. When pollen starts coming out in the spring, the queen starts laying more eggs. When the nectar flows, the bees draw out more comb.

If the hive becomes congested, that is incoming nectar competes for cell space with the queen's desire to lay more eggs, the colony will begin the preparations to swarm. When the old queen is too old, the colony will supersede her. When the nectar flow decreases in the late summer, the queen slows down her productivity.

Bees operate in response to their environment. Unfortunately, so do beekeepers. Once we see swarm cells, we add more brood boxes. Once we see the upper brood chamber filling up with nectar, we add our supers.

This is all wrong, wrong, wrong.

As a beekeeper, you cannot live in the reactive mode, you need to be proactive. Which means before the colony finds themselves with no other option but to swarm, you need to provide the room that will alleviate swarming. Before the nectar comes in, you need to be proactive and supply the colony with honey supers. Before mites reach what is commonly referred to as the "economic threshold," you need to treat for mites.

With bees, you cannot wait until the colony is asking for more room, you need to provide it. If you wait until they ask (as in when they start building swarm cells), you're really too late. The best you can do is to keep the situation from becoming a problem. This is a reactive mode. You need to be proactive.

And I have to learn this principle every year. Every year I believe I have the time in the spring to assemble all my frames, paint old boxes, etc., etc., etc.

But then time flies when I procrastinate, and the next thing I know, the bees needed those supers last week.

Upon routine hive inspections, I find swarm cells. I check my notes and this is an older queen. She did really well last year, but this year she's a bit slower and they're planning to swarm. Young queens reduce the swarming impulse.

So when should you requeen? Before the former queen gets too old! When was that? Last fall (for those of you, like me, who like to make fall splits). Or if you requeen in the spring, when should you have ordered your queen (about six weeks ago, at least).

Procrastination will kill you. Keeping bees in the reactive mode will frustrate you. Be proactive.

My point is very simple: anticipate what the bees will need before they ask. Provide them with the resources (supers, etc.) before they need them. Be proactive. Those who operate in the reactive mode are always chasing their tail, always a day late and a dollar short.

Be proactive, not reactive.

In the first chapter I also hit on the idea of luck. Luck is simply experience and preparation meeting opportunity. Opportunities come along every day, but if we're not prepared, then we squander those opportunities. Experience is what we gain so we can recognize those opportunities the next time.

And will there be a next time? Doesn't opportunity only knock but once? I don't think so, but there are no guarantees it will come around again.

I also hit on the idea of fear. Sometimes we are fearful of expressing our goals because someone will come along and belittle us, tell us we're too ambitious. They'll criticize us, call us crazy and generally demean us right out of our hopes and dreams. Sometimes we're even fearful of expressing goals to ourselves. We are afraid of failure, and so afraid of failing that we fear that little voice inside of our heads that continues to remind us of our self-worth.

We are afraid of disappointing our own hopes and dreams. We feel that if we cannot live up to our own expectations, we certainly cannot live up to the hopes and expectations of others. We are afraid of failing. And so most people don't even try.

Philosophically, if we try and fail, we can be forgiven. If we fail to even try, then there is nothing to forgive. Better to love and have lost, then to never have loved at all. But to love and lose hurts. We hate the idea of failing. Failure is the "F-word" of our generation. We are a nation of winners, or so we want to be.

But is it the fear of failure that will keep us from attaining our goals? Or is it the fear of success?

If you're a small beekeeper with four hives, most people think of you as odd. Very few people keep honeybees anyway, and if you do, you're different than most people. With four hives you're more of a novelty. Making the move up to twenty-five hives means you're serious about keeping bees.

With twenty-five hives, if you're diligent about keeping track of the details, it's very likely you're going to be marketing over a thousand pounds of honey (and that's a conservative estimate). You'll need more outlets to market your honey and you'll soon develop loyal customers who are now seeking you out, believing you are always going to have honey on hand to meet their needs. They will come to expect you to have honey (and little do they understand the seasonal nature of beekeeping).

However, the pressure to perform and meet other's expectations is sometimes too much for some people. These people don't really fear failing, but they begin to fear success. They ask: How will my life change if I'm suddenly a successful beekeeper? What will other people begin to demand from me? How will other people perceive me, judge me? Will they accept me? And the possibilities are scary!

And it's not just beekeepers, but it works in every walk of life. There is something about succeeding that bothers people. If you succeed, your world will change. People will begin to raise their expectations of you. Then the real pressure comes to bear. You no longer keep bees for the fun or it, you're keeping bees because people expect you to and you feel the pressure to live up to their expectations.

Beginning beekeepers will call you with questions and they want answers. Groups looking for a speaker will call you to give presentations. People will call you to remove colonies from inaccessible areas as if you yourself could sprout wings and reach a second-story chimney.

Your life will change if you are successful. Isn't it better to fly below the radar, simply carry on in the mundane and never really achieve our dreams? Isn't it better to simply have a 9-5 job and after dinner you retreat to the easy chair to vegetate in front of the television and surf those 60,000 channels on the cable until the ten-o'clock news (provided you haven't fallen asleep before then)?

My response is simply, **"NO!"**

Life is too short not to fulfill your dreams. You have a right to be successful if you're willing to put in the work and the effort. And sometimes it is not just a special skill you need to succeed. All you really need to succeed is the persistence to give it one more try, and if that doesn't work, one more try. In more cases than not, you find success when you keep knocking on the door.

In the Bible, Jesus said, "Knock, and the door will be open to you." If you understand the original languages in which Jesus spoke, there is implied a continuation of action in his word, "knock." It literally means to knock and keep on knocking until that door is open. And the greatest temptation will be to knock once and call it quits. The second-greatest temptation is to settle for too little. The and perhaps the third-greatest temptation will be to be settling for the path of least *persistence.*

Success is never as hard as we make it out to be. You just got to keep at it. And let me give you this warning: Success is relative. Your target will always be changing. The bar is always on the rise. When you reach one level, you'll discover there's another level above it. Success is really a never-ending ladder that you climb one rung at a time.

And then to top it off, there are a host of people who will resent you when you succeed. In a nutshell, you are leaving them behind as you climb this ladder. Misery loves company and they'd love to have you stay with them in their misery. They resent the fact that you are leaving them behind as you continue in your success. They will criticize you behind your back, spread malicious gossip, tell others that success has gone to your head and that you've gotten "arrogant."

When others complain to me and criticize someone else who has succeeded, my response is to listen, never to refute, then to sum up their comments with, "Yes, but it's hard to argue with success. They did something most of us only wish we could do."

But do you really wish for success? On the outside we say "Yes!" even with enthusiasm. But on the inside, we may not be so certain. Do we really want the changes that come with success? Are we really ready to embrace how people will see us when we succeed?

The biggest problem with the fear of success is the expectations other will have of us. It is better (as most of us believe) to be a low-expectation person, bumbling along beneath the radar, perhaps verbalizing our desire to be successful, but secretly, in our heart of hearts, we don't want the expectations that go along with success.

Better to tell everyone how we want to be a big-time beekeeper than to actually do the work it will take to become that big-time beekeeper of our dreams.

I watch and listen to a lot of people in my daily work. I listen to people talk about their dreams, their hopes, their aspirations. Then I listen to them complain about how the they don't have the time, they don't have the energy, they don't have the money, they don't have the _____ _____ (you can fill in the blank with whatever excuse you use).

Most of these things are easy to overcome. And yet they easily become the excuses we use to prevent us from attaining our goals. It seems easier to use the excuses so we don't even have to try, rather than ignore the excuses, try, fail, then have to explain ourselves as to why we failed.

I knew a man who always wanted to open a business that catered to college students. We live next to a college town and the business he wanted to start was perfect for college students. Day after day, he kept telling everyone who would listen about his dream. But he conditioned his dream on the statement, "But I don't have the money. If only I could get a loan."

Someone asked him why he didn't apply for a loan. He said the bank wouldn't loan him the money. Now, you see, the problem wasn't his fault; it was the bank. And like so many people, he never actually went into the bank and asked for the money, he simply presumed the bank would not loan him the money. Rather than find out, he simply used the bank as his excuse why he couldn't reach the levels of success he kept talking about.

What made this statement odd was all of the "toys" he bought for himself. And most of these items he financed with credit cards. He had a boat, an extra pick-up truck, a four-wheeler he used for hunting, the big-screen plasma television, etc., etc., etc.

I always thought (but to myself of course) that if he saved his money rather than spend it on toys and expensive luxuries, he would soon have the money to start this wonderful business catering to college students. If money was his principle obstacle, then if he simply saved his money, he'd have enough to launch his business. Then he'd have more money to spend on toys when the business is successful!

He kept up this "If only..." talk for some time, when one day, one of his buddies said, "This sounds like a great opportunity. We're not getting any younger. I have some extra money to invest. How about I loan you the money and you can get this new venture off the ground? Or if you want, I'll give you the money and we can be partners."

The man who wanted to start the business froze. Suddenly, the obstacle to this opportunity was removed. Now it was time to "fish or cut bait." To mix in another metaphor, he had to "milk it or move it." Now it was time to either seize the day or let it go.

He let it go.

And we never heard him talk of this business idea again. People who fear success are like this. They offer excuses why they cannot succeed. Then when someone comes along and remedies the excuse, another excuse rises to the surface. If that excuse is remedied, then it's something else that gets in the way.

People who can only offer excuses and refuse to remedy those excuses do not really want to fulfill their dreams. They're simply people who talk a good story. If you try and help them, they'll find another excuse, or they'll find reason to criticize your help or blame your help on their failure if they do try. Some people will talk about hopes and dreams and success, but in reality, they just want to talk. Successful people are about action and how they are working to remove the obstacles and overcome the challenges that hinder the progress.

When asked why they are not removing those obstacles and overcoming the challenges, unsuccessful people will finally admit: It's too much work.

Success is work. Right after we were married, my father-in-law gave me a very significant piece of advice I mentioned in a previous chapter:

"Nothing important merely happens."

My father-in-law was very successful, but he worked hard. Life takes work. You get out of it what you put into it. And if you're not willing to step up to the plate and take a few swings at some pitches, running the risk of maybe striking out, then sit down in the dug out and shut up. Either you step up to the plate or you warm the bench. Your actions will always speak louder than your words.

There is another man I know who has several opportunities available to him every year. But he just can't seem to get organized in time to take advantage of the opportunities. If he has time, the weather isn't right. If the weather is right, he comes down with some mysterious disease that keeps him in bed for three days. Then he makes a remarkable recovery when the rains come, and of course, since it is raining, he is prevented from moving forward and working his bees.

It's always something.

It's always something that keeps him from succeeding. There's always an excuse. And it's not always the big things. It's like he has the opportunity, but he shoots himself in the foot and spends the next week limping around.

Opportunity knocks and he finds reason to suddenly become deaf and he can't find the door. He does a remarkable job of purposefully undermining himself. And then I wonder if this person really wants to succeed or does he just want to talk the talk?

There are a couple of beekeepers I know who ask me for advice. Usually I couch my advice in terms of "This is what I'm doing now," rather than, "Here's what **you** need to be doing now." I don't want to tell them what to do, I find it best to share what I'm doing. I'm not going to talk the talk unless I can walk the walk. I'm not going to tell someone to do something I'm not willing to do myself. And I've felt the backlash from those who resented my attitude of "here's what you need to do."

We each must do our own thing and I found it comes off negative when I tell people what they need to do. And so much of life is the inconsistency of people who do just the opposite of what they say for you to do.

The best place for advice is from those who talk the talk and walk the walk, and do it consistently.

What I've found is we all need to find our own way, but we can still learn from others. Rather than become too paternalistic and overbearing, I simply offer what I'm doing or how I would do it if I faced the same problem. Then they are free to choose their own path without recriminations from me.

There are also people who simply cannot ask for help. Call it pride, if you want, but they just cannot ask for help. They become their own enemy because they know they need outside help but they have too much pride to ask. It is the appearance of looking ignorant or weak. But if this is your problem, then isn't your lack of success making you look weak?

Perhaps the most used excuse is time. I've heard it quite often, "I just don't have the time to take care of twenty-five hives of bees." We all have the same amount of time. We all have twenty-four hours each day. It's what we try and put into those twenty-four hours that gets us into trouble.

So if you really want to take care of twenty-five hives, you will find the way. If you prefer to watch sports on the 60,000 channels available on the cable television, that's what you will do with your time.

We all have priorities and your actions will speak louder than your words. Your actions will tell us what are your major priorities in life.

And I know how we all get busy. We're all busy. But it is about priorities. And for some beekeepers, their bees are not their priority and so other things come before the bees. When opportunity knocks, there is something else to take care of. And I don't mean to sound mean.

We all have things to do. There are times the weather interrupts my plans. There are times my family needs me and my family comes before my bees. We all have priorities, but some people, it seems like their bees are their last thing to do.

But then I wonder why they keep bees if they never make them a priority. In the spring time, I share what I'm doing to prevent swarming. But they don't do it. Their bees swarm and their honey crop flies off with that swarm. I share how I'm staying up late at night extracting my honey. But they don't have time, plus that bee suit is too hot, so they wait until the fall to harvest their honey. But the bees have consumed a lot of the honey so their crop is small. Then, despite a smaller than expected honey crop, they complain because they don't have anywhere to sell their honey. And when they have honey to sell, they complain because someone else (usually me) has already beat them to that market.

I like to make fall splits. Other beekeepers want to wait until spring to make their splits, but by the time they get around to ordering a queen, all the queen producers are sold out. I tell them I'll give them one of my swarms, or better yet, I'll just refer them to one of my swarm calls.

But they never seem to have the boxes ready when I refer the swarm call to them. They are not prepared and they have not prepared their hive bodies and frames to receive that swarm.

Then they complain how they never get good bees or collect a good honey crop, or how I take all the swarms in the county.

During one of the Christmas seasons, we were swamped at the church. The season is always busy and we hosted extra services including two on Christmas Eve. I got to feeling sorry for myself, complaining to a church member how busy I was and how I had so much work to do.

Her response was not very kind, but it was truthful. When I said I was so busy and had all these sermons to preach, how Christmas always sneaks up on me and it is here before I know it, she flatly said, "I don't know why you're so surprised about Christmas coming so soon. You had 364 days to prepare for it."

Ouch. It hurt.

And the same is true in beekeeping. And I'm as guilty as anybody when it comes to not being ready, not being prepared, not taking care of the little details that have to be done long before the major things come upon us.

And by now I know that every spring I've got to work my hives to prevent swarming. I know I need to get the supers on. I know all these things and basically I have a year to get ready for them. And then some emergency pops up, and yes, I have days when I'm just too tired or my children have a special even planned. And I confess I'm not the most organized person on this earth.

But I'm getting better. I'm learning that I need to be prepared for the opportunities. I'm learning and re-learning I cannot procrastinate. The bees won't wait for me. I have learned that there are some days when I say, "Oh, I think I'll let that wait until tomorrow," and tomorrow's weather changes and makes it impossible to tend my bees.

Do not put off for tomorrow what needs to be done today.

Much of our frustration is self-generated. Secretly, we know that if we succeed, then people will expect more from us, and we'll be expecting more from ourselves. It's easier to live with the excuses.

But it's not near as much fun.

Excuses are easier. But if you don't want to discover your hopes and dreams, then why do you tell everyone of your hopes and dreams? Why not compromise your desire and settle for a mediocre level? At least you'd be more honest!

And not everyone is cut out to keep twenty-five hives of bees. And that's okay. There is nothing wrong with keeping four hives of bees is that's what you want to do. There's nothing wrong with keeping four hives of bees if that's all the time and energy you have to devote to their care.

If you remember, at the outset of this manuscript I challenged you to identify your purpose. Why do you keep bees? Why do you want to move up to twenty-five hives? Maybe, if your level of frustration is great, you need to revisit your purpose. Or maybe you need to revisit your motivation? Instead of cutting back to four hives because you can't make twenty-five hives work, maybe you need to look at yourself and see what needs to be changed. If your purpose has good intentions, are you living up to those expectations?

If you tell me four hives is your limit, I will admire and respect your honesty. But if you're just going to tell me all the excuses why you can't be successful, then there's nothing to respect. You're not even honest with yourself.

If four hives is right for you, then look me in the eye and say proudly, "I have four hives." And don't apologize. I have more respect for a beekeeper who looks after four hives and does a good job with four hives, then someone who simply fools around twenty-five hives and does a poor job.

It boils down to quality, not quantity. I'll bet the beekeeper with four hives and does a good job harvests more honey than the beekeeper with twenty-five hives and fails to keep them from swarming or falling to the perils of the wax moth.

As we talk about moving from a few hives on a hobby level, upwards to twenty-five hives, things will change. We need to embrace a more business-like structure, a profit-motivated mindset (and there's nothing wrong with making money), and a growth potential ready to seize opportunities.

It really means change. Expectations will be higher. People will demand more from us.

But the real culprit in our lack of success is ourselves. As the comic strip Pogo once said, "We have met the enemy and the enemy is us." If you aren't willing to step up and do the work, who will?

There is an old story I love to tell from time to time. In this village is a wise old man who knows everything. People come from all around the area to ask questions and to seek his counsel. He is widely respected for his wisdom.

But in thc village is a sullen, insolent young man that resents all the attention the wise old man receives.

(Remember what I said earlier about other people who resent success?)

So the brash young man decides to fool the old man and embarrass him, to prove to the rest of the village who is really the wisest person. The young man planned on taking a pigeon and bending the bird's neck, tucking its head under its wing. Then he would hold the bird in his hand using his thumb to secure the bird's head under the wing. When you do this to a bird, it remains motionless and perfectly still.

The young man planned to hold the motionless bird behind his back, then, in front of all the villagers, he would ask the old man to predict if the bird was alive or dead.

If the old man said the bird was alive, the young man would quickly crush the bird and kill it. The old man would be exposed as a fool. If the old man said the bird was dead, then the young man would pull the bird out from behind his back, lift his thumb off the bird's wing and release it. The bird would immediately take to flight and the old man would be exposed as a fool.

The insolent young man knew his plan was foolproof. So one day when a crowd gathered in the village to ask the old man a few questions, the young man stepped forward with the pigeon secured in his hand behind his back.

He asked the old man his long awaited question: Is this bird alive or dead that I hold behind my back?

The old man pondered his question. The villagers waited in rapt expectation. A sly smirk began to draw across the young man's face. He had the old man exactly where he wanted him. He awaited the answer so he could show everyone who was the better man.

He was ready to squish the bird if the old man said it was alive; he was ready to release the bird unharmed if the old man said it was dead. This was a no-win situation for the old man and the young man felt there was no way he could lose. It was fool-proof.

Finally the old man gave his answer. He said, "The answer to your question lies within your own hand." The young man knew he had been had and he sulked away without further comment.

You want to move up to twenty-five hives of honeybees? You can offer all the excuses in the world, but the truth is this: Your success lies within your own hands.

You will determine your own level of success, largely by how much energy you are willing to put forth. How much passion are you willing to invest in this enterprise? How much knowledge to you need to gain? How is your bank account?

There is a simple equation which bears repeating quite often: You will get out what you put in. And like Pogo says, you really are your own worst enemy. Too often we are not willing to put forth the effort that is required of our dreams.

So how do we overcome our worst enemy? I think the right word is PASSION! We need to be passionate about our bees. We need to inject energy. We need to be willing to invest lots of energy if we want to receive lots of joy. Passion is a great word, it is an energizing word.

There is also another word to live by and that's the "hunger factor." How hungry are you? How bad do you want to keep bees? Do you have the energy to hunt down those excuses and kill them? Do you hunger more for a feast of success or are you satisfied settling for a snack of excuses? If someone came along and said, "You can't do this," how much are you willing to show them?

There is a story of a famous piano player who played a concert, then greeted his adoring fans afterward. One female fan simply gushed with enthusiastic accolades, "Oh that was wonderful. Why I'd give half my life to play like you."

The pianist was unimpressed. He simply said, "Ma'am, I gave my whole life to play like that."

While keeping bees does not require your whole life, it is your passion that makes it a priority. It's not enough to have knowledge. When beekeeping is a priority in your life, you will find success. Passion overcomes the excuses. But you have to hunger for success.

Hunger is something that is developed. How do you develop your hunger and passion for keeping bees?

Like the old-fashioned milk stool that had three legs, there are three legs, or three parts, to developing a passion and a hunger for keeping bees.

The three parts are **belief, study** and **action**. If you have all three, you will know what it means to be passionate about keeping bees. And like the three-legged milk stool, you need all three. If you only have two, the stool will fall over.

The first leg is belief. Do you believe yourself to be a beekeeper? Do you believe you can keep bees, or more importantly, learn about bees to keep them successfully? If you think of yourself as too stupid or too clumsy, or too lazy to keep bees, then forget about keeping bees. Move onto something else and save yourself the embarrassment and the financial losses with trying to keep bees.

In one of the Star Wars movies, Master Yoda is trying to get Luke Skywalker to use the force. Luke is unsuccessful, and he complains how he just can't get it. Yoda urges him on. Luke whines how he's trying.

Yoda cuts through all the excuses:

"Do not try. There is no try. Do."

Nike shoe company has coined that term,

"Just do it."

To believe yourself to be a beekeeper is the first step. And this doesn't mean you're going to try to keep bees. You are going to do it. Do not try. Do.

<u>The second leg is study</u>. Your study will include reading. Most libraries have some ancient books, which are okay because bees have not changed over the years. But beekeeping has changed. Those old books will not include the latest challenges like mites and small hive beetles.

If you stop in at your local retail book store, do not be surprised to find their shelf on beekeeping will be empty. There is just not enough demand to keep these books in stock at the local retail level.

My suggestion is to go to the Internet at www.amazon.com and search their web site for books on beekeeping.

There are two magazines out, *Bee Culture* and *American Bee Journal*. Both are excellent, though each one seems to write for a different audience.

There are host of web sites, plus two really good forums on the Internet. www.beesource.com and www.bee-l.com both have places to log in and join in on the discussion.

Make every effort to study what is happening now. Stay current.

Your first leg is belief. Your second leg is study. But without the third leg, your milk stool will not stand. You need action.

The third leg is action. A good aim is worthless if you're not going to pull the trigger. A lot of people study on how to swim, but until you get into the pool, until you are willing to take action, you will never really know how to swim.

The same principle works in beekeeping. Believe all you want. Study all you can. But until you take action, you're not really keeping bees. You talk all the talk you want to talk, but until you actually walk the walk, you're just talking.

The action phase is often rife with fear. Do I have what it takes to care for twenty-five hives of bees? Will I find the time? Do I have the time? Do I have the energy? Will my spouse understand? Where will I sell all that honey?

Many of these questions have no answers until you step into beekeeping and find out for yourself. Then you'll also find that one answer works on one day in one situation, then it won't work a week later in another situation. You just have to do it. Don't talk about it; do it. Have courage! Be confident!

Courage comes from wanting to do it well.

Security comes from knowing you can do it well.

Confidence comes from having done it well.

Beekeeping With Twenty-five Hives

Chapter Fourteen:

Concluding Thoughts

As you think about increasing the size of your apiary, either by buying new equipment, expanding to a new location or making splits, there is always a great deal of fear and trepidation. If you didn't feel some apprehension, then I'd worry. But if you're just a little hesitant to make this kind of leap of faith, then don't worry. Those feelings are normal.

But perhaps you're thinking, "Maybe I'll do this when I have time," or "Once I get the car paid off," or "When I find a market for the last year's honey." And all these statements might hold a great deal of validity.

Sometimes we need to take care of some things first, then move into that which is not so pressing. But if you're just putting it off because you fear making the decision, then your indecision has become your real decision.

I'll tell you a story about a man who, along with his contemporaries, graduated from high school and went to work at the local meat packing plant. This was several years ago when wages and benefits were fantastic (since that time labor and union relations have soured this industry and it's been taken over by low-wage, immigrant labor). Back in those days, everybody aspired to work at the packing house. And also in those days, businesses treated their employees with respect to reduce turnover.

This particular young man went to work with his buddies who also graduated from high school that same year. But he aspired to do other things. He wanted to go to college. The security and the benefits of working at the packing house were a tough tie to sever. There was so much to give up. So he began asking the advice of his co-workers what they thought of his leaving the packing house to attend college.

One old boy said, "College? How long with that take?"

The young man responded, "Four years."

"Four years?" came the reply. "How old will you be in four years?"

The young man flatly responded, "I'll be twenty-two." Then after a moment's reflection he added, "But I'll still be twenty-two if I stay here and work for four more years."

A lot of people put off great plans because it's going to take them some time to get where they want to go. You may have two hives. You may aspire to have an apiary of one-hundred hives.

But it's going to take you six years (provided you followed my advice to limit your expansion to doubling each year, and if you doubled each year moving from two to four, four to eight, eight to sixteen, sixteen to thirty-two, thirty-two to sixty-four, and sixty-four to one-hundred and twenty-eight).

But if you put off your aspirations, you're still going to be the same person in six years if you stay at two hives. And maybe you'll find that when you reach fifty hives, fifty hives is all you can handle. And it may take you a few years to learn how to work fifty hives before you make the jump to one-hundred. But if you put off expanding until (fill in the blank) you'll probably find that time will never come.

Let me leave you with two pieces of advice. The first piece of advice is to "WIN." To "WIN" is to think long and hard about "What's Important Now." And right now, maybe getting your spouse through school is what's important now. Maybe buying a new car is what's important now.

But somewhere your beekeeping aspirations will be ready to rise to the top of your "What's Important Now" list. And if you don't take care of what's really important now, if you don't lay the important foundation of family and faith, then there may be no future option to raise honeybees. Take care of what's important now.

The second piece of advice is to not wait too long. In five years, you will be five years older. In five years there will only be three things that will greatly change your life in significant ways. Those three things are 1) the books you read, 2) the people you meet, and 3) the dreams you dream.

Along these lines, remember this as well. Those who don't read books are no better off than those who can't read. And those who don't read books and think it doesn't matter are the most ignorant.

When you surround yourself with successful people, successful people will always tell you that you can do something. It's the people who never accomplished anything that will always discourage you from to trying to achieve great things. Hang out with successful people. And if you don't dream dreams, you'll never know how far you can go.

Twenty-five hives is a lofty goal, but it may be a small stepping stone to something greater. In this manuscript I have laid out a lot of ideas. You don't have to do them all. My advice is to pick one and modify it to fit your circumstances. Revise my ideas to fit your goals. Or totally reject me and do it your own way!

But above all, follow your dreams. Let nothing step in your way.

About the author:

Grant F.C. Gillard began keeping honeybees in 1981 following his graduation from Iowa State University from the College of Agriculture. He started out with twenty hives on the family farm in southern Minnesota and now resides in Jackson, Missouri where he tends around 200 hives...for now.

He sells honey at several local farmer's markets as well as raising his own locally adapted queen honeybees. He is a husband of twenty-six years and father to three grown children.

He pastors the First Presbyterian Church in Jackson, Missouri, as his "day job." He frequently threatens to retire to devote his full energy to beekeeping, but secretly, he enjoys the ministry and is greatly appreciated by his congregation.

After serving for the past nineteen years in this position, he has become more of a community chaplain and is often simply called, "The Bee Guy," or "The Honey Dude," depending upon which generation recognizes him at Wal-Mart.

He is eternally grateful to members of his congregation who have graciously allowed him to dabble in this hobby, and for his restraint of not turning every sermon into an illustration on beekeeping. He is a past-president of the Missouri State Beekeepers Association.

He is a frequent conference speaker and may be contacted at: gillard5@charter.net

Contact him regarding his availability for your next event.

Other books of interest may be found at:

www.CreateSpace.com

and

http://www.Smashwords.com

Or visit Grant's personal web site where you can look at his other publications and read sample chapters:

www.grantgillard.weebly.com

(click on the "My Books" tab at the top)

Grant also blogs under revgrant1 at:

www.expertscolumn.com

and

www.xomba.com

You can find him on Pinterest and Facebook, or just jump on any search engine and "Google" him.

https://www.createspace.com/4106626

Keeping Honey Bees and Swarm Trapping

A Better Way to Collect "Free" Bees

https://www.createspace.com/4111886

A Ton of Honey

Managing Your Hives for Maximum Production

https://www.createspace.com/4107714

Free Bees!

Removing and Retrieving Honey Bee Swarms

https://www.createspace.com/4044187

Beekeeping 101: Where Can I Keep My Bees?

https://www.createspace.com/4043781

Why I Keep Honey Bees

(and why you should, too!)

https://www.createspace.com/4044721

Honey! It Turned to Sugar

Dealing with Granulated Honey

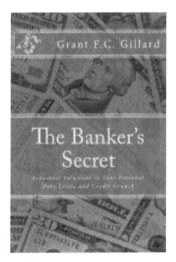

https://www.createspace.com/4111285

The Banker's Secret

Personal Finance and Debt Management

https://www.createspace.com/4147010

Better Luck **THIS** Time:

Making Good Luck Happen